Preaching Spanish Nationalism across the Hispanic Atlantic 1759–1823

Preaching Spanish Nationalism across the Hispanic Atlantic 1759–1823

SCOTT EASTMAN

Louisiana State University Press
Baton Rouge

Published with assistance from the Spanish Ministry of Culture
Published by Louisiana State University Press

Manufactured in the United States of America
First printing

Designer: Laura Roubique Gleason
Typefaces: Minion Pro, text; Bodoni, display
Printer: McNaughton & Gunn
Binder: Acme Bookbinding

Library of Congress Cataloging-in-Publication Data
Eastman, Scott, 1971–
Preaching Spanish nationalism across the Hispanic Atlantic, 1759–1823 / Scott Eastman.
p. cm.
Includes bibliographical references and index.
ISBN 978-0-8071-3957-8 (cloth : alk. paper) — ISBN 978-0-8071-3958-5 (pdf : alk. paper) — ISBN 978-0-8071-3959-2 (epub : alk. paper) — ISBN 978-0-8071-3960-8 (mobi : alk. paper)
1. Nationalism—Spain—History—18th century. 2. Nationalism—Spain—History—19th century. 3. Nationalism—Religious aspects—Spain—History—18th century. 4. Nationalism—Religious aspects—Spain—History—19th century. 5. Church and state—Spain—History—18th century. 6. Church and state—Spain—History—19th century. 7. Catholic Church—Spain—Clergy—History—18th century. 8. Catholic Church—Spain—Clergy—History—19th century. 9. Nationalism—New Spain—History—19th century. 10. Nationalism—Religious aspects—New Spain—History—19th century. I. Title.
DP203.E37 2011
320.54094609'033—dc23

2011020451

The paper in this book meets the guidelines for permanence and durability of the Committee on Production Guidelines for Book Longevity of the Council on Library Resources. ♾

To Sabina

CONTENTS

ACKNOWLEDGMENTS

What is Spain? A collection of regions with distinctive, primordial roots and traditions? A backward state that only transitioned toward modernity in the late twentieth century? A memory of lost glory, couched in imperial grandeur? When I began my research, I traveled to Madrid armed with a number of preconceived notions concerning nineteenth-century Spain. I assumed that Spain had failed to nationalize, to turn their peasants into Spaniards. I assumed that the vestiges of the Old Regime, empire and religion, mattered little to liberals. I assumed that I could craft a research project grounded in documents housed in the capital city's archives. Having read the most important works on nationalism in graduate classes, I assumed that I would focus, top-down, on politics. As Eric Hobsbawm reminds us, although history from below is crucial, nation building must be analyzed above all from the perspective of the government. I never imagined I would spend the majority of my time reading sermons and pastoral instruction, exploring the religious sensibilities and nationalist aspirations of Spaniards on both sides of the Atlantic as they navigated the currents of modern social and political thought.

With a great deal of support and guidance from José Álvarez Junco, I began to sort through documents in the Colección Documental del Fraile, housed in Madrid's military archive, and shaped the beginnings of this book. Through a Fulbright grant, I spent nine months in the dusty, old room on the first floor, underneath a larger-than-life portrait of Franco on horseback (kept largely out of sight on the second floor). My initial presentation on the topic of religion and identity, given at the Universidad Autónoma in Madrid, as well as subsequent talks at Complutense and at the Universidad de Valencia, demonstrated to me that the issues I had looked into remain the subject of vital debates, with great contemporary significance, not at all limited to the halls of academia. Returning to study at the University of California, Irvine, I broadened my analysis to include the viceroyalty of New Spain, and Puebla in particular, as a case study to balance out my examination of peninsular Spain. With funding from U.C., Irvine, and Creighton University, I made multiple trips to Mexico and traveled to Valencia in order to understand the region and the nation from different angles. Building on an increasingly important literature on revolutions and independence in the Americas, this book is the product of the renewed interest in Atlantic world history and has been influenced by the methods of scholars who truly have globalized historical methodologies.

First and foremost, I would like to thank Kara and Sabina Eastman for their patience and understanding throughout such a long process. Without their help, this would not have been possible. I also would like to express sincere appreciation to everyone I worked with at Irvine, especially Carolyn Boyd, who is an outstanding mentor. Her feedback on all aspects of my work helped me to write a much stronger and more coherent monograph. She has inspired me with her own work on national identity and through her contributions to the field of modern Spanish history. Jaime Rodríguez helped me to connect my research on Spain with my work on nineteenth-century Mexico, and his tireless commitment to scholarship continues to bridge the historiographical divide between historians of Spain and Latin America. I greatly appreciate Tim Tackett's help with an early version of chapter 2, part of which was published in Spain in the journal *Historia y Política*. Kavita Philip also provided me with insightful advice as I wrote my introduction and developed my argument. I owe a great debt to LSU Press, and in particular to Alisa Plant, who patiently guided the project through its final stages and revisions. I must thank all of the archivists who facilitated this research, especially those who work at the Servicio Histórico Militar, the Archivo Diocesano de Valencia, the Colección LaFragua at the Benemérita Universidad Autónoma de Puebla, and the Biblioteca Valenciana. Finally, I could not have completed this project without the invaluable comments (and documents) provided by colleagues, notably Carmen Aguilar Guzmán, Gregorio Alonso, Brian Connaughton, Ivana Frasquet, Chris Gerteis, David Gies, Amy Lyons, Gabe Paquette, Allyson Poska, Natalia Sobrevilla Perea, Nigel Townson, and Clint Young.

Preaching Spanish Nationalism across the Hispanic Atlantic 1759–1823

INTRODUCTION

In 1812, during the War of Independence in Spain, the Capuchin friar Rafael de Vélez warned that "a new revolution of ideas, a war of opinion" had just begun in Spain. "The people," he feared, would embrace these new principles and "blindly follow those who present themselves as the restorers of their rights." He urged his parishioners to arm themselves in defense of the *patria* (homeland), yet he insisted that the true battle would be fought against the false philosophies emanating from France. Revolutionary pamphlets were the "arms that had defeated a multitude of peoples and nations seduced by the liberal ideas of reform and enlightenment." Vélez bemoaned the freedom of the press that had allowed such printed materials to circulate, hearkening back to the first days of the uprising against the French, when all periodicals were suffused with "piety, devotion and a saintly enthusiasm."[1] Written as a diatribe against the legacy of the French Revolution, the work of Vélez, and that of many others, illuminates the profound impact of early liberalism upon competing conceptions of Spanish identity. The true meaning of Spanishness, especially concerning religion as a marker of the collective, had become increasingly contested within an interconnected political culture across the Hispanic Atlantic world.

Many scholars interpret the inheritance of the wars of independence, bequeathed to a generation of nineteenth-century nation-builders in Spain and in the Americas, as one of strife, reaction, and entrenched conservatism—in sum, as an obstacle to be overcome. For example, Jean-René Aymes states that the initial Spanish uprising in 1808 was driven by a defense of honor and of God, King, and Country. Juan Pablo Fusi likewise insists that "the ideological mobilization of the most reactionary sectors of the Church . . . made the Catholic faith the essence of Spain . . . and identified Catholicism with the nation and the Spanish Monarchy." Historians of New Spain also claim that a hegemonic conservative clerical ideology endured well into the era of postindependence Mexico. Anthony Marx writes that the Catholic church in Spain remained a bulwark against Enlightenment ideas and failed to unify Spaniards in an age of growing secularization. Michael Burleigh interprets the period in terms of a "fusion, whether in Spain, Germany or Russia, of counter-revolution, nationalism and religion." And historians such as Charles Esdaile maintain that the ideological polarization of 1812 inexorably led to further conflicts that climaxed in the twentieth century with the Spanish Civil War.[2]

While a copious literature has focused on the counterrevolutionary theology of priests such as Vélez during the wars of independence, this book recovers the radical notions of popular sovereignty and the deeply rooted culture of liberal nationalism that emerged alongside it within a Catholic public sphere in Spain and New Spain. By 1808, Spaniards had challenged the hegemony of Old Regime discourse as the "people" became the embodiment of a reawakened nation. Using allusions to the biblical captivity of the Israelites in Egypt, clergymen likened the people of God to *el pueblo español*, the Spanish people, who had become the chosen nation struggling to uphold the divine sanctity of the embattled Catholic faith. New discourses of national identity, preached by reformist clerics and spread through pulpits and plazas as well as through the channels of print culture and salon society, threatened the privileges of social hierarchy and unfettered royal power, the twin pillars of absolutism. Fundamentally altering Old Regime patriotism, the language of a liberal Spanish nationalism found a ready audience among those disparaged by the likes of Vélez as unsophisticated rabble. While Vélez feared that this new revolution would alienate and divide Spaniards, and compared the assembly in Cádiz to legislators in Paris in 1789, Spanish nationalists, unlike their French counterparts, reaffirmed their adherence to the church by grounding national identity and citizenship in their common Catholicism.[3] In addition, they legitimized their program of change by referencing Hispanic traditions of representation and liberty. In no way did they seek to break completely with the past; rather, they appealed to history to justify their claims. Revolutionary liberalism, as a hallmark of modernity, appeared to Spanish advocates as complementary to both tradition and faith. Historians who insist upon viewing the amalgamation of religion and nationalism as a retrograde phenomenon within the Spanish-speaking world have downplayed the role of liberals, lay and clerical, in the making of a Spanish national identity couched in religious essentialism. Those who seek to disentangle a secular identity from older, religiously based solidarities gloss over the fact that modern nationalism in the Hispanic Atlantic world was predicated upon Catholic imagery and identification.[4] Indeed, this study demonstrates that the success of a nascent liberal nationalism depended in large part upon the incorporation of religion and the active participation of a significant segment of the clergy in its service.

Local notables as well as village curates and soldiers, elites and peasants alike, understood their loyalties to provincial authorities, the church, and the Spanish Monarchy in complex terms. In peninsular Spain, prominent Spaniards cooperated with the French during the War of Independence while others resisted. Although some Americans single-mindedly pursued emancipation from the metropole, others reacted to events in Europe by emphasizing metaphorical bonds of familial kinship and by pressing for increased autonomy and equality under a representative constitutional government. Furthermore, reformist partisans as well as traditionalist practitioners of Catholicism struggled to define a faith fraught with historical significance in the midst of a war against a people perceived as embodying the "atheistic" legacy of the French Revolution. This transatlantic study challenges conventional explanations of these conflicts by exploring the common language and culture that underpinned local and national identities during simultaneous "wars of independence," as the Spanish fought against the French in the peninsula and civil wars broke out in Spanish America by 1810. Expressing both locally centered worldviews and a plurality of nationalist visions, the vibrant political cultures of the early-nineteenth-century Spanish Monarchy displayed tensions between Old Regime paradigms and variants of liberal ideology as armed forces battled for control of the Iberian Peninsula and the Americas.

By the early 1820s, the modern Spanish constitutional system had exerted a great deal of influence from Brazil to southern Europe, and an enduring popular culture sustained often vitriolic debates over freedom and natural rights.[5] In 1810, Álvaro Flórez Estrada wrote that the "revolution" in Spain was a transformative event in contemporary history that would "change the entire political system of Europe."[6] In a sermon celebrating the reconvening of the Cortes in 1820, a priest similarly intoned: "It appears that divine providence has destined the Spanish Nation to be a shining example to the whole world in this century."[7] Attempting to repair the damage caused by a decade of internecine warfare in 1820, American and peninsular deputies in Madrid embarked upon renewed negotiations in order to find common ground with those who had risen up against Spanish authorities in the New World. Yet contemporary historians, such as Roberto Breña and Josep Fradera, present the entire epoch as one of failure and premature experimentation.[8] Fradera writes that the utopian aspects of early Spanish liberalism indelibly weakened the project as a whole, viewing the period as "an exceptional and peculiar moment."[9] In contrast, this work sheds light on the contingent aspects of an era that ended only with internal dissent magnified by the concerted policies of the Holy Alliance and external intervention. It took one hundred thousand French troops to end the Trienio liberal in April 1823, and cultural and political ties between the historic Spanish kingdoms did not cease with American independence. Many in Peru as well as Mexico reimagined their new nations with Spanish princes sitting on autonomous New World thrones, presiding over states that were, in many ways, the mirror image of the Spanish constitutional regime of 1812. Likewise, demands for popular, consensual governance did not end with Fernando's restoration in 1823, and radical liberalism informed the spirit of politics as well as debates over social and economic questions in peninsular Spain and the Americas throughout the course of the nineteenth century. Thus, methodologically, this book emphasizes the common origins of Hispanic liberal nationalisms, grounded in Catholic reformist rhetoric, as potentially unifying discourses utilized to construct the foundations of nations-in-the-making in Spain and in New Spain. Local experiences of revolution and political participation, which were remarkably similar from Valencia, in peninsular Spain, to Puebla, New Spain, illustrate the ways in which supraregional identification with the nation-state often supplanted local grievances and concerns while providing a bridge between particularist identities deployed in the Old World and in the New. It is important to note that lawmakers did not erase an imperial legacy with a simple stroke of a pen, as Jeremy Adelman points out, and that coherent nations did not immediately arise from the ashes of empire.[10] Significantly, a popular nationalist idiom had surged across Spain and New Spain that elided class and regional difference. A discourse of Spanish nationalism took hold on both sides of the Atlantic between 1808 and 1820 that served as a template for all competing ideologies in the decades that followed.

MODERNITY, NATIONAL IDENTITY, AND CONSTITUTIONALISM

In the aftermath of the Enlightenment, when the wars of the French Revolution reached the Pyrenees, until 1823, when the "sons of St. Louis" invaded to suppress a liberal revolution, the Spanish Monarchy experienced the ravages of war across the Americas as well as the peninsula. During this period, as Spaniards fought the French (1793–95, 1808–14) and civil war engulfed the Americas (1810–25), liberals promulgated the Constitution of 1812 twice, in March 1812 and again in March 1820. In March 1814, as King Fernando VII returned from captivity in France, reactionary elites delivered an influential manifesto that condemned constitutional government as an attack on royal sovereignty. Although Fernando VII issued a royal decree declaring the Constitution null and void in May 1814, he subsequently swore allegiance to the charter following a military revolt in 1820.

The Constitution of 1812 limited the powers of the king, ended seignorialism, privileged a national legislature, and established modern ideals of national sovereignty and representative government. In Spanish America, constitutional reforms included an end to Indian tribute and the establishment of *ayuntamientos* (municipal councils) for each town of more than one thousand inhabitants.[11] While constitutional architects in France and the United States limited the public role of religion, Spanish liberals guaranteed the exclusivity of the Catholic faith and proclaimed the transatlantic territories of the monarchy a unitary Catholic nation, placing religion at the center of nationalist narratives. How did Hispanic liberals come to enshrine such seemingly contradictory notions in the context of revolutionary legislation intended to remake the fabric of society and the institutions of government? According to one priest presiding over the sacralization of the reinstated Constitution in 1820, the new code of laws represented the triumph of both ancient traditions and modern constructions of the nation-state: "The Prince, in association with the Representatives of the people, will make just laws, will hand down correct decisions [and] will avoid injustices, violence, seduction, fraud, and the disturbance of order and tranquility. The aforementioned people will enjoy the sweetness of peace [and] will conserve the holy Religion, marked by the Codes of our ancient and modern institutions."[12] Consecrating a liberal constitutional monarchy in the name of religion seemed both appropriate and self-evident to its proponents in the early nineteenth century. Yet contemporary theorists such as Anthony Giddens have tended to reify religion as an artifact of the Old Regime, and nineteenth-century liberalism as a harbinger of modern political systems, establishing a dichotomy between tradition and modernity in historical discourse.

Modernity has been defined as the forces of ineluctable progress moving societies toward secularism, empirical scientific inquiry, developed industrial capitalism, centralized state bureaucracies, and democracy. Giddens defines modernity as a process of "disembedding" from traditional mores and cultural norms.[13] François-Xavier Guerra likewise emphasizes both the political and social dimensions of modernity and highlights the revolution in individual consciousness that had occurred by 1810 in the Hispanic world. The Enlightenment, as the bearer of modernity, provided the ideological foundations for the new rhetoric and political sociability of patriotism and nationalism. Taking a macrohistorical point of view, Guerra narrates the widening divisions between the mental universe of modernizing elites and traditional rural society.[14] This historical tendency also can be traced to historians who have viewed peasants and the landless poor as "prepolitical" actors on the modern world stage.[15]

The demarcation of a boundary between tradition and modernity lends credence to analysis based upon modernization theory. For example, Guerra argues that the imposition of modern liberalism and representative forms of government upon the stratified corporative bodies of the Old Regime created fundamental tensions within traditional society.[16] This assertion relies upon an implicit understanding of modernization and its consequences. Traditional societies, accordingly, cannot withstand the pressures of modern structures and worldviews that conflict with older ways of doing things.[17] Modernization theory underpins much of the literature on nineteenth- and twentieth-century history and on national identity in particular. Eric Hobsbawm and Benedict Anderson, among many others, theorize that identity transitions in stages from religious modes of thought to identification with the nation.[18] The former must yield to the latter because tradition cannot coexist with modernity.[19] Liah Greenfeld, writing from a sociological vantage point and influenced by the ideas of Max Weber, contends that modernity should be defined by nationalism rather than nationalism being defined by its modernity.[20]

Many historians plainly state that the nineteenth-century Spanish Monarchy "failed" in its efforts to modernize and nationalize.[21] Successive liberal governments could not transform Old Regime structures and political relationships and continued to incorporate Catholicism as a locus of identification. According to one scholar, this constituted a failure as well because "Catholicism did not engage secular loyalty to the same extent it would in France or that Protestantism would in England."[22] Fin-de-siècle liberals such as Joaquín Costa argued that "the survival of feudal structures in the countryside and the predominance of the old aristocracy, and their values" impeded a bourgeois revolution.[23] Ernest Gellner points to

Spain as an example of a "retarded exception . . . having retained at a remarkably late date a nationalist regime which incorporated the endorsement of absolutist Catholic claims in its image of the nation."[24] Hobsbawm opines that "nineteenth-century Spain was not exactly in the vanguard of ideological progress."[25] Borja de Riquer i Permanyer argues that the responsibility for the failure to create an inclusive national identity "falls in any case on the men who dictated such norms, on the nineteenth-century political class, on the groups that led the liberal revolutionary process."[26] Historians have construed the fragmentation of national identities by the later nineteenth century as the logical consequence of the failure of Spanish nationalism.[27] Furthermore, many historians have asserted the primacy of late-nineteenth-century mass movements, linking the advent of separatism in peninsular Spain and the origins of revolution in Mexico to a legacy of political polarization inherited from the first decades of the century.[28] For example, the Mexican liberal José María Luis Mora viewed the struggle for independence as "pernicious and destructive to the nation."[29] This type of historical narrative has been tremendously influential, whether seen in terms of sociologically informed national studies, economic analysis, or general works on nationalism.[30]

More recent scholars and cultural historians have challenged these ideas.[31] Foregrounding cultural aspects of nationalism has resituated questions of political failure and the role of the state in fostering national identity.[32] Prasenjit Duara focuses on the fluidity of identities and relationships that often betray resemblances between premodern and modern modes of consciousness.[33] Dipesh Chakrabarty similarly questions definitions of the word "political," with its exclusionary connotations based on historicist ideals. For example, in looking at nineteenth- and twentieth-century Bengal, Chakrabarty argues that "the political sphere in which the peasant and his masters participated was modern . . . and yet it did not follow the logic of secular-rational calculations inherent in the modern conception of the political. . . . Theirs was not a 'backward' consciousness—a mentality left over from the past, a consciousness baffled by modern political and economic institutions and yet resistant to them."[34] He suggests that the paradigms of political participation and popular worldviews that operated in colonial India were different from those in effect in secular, bourgeois Europe.

From a transnational perspective on the Atlantic world, however, Europe can no longer be understood as a secular entity that stands apart from colonial outposts. During this crucial era, Spanish identities were forged, not simply in a single secular historical time, but during the period of flux and transition between absolute monarchy and liberalism that was often "out of joint with itself."[35] The Spanish Monarchy does not represent a unique case; a considerable body of research demonstrates that nationalists across the states and multiethnic empires of the nineteenth-century Atlantic world similarly constructed particularist identities upon the foundations of religious tradition.[36] Processes of nationalization were at work in all of the territories of the Spanish Monarchy that laid the basis for a "mixed modernity," meshing Enlightenment ideals of progress and reform with the doctrines of Roman Catholicism.[37] This book compares emergent patterns of identification in Spain and the viceroyalty of New Spain, focusing on a lingua franca of liberal Spanish nationalism. Many ardently fought for a transatlantic nation-state encompassing peninsular Spain and the Americas, demonstrating that national identities, far from concrete outcomes of the forces of modernization, developed in an atmosphere of fluidity and negotiation rather than one of consensus and stability.

COMMUNICATING IDEOLOGIES OF NATIONALISM ACROSS THE SPANISH MONARCHY

From the optic of the nation-state, this is a transnational history of Spain and Mexico at the onset of the modern age. More accurately, this is a study of transatlantic culture and political mobilization at a moment of discord and strife. Napoleon's invasion of peninsular Spain in 1808 brought on a crisis for the Old Regime state and its legitimating rhetoric. Across the Hispanic Atlantic world, a common culture forged above all in the forms and symbols of religious belief linked the Americas to the metropole and elites to peasants and indigenous actors, providing a shared language through which emerging collective identities could be constructed and articulated.[38] Tracing the development of nationalism in the period during which the vocabulary of nationality and the idea of popular sovereignty were first articulated highlights the artificiality of a distinct divide between the early modern and modern periods and also elucidates both the continuities and disjunctures between eighteenth-century patriotism and nineteenth-century nationalism. If, as Guerra maintains, the Spanish polity was one of extraordinary coherence in 1808, and Spanish patriotism had a ready audience in all territories of the monarchy, both Spain and Spanish America must be studied in order to fully comprehend the divergence that took shape by 1821.[39] Unlike imperial codification, which differentiated between the populations of the metropole and subjects in colonies, the Constitution of 1812 laid the foundation for a nation stretching across the Atlantic composed of all Spaniards residing within the boundaries of *las Españas* under the banner of the Bourbon Monarchy.

Scholars tend to research contemporary nation-states through the lens of national histories.[40] Studies of Spanish national identity have obscured the importance of the *Ultramar,* the overseas territories, and the Americas seldom merit discussion.[41] Few historians have plotted the transformation of Spanish nationalist discourses in different parts of the Spanish Monarchy from the late eighteenth century through the 1820s, when constitutional government was reinstated and Spanish America definitively broke away from the *madre patria,* the motherland.[42]

As Spaniards on both sides of the Atlantic constructed the institutional foundations of a new government, the emergence of the public sphere ushered in a new political culture. While news had circulated in official publications such as the *Gazeta de Madrid* under the Old Regime, a de facto freedom of the press accompanied the turmoil and chaos of 1808. Periodicals such as the provocatively titled *El Robespierre Español* espoused revolutionary notions of national sovereignty, capitalizing on the burgeoning market for new ideas. In cities such as Valencia, local governments fell to new ruling coalitions that promised to end Napoleonic tyranny. Countless publications surfaced to advance competing interpretations of the events. Juan Rico, a Franciscan living in Valencia, and a leader in the provincial *junta,* an ad hoc committee formed in times of crisis, pronounced the period a revolutionary war of independence waged by the Spanish people against the French Empire.[43] Similarly, between 1810 and 1814, residents of New Spain forged a liberal governing regime as they faced an armed insurgent campaign that threatened to derail the constitutional political process. Across the territories of the monarchy, Spanish nationalism coalesced around the radical premise that the people formed the nation.

The distribution and reception of ideas is a central concern for historians of nationalism. Precisely how new ideas emerge, circulate, and gain acceptance continues to be a topic of contention, especially regarding the age prior to mass communication. Several factors point to the importance of religious sources for nationalist sentiment and to clerics as unique intermediaries between citizens and the state. The clergy, from bishops to local curates, certainly acted as one of the main channels of communication for the popular classes, a largely illiterate and rural population, and provided what Peter Guardino terms "a vital and effective ideological content" to discourses of identity during the wars of independence across the Spanish Monarchy.[44] Clerics also played pivotal roles as political figures, and as such advocated liberal as well as traditional conceptions of the nation and state. One-third of the deputies in the Cortes of Cádiz—the elected body that first defined the parameters of liberalism as the basis for representative government in the Hispanic world—were clerics. Charismatic ecclesiastics were the main protagonists in the war efforts of 1793–95 and 1808–21, and the priests Miguel Hidalgo y Costilla and José María Morelos, among many others, led the initial insurrection in New Spain. Recent research, however, has debunked the nationalist mythology that a majority of New Spain's clergy supported the insurgent efforts, and estimates indicate that 80 percent remained loyal to the monarchy.[45]

Historians are divided over the role played by clerics in peninsular Spain. William Callahan argues that "for the majority of the secular and regular clergy, the struggle against Napoleon was a sacred war, a 'Holy Crusade' against an invader for whom no epithet was too harsh." He notes that even among the upper echelons of church hierarchy, "few churchmen [remained] sympathetic to the monarchy of Joseph Napoleon."[46] John Lawrence Tone maintains that the rural-urban divide in Spain to a large extent determined the position of a particular cleric. He insists that "in most urban environments, for example, Madrid, Granada, and Málaga, most ecclesiastics actively supported the French regime."[47] If, as José Álvarez Junco contends, one of the central historiographical problems concerning the wars of independence consists of distinguishing between the rhetoric of liberal deputies ensconced in Cádiz and that of the combatants in Spain and the Americas, the role and influence of clerics must be reassessed.[48] While the church may have maintained a virtual monopoly over the means of communication until 1808, the clergy, both before and after Napoleon's invasion, articulated a plurality of views on politics, identity, and the role of religious institutions in a changing society. Clerics at all levels of church hierarchy established foundational narratives of national identity, and their ideas dovetailed with those of journalists, playwrights, poets, and governing officials acting independently of church strictures.

Moderate and liberal priests are rarely cast in historical accounts as typical nineteenth-century Hispanic clerics, however. On the contrary, historians tend to characterize Spanish churchmen as "all-powerful" and able to arouse the "fanatic fury" of Spaniards all too ready to follow their lead. In this view, churchmen embodied the reactionary spirit of modern Spain.[49] According to José Mexía, an American deputy to the Cortes, "The influence of any ecclesiastic, I am not speaking now of a bishop or an archbishop, but of a simple ecclesiastic of average comportment, has more force than 20 regiments, particularly in the Americas; and with the addition of virtue, they dominate in the hearts of all people, especially in those countries known for the religiosity of their inhabitants."[50] Other accounts likewise suggest that religion continued to represent a primary marker of identity in the early nineteenth century, and that the clergy had considerable impact on the communities they served. A chaplain accompanying the British army in Spain, after sitting through a sermon in Ciudad Rodrigo, concluded that "the preacher was eloquent and impressive, and his audience sensibly affected."[51] He delineated the centrality of Catholicism to the war effort and the profound "religious prejudices" faced by the English, noting: "When any officer announces himself an Irishman, there is an immediate exclamation of pride and joy, 'Es Católico, es Irlandés'; and he is thenceforward treated with the warmest cordiality of friendship by every member of the family."[52]

Influential contemporaries as well as foreign travelers often denigrated the visceral religious extremism propounded by zealous clerics. For example, José Blanco White, a vocal critic of the church who fled to England in 1810, stated: "The influence of religion in Spain has no limit, and divides its inhabitants into two classes: fanatics and hypocrites."[53] The chief of police in Madrid in 1809 insisted that "there are frequent and repeated warnings in court and in the provinces of the 'incalculable damage that some fanatical priests cause to public opinion and to the public spirit' that inspired their penitents to utter the 'most detestable' maxims."[54] One cleric, who collaborated with the French authorities in Spain, leveled similar charges of extremism against the church, purporting to be horrified at the "voices of ignorance and the abuse of the fanatics."[55] The trope of religious fanaticism and excess, first articulated during the sixteenth century in debates over the treatment of the indigenous peoples of the New World, continued to mark the discourse of foreign observers as well as Spanish critics during the nineteenth century.

The idea that the Spanish clergy symbolized the reactionary nature of the "Spanish character" has been embedded in much of the historiography on the War of Independence.[56] Even some twentieth-century studies uphold a teleological vision of the church as apocalyptic and atavistic. One historian contends that "blind patriotism, preached and experienced with religious messianism, will be converted into the principal ingredient of

Spanish religiosity during the war."[57] Echoing a construction of Spaniards as innately and fervently religious, other historians replicate the essentialist vision of a supposed Spanish character first fomented by the clergy during the War of Independence. For example, one scholar argues that the discourse of the clergy, "creating a state of exaltation and of furor[,] . . . will bear fruit in the War of Independence and will culminate in the formation of a fanatical, intolerant, and aggressive spirit that will constitute one of the essential constants of the modern Spanish soul."[58] Similar interpretations are used to suggest that the political-religious ideology of National-Catholicism in Spain was based in the Catholic reactionary sentiment of the early nineteenth century, rooted precisely in the War of Independence. Such scholarship minimizes the role of liberal clerics who advocated reform and steadily lost ground to the forces of reaction in the church even as liberals came to power during the reign of Isabel II.

Historians studying the nineteenth-century Spanish Monarchy have begun to interrogate the synthesis of religious ideals within specifically Spanish nationalist ideologies. José Maravall finds that sectors of the clerical representation at the Cortes of Cádiz developed a doctrine of "liberal Catholicism" that played an important role in the articulation of the Constitution of 1812 and the construction of the nation.[59] Álvarez Junco advances the notion of "a fusion of religious and political identity" during the early nineteenth century.[60] Building on such works, José María Portillo Valdés develops an argument based upon a juridical and political transition from a Catholic monarchy to a Catholic nation during the period 1780–1812. Educated in the era of Enlightenment and eighteenth-century Atlantic revolutions, the architects of the Constitution of 1812 drew upon Catholic as well as liberal principles to consecrate a unique vision of a Hispanic nation.[61] Similarly, in the case of Spanish America, D. A. Brading maintains that "the invocation of historical and religious themes in patriotic rhetoric served to bridge the chasm dividing the elite from the masses."[62] Competing discourses of identity grounded in religion show that Europeans and Americans were not simply bearers of modern secular ideology but that they propounded complex and often contradictory nationalist projects.

This study centers on the ways in which actors within the public sphere, especially the clergy, articulated nationalism and the horizontal bonds of loyalty between the people and the state. Spaniards generally enjoyed freedom of expression beginning in 1808, but clerics also exploited the independent print media, gaining access to the public sphere in myriad ways, from publishing sermons to writing polemical pamphlets and establishing newspapers. The voices of the religious echoed from church walls, rang through public plazas, and were impressed onto the printed page. While historians agree that a majority of clerics continued to advance the ideals of absolutist monarchy during the epoch, it is paradoxical that a nationalist idiom preached from the pulpit merged a largely religious identity with the radical proposition of the sovereignty of the people.[63] During this transformative era, the clergy drew upon both the traditional language of hierarchy and order as well as the template of liberal nationalism, which sought to overturn absolutist power and monarchical privilege, in constructing sermons, religious instruction, and public pronouncements. Foregrounding religiosity provides a unique perspective into the competing discourses of Spanish, American, and Mexican identity and suggests possible reinterpretations of the origins of Hispanic nationalisms. Within the context of the Spanish Monarchy, Catholicism and the revolutionary ideology of liberal nationalism were intertwined, serving as the principal legacies of the period.

CONCLUSION

In sum, this is a book about the inherently incomplete process of the formation of national identity. Nationalism, as a set of discursive practices, represented an amalgamation of the culture and politics of the eighteenth-century Enlightenment and nineteenth-century liberalism. The task for historians, therefore, "lies in discerning the continuities and discontinuities of political cultures in which linguistic meanings are never entirely stable, never entirely fixed."[64] How were the foundations of nationality and citizenship articulated in the discourse of the time? How were these ideas received?

Documents housed in Madrid and Mexico City in the National History Archive, the Military Service Archive, and the national libraries of Spain and Mexico form the majority of evidence. In addition to macrohistorical analysis, municipal perspectives must be recovered in order to understand the urban revolutions of cities such as Valencia, Seville, and Puebla. Diocesan archives and municipal records, including letters, memoirs, and local edicts, are thus used to demonstrate the impact of nationalism at a local level. Royalists held onto the city of Puebla but failed to prevent insurgents from taking other significant towns and rural zones in the province, which was New Spain's second-most important economic region.[65]

Valencians followed a similar pattern. Local militias defeated invading French forces under Marshall Moncey in 1808, inspiring a torrent of nationalist sentiment in the region, but the city eventually fell to Napoleonic troops in January 1812. In both cases, nationalist discourse surged into the public sphere and provided a foundational mobilizing rhetoric of popular involvement in a nationalized struggle.

The Hispanic Enlightenment serves as an entrée into the discursive analysis of national identity in chapter 1. Men and women of letters, known as *luces* or *letrados,* visualized reason and faith as the wellsprings of a regenerated monarchy. By 1793, the violence and warfare of the French Revolution had swept the Spanish Monarchy into conflict with France. The subsequent French invasion of northern Spain precipitated a decisive turn toward reactionary patriotic calls to arms. Portraits of prominent clerics provide a corrective to stereotypes of fanatical churchmen bent upon upholding an archetypal absolutism. Significantly, the language these clerics used conferred legitimacy on the premise of national sovereignty and liberal ideals of constitutional government.

In chapter 2, I explore the ways in which clerics utilized Spanish nationalist rhetoric to mobilize soldiers at the local level to fight the French and to defeat *afrancesado* collaborators during the "revolution" of 1808. In Valencia and Seville, liberal uprisings displaced Old Regime notables and municipal authorities. By 1812, nationalist narratives of a unanimous uprising against the French had been profoundly influential. The Constitution of Cádiz established the principle of national sovereignty and united the territories of the monarchy into a transatlantic Spanish nation under the banner of Catholicism, drawing on the growing mythology of popular resistance. Thus the legal consecration of the people as the nation in the Constitution of 1812 built upon an extant nationalist language imbued with the spirit of earlier municipal revolts.[66] Clerics and nationalist supporters of the government exalted the unity of previously divided kingdoms. Typical of such rhetoric was the sentiment expressed by Juan Antonio Posse in 1812: "Now Galicians, Andalusians, Castilians, etc., we are Spaniards, and all men from both hemispheres are Spaniards."[67] The Atlantic had been erased as a geographical and political barrier, with declarations of unity proffered from all sides of constitutional Spain.

The emergence of the public sphere in the Spanish Monarchy is examined in chapter 3. Public discourse and the political sociability of salons, popular culture, and the print media firmly established a new cultural geography that flourished beginning in 1808. Although not generally construed as actors within a public sphere epitomized by rational-critical debate, clerics and missionaries nevertheless played a central role in defining the liberal state and the constitutional government inaugurated in 1812. The Catholic public sphere encompassed the spaces of exchange and dialogue created across the Spanish Monarchy, including the church as a defining arena of political contestation, and allowed for the transmission of new discourses of identity.

In chapter 4, religion, gender, and race inform questions of inclusion and exclusion as defined by citizenship. Religion provided for inclusive notions of national citizenship yet also sparked political debate over the historical legacy of the Inquisition and the meaning of Spanishness in 1813. In Spanish America, ideologies circulated within the public sphere that increasingly emphasized a particularist national heritage tied to indigenous roots, driving a wedge between peninsular Spain and American autonomists and separatists. In chapter 5, I discuss the pronounced change in collective identification in New Spain between 1810 and 1821. Americans who had preached the sanctity of Spanish nationalism from pulpits and in the press tended to abandon the inclusive rhetoric of a united transatlantic nation by the 1820s.[68] The city of Puebla provides a clear example of the tensions between the warring factions. Many American *ayuntamientos* proclaimed the Constitution of Cádiz in both 1812 and 1820 as they forged revolutionary political regimes while staving off insurgent military campaigns. Mexican nationalism had roots in a common Spanish nationalist idiom and centered identity on religiosity and a defense of liberty and the law, mixing a particularist ethnic discourse with the universal values of liberal constitutionalism. In the final chapter, I describe the enduring culture of liberal nationalism in Spain and in New Spain. Songs, poems, plays, and catechisms espoused competing visions of national identity yet drew upon the shared language of popular sovereignty and a civic nationalism first articulated in the period 1808-12. Particularist nationalist ideologies deployed by the 1820s, grounded in Catholic rhetoric and religious imagery, upheld the liberal promise of national sovereignty. Accordingly, the people possessed the natural right to govern and elect representatives to rule in their name.

Placing culture and the sociopolitical matrix of the Spanish state into the larger theoretical framework of national identity complicates the conventional wisdom that equates the nation with modernity in Europe and across imperial boundaries. An emergent Catholic public sphere provided the opening necessary for the process of nationalization to take root, and Catholicism continued to provide social cohesion in profoundly religious societies. Accordingly, this project analyzes history not as a state-sponsored elite project, but as a reciprocal engagement between classes and competing ideological dispositions. Religious instruction, sermons, songs, and periodicals—aspects of oral and print culture—formed integral parts of the politics of the time. Such documents reveal the origins and contingencies of Spanish nationalism across the diverse territories of the monarchy at the beginning of the nineteenth century.

Eric Van Young notes that "we know virtually nothing of the politically tinged homilies [priests] must have delivered, the impassioned Sunday sermons."[69] The lens of Catholicism and sermons in particular are a window into collective representations and the *mentalité* of the people who participated in the defining events of the time, which are not shaped by elite political powers and state institutions alone. Religion and tradition were bound together within a burgeoning nationalist script, challenging the logic that nations were constructed out of the ashes of a confessional society.

1

THE PEOPLE OF GOD

Patriotism, Enlightenment, and Religion

At the height of the Hispanic Enlightenment, during the reign of Carlos III (1759–88), *letrados* on both sides of the Atlantic interrogated the essence of identity and the meaning of place. As reformist thinkers challenged political, social, and economic norms and monarchists sought to maintain absolutist prerogative, questions of loyalty became a paramount concern. These issues hinged upon emotional bonds as well as reason, the hallmark of enlightened sensibility. In New Spain in 1778, the cleric Francisco de S. Cyrilo called upon parishioners to "reflect upon what Mexico is."[1] He proclaimed it to be among the most admired cities, having been rebuilt completely and restored to its former glory, with considerable support provided by the nobility, after the depredations of the initial Conquest. Given in honor of Our Lady of Guadalupe, his sermon privileged an aristocratic Spanish legacy inscribed in religious terms. He viewed Mexico City as a font of Catholicism, an outpost of devotion in a new world. In peninsular Spain, writing in the 1770s, José Cadalso also offered insights into the nature of political identification. Bitterly disparaging the nobility for having detached themselves from a sense of place, he asserted that nobles across Europe, to the detriment of their respective countries, lacked an animating spirit of patriotism and the heroic capacity to defend their homelands. He famously argued that there were no patriots in Spain, that the majority of Spaniards remained tied to superstitious notions of the miraculous and obsolete interpretations of their faith. While clerics in the Americas venerated the region within the larger framework of the monarchy, many peninsulars expressed disdain for localism and for what Cadalso referred to as a "blind" love of country. He explained that patriotism must be properly channeled in order to avoid "reverence for the ridiculous and deprecation of the respectable."[2]

Yet their epistemologies were not mutually exclusive, as both presented the commingling of reason and faith as the path toward enlightenment.

In the late eighteenth and early nineteenth centuries, subjects of the transatlantic Spanish Monarchy began to envision an inclusive *patria* as an artifact of a unique history and cultural patrimony. American and peninsular ideologues shaped the foundations of patriotic rhetoric as Bourbon ministers embarked upon a course of reform that would reshape the parameters of the state. While religion informed such discourses, the defining event of the age—the revolution of 1789—transformed the development of Enlightenment ideas across the Spanish Monarchy.[3] When the conflicts of the French Revolution spilled over into Spanish territory in 1793, and Spain declared war against the "barbarous French Nation," Spanish notables, with a great deal of support from the clergy, established a patriotic script that would be deployed again, on a much larger scale and with a different emphasis, in the aftermath of the Napoleonic occupation in 1808.[4]

THE PEOPLE OF GOD

In constructing Spanish identity, the clergy played a fundamental role in transforming the discourse of *el pueblo de dios* and *el pueblo católico* into that of *el pueblo español*. They posited the essentialist notion that all Spaniards were Christians and, as each term had the exact same meaning according to church doctrine, moved seamlessly from using one to the other.[5] In 1778, a cleric preaching in Cádiz dedicated a sermon to King Carlos III with the refrain: "Long live this Happy Nation! Long live the people of God! Long live Blessed Spain!"[6] Thirty years later, a Catalan ecclesiastic writing to the governing *junta* juxtaposed commonplace religious rhetoric with the language of national sovereignty, signifying that each term conveyed the same meaning: "Rejoice, Ministers of the King, now that you can direct your words tranquilly to the chosen people, to the Catholic people, *to the Spanish people*."[7] The chosen people, following in the path of the ancient Israelites, were by definition the Spanish people, the people of God.

Between the reign of Carlos III and Napoleon's invasion, prominent clergymen of various ideological persuasions modified the use of Catholic imagery and the conception and expression of Spanish patriotism, effectively forging the basis of an inclusive transatlantic nationalism. The conservative bishop of Santander, Raphael Thomás Menéndez de Luarca, the

Capuchin Miguel de Santander, and the theologian Joaquín Lorenzo Villanueva, among many others, were protagonists in both the War against the Convention as well as the War of Independence, and each manifested the shifting ideological positions characteristic of the time. While many historians identify Fray Diego José de Cádiz as the archetypal missionary of the age and focus on his reactionary ideology, these three figures represent the varied political views of the clergy.[8] From the halls of Spain's great cathedrals to its local parishes, important religious leaders as well as local priests manifested their political views and were integral to the elaboration of the various strands of Spanish patriotism.

Of the approximately 148,409 priests and religious in peninsular Spain at the end of the eighteenth century, regulars outnumbered the secular clerics active in parish work by more than two to one. Religious orders counted 53,098 members in addition to 24,471 nuns compared with only 22,000 curates.[9] In the viceroyalty of New Spain in 1810, there were 6,827 male diocesan and regular priests, mostly of Creole origin. In Mexico City, male and female religious comprised 1.5 percent of the population, compared to 2 percent for Madrid.[10] Despite the dominant notion that the Spanish church was an artifact of Old Regime conservatism, missionaries were unusually free to express their ideas, and male and female ecclesiastics played influential roles within Hispanic society. According to Antonio Domínguez Ortiz, missionaries "had as their ordinary audience the entire populace, without class distinctions,"[11] and this promoted the circulation of dissenting ideologies and of controversial opinions within an emergent public sphere. That dissent could exist in Old Regime Spain is evinced by the fact that the two most renowned missionaries of the time, Miguel de Santander and Diego de Cádiz, strayed from accepted church doctrine. Santander praised the efforts of Diego de Cádiz, and the two Capuchins shared a friendship and corresponded throughout their lives. Diego de Cádiz promoted the publication of Santander's sermons and wrote the prologue to an 1800 edition of his work. Despite their divergent ideological positions, they shared a desire to curb the abuses of royal power, to reform the country's moral shortcomings, and to avoid the anarchy and disorder that had plagued revolutionary France.[12] Diego de Cádiz even faced the wrath of the state when he spoke out against enlightened fiscal policy in the mid-1790s.

In a travel account first published in the early 1790s, the Englishman Joseph Townsend portrayed the emotional attachment that Spaniards felt toward church fathers. Yet the faithful—in his view a discerning and perceptive public—questioned aspects of church dogma. Townsend described the friar Diego de Cádiz preaching in the main square of Cartagena to more than ten thousand people on several successive nights: "This man . . . was constantly attended by a guard, to prevent his clothes from being torn from his back for relics. What he spoke was heard with the most profound attention. . . . One sermon, however, had a pernicious tendency; yet so deeply is a sense of honour, of gratitude, and of filial piety impressed on the human heart, that few appeared to relish his doctrine, or to be convinced by his arguments; but most of his hearers seemed to shudder with abhorrence, when he endeavoured to persuade them, that in cafes of heresy, they were in duty bound to accuse, at the tribunal of the inquisition, their nearest and their dearest friends."[13] Townsend maintained that Spaniards did not blindly accept and obey the word of priests and missionaries, yet he also conveyed a sense of the power and importance of religion in their lives. The reception of such sermons, mediated by cultural norms and the political structures of the time, played a critical role in the development of Spanish national identity.

PATRIOTISM UNDER THE OLD REGIME

Patriotism provided a linguistic repertoire for the construction of nationalist discourses. David Bell contends that patriotism signifies "an emotional attachment to a place thought of as 'home,' and more specifically . . . to that territorial entity whose rulers possess final coercive authority over the persons living within it."[14] Within the context of Indian history, C. A. Bayly defines patriotism as "the sense of loyalty to place and institutions which bound some Indians, even in the immediate pre-colonial period, to their regional homelands." These "'old patriotisms' . . . were neither unchanging antique identities, nor monolithic manifestations of popular resistance. Rather, they constituted a set of distinctive doctrines, ideologies and patterns of communication." He further argues that "old patriotisms created conceptual realms, clusters of institutions and popular sentiments which facilitated the rooting of later nationalism."[15] Thus Bayly challenges the idea that Indian nationalism was purely modern and derived primarily from European forms. If such claims successfully complicate earlier understandings that give primacy to the colonial origin of nationality in India, then both colonial and postcolonial nationalisms must be conceptualized as building upon earlier loyalties and ties. In the Spanish Monarchy during the early nineteenth century, patriotism built upon older forms of identification based on hierarchy and loyalty to the figure of the king and provided a leitmotif for subsequent nationalist narratives.

As historians such as D. A. Brading and Jorge Cañizares-Esguerra argue, late-eighteenth-century patriotism in the New World was a territory staked out in large part by Creole clerics.[16] These clerics constructed narratives examining the origins of colonial societies and emphasized the importance of indigenous civilizations prior to the arrival of the Spaniards. Cañizares-Esguerra contends that "patriotic epistemology . . . cannot be ascribed solely to Creoles. Spanish bishops who served terms in the colonies, for example, were among its leading representatives. The discourse of patriotic epistemology appears therefore broadly clerical rather than merely Creole." That Spanish bishops embraced patriotic texts written by Creoles provides evidence that the language used "was a reflection of aristocratic, racialized longings of members of ancien régime polities" and did not look to supplant the old order.[17] Patriotism thus appears as an effort to affirm a group identity embedded in the status quo, in contrast to nationalist rhetoric, which fundamentally posits the idea of equality within a national community of citizens.

Historians have not thoroughly examined the links between American patriotic discourses and peninsular thought that worked to delineate the parameters of national identification in the Hispanic world.[18] Few studies have analyzed the concurrent development of nationalist discourses in Spain and in the Americas. Benedict Anderson maintains the primacy of colonial nationalism without even mentioning the impact of the Napoleonic invasion of Spain and the promulgation of the Constitution of Cádiz.[19] Anderson highlights the role of Creole functionaries and the rise of print capitalism in the development of nationalist consciousness while neglecting the rise of liberalism throughout the Spanish dominions and the paucity of printing presses in peripheral areas as well as in zones occupied by insurgents.[20] He separates processes fundamentally tied together by political events, governing structures, and a syncretic culture. The origins of nationalism cannot be attributed solely to New World elites within the colonial system or to European philosophes, but can be found in the interstices of the links between colony and metropole, and in relationships between subjects and sovereign, citizens and government.

Sermons and public religious discourse shed light on links between Spanish and Spanish American patriotism and particularist nationalisms that have too often been viewed as peripheral to the larger currents of contemporary nationalisms.[21] One historian of New Spain notes that the identity of *novohispanos,* the people of New Spain, as members of an integrated Spanish state has not been adequately studied.[22] Likewise, historians studying European nationalisms have only recently foregrounded the imperial relationship with the metropole. In order to expand on this historiographical tradition, ideas and practices that unified the territories of the Spanish Monarchy as well as the fractures and disjunctures that displayed regional differences must be taken into account. American and Spanish identities have been presented as mutually exclusive or oppositional. Yet Catholicism and the language of national sovereignty provided a unifying idiom for Spanish national identities during the transition from the Old Regime to the period of liberal ascendancy. Nationalist discourses took shape around words such as *patria, nación,* and *pueblo* that incorporated both the radical connotations of revolutionary thought and the religious imagery of the Catholic world.

Antonio de Capmany's 1778 definition of *el pueblo,* associating the people with the working classes and the peasants, corresponded closely to the contemporary French usage of the term. Under the pseudonym Ramón Miguel Palacio, the Catalan Capmany wrote a discourse in defense of the political, economic, and cultural traditions of artisans and trade guilds. He identified the people of Spain with the popular classes and praised their admirable customs and traits: "What kind of thing is the people? In Greece and in ancient Rome, it signified the entire Nation, but among us, that are neither Greeks nor Romans, it signifies only a part of the nation. . . . The people, who are the most numerous class and the only one that works, form the physical force of a Nation. They also form the moral force in another sense, because the true character and the customs of a Nation are found in the private life of the most numerous class, that is the people; and the reason is that only with the people are these customs natural, constant and uniform."[23] As the term *el pueblo* took on respectable, rather than pejorative, connotations, Capmany conceptualized the culture of the popular classes as a specifically national heritage.

Similarly, the *patria* came to be an object of veneration. While in the seventeenth century the term simply denoted the place of one's birth, Enlightenment texts constructed the *patria* as a mythical homeland to be defended at all costs. Significantly, phrases such as "love of the fatherland" became commonplace and attached notions of duty and service to the idea of a belonging to a larger community. *Patria* came to be understood as an ideal manifestation of the state, endowed with neoclassical attributes. Because the definition was inseparable from ideas of liberty and freedom, the *patria* was worthy of respect and devotion, and to die in its defense was the ultimate honor.

In France, the terms *nation, patrie,* and *peuple* were linked through the new ideology of nationalism, which posited the nation as the people and transformed *patrie* into a term of emotive and sentimental power. By 1793, the *New Dictionary* had incorporated a legalistic framework into its definition of the people, mirroring that of the nation.[24] Used interchangeably, the terms "people" and "nation" came to have a new meaning in the context of the French Revolution. Thus the cleric Sieyès wrote in 1789 that "we can be free only with the people and by the people."[25] He equated liberty with representative government and implied that they were inextricably tied together. In Spain during the wars of the French Revolution, however, few patriots made such connections. Juan Pablo Forner, for example, writing in 1794 in *Amor de la patria,* denounced the pretensions of a sovereign people: "The origin of their decline [Athens and Rome] was in the inability of the people to manage the interests of the State effectively." He firmly maintained that "a Democracy is a battleground."[26] Spanish patriots such as Forner distinguished themselves as enlightened aristocratic elites, alluding to classical antiquity in order to extol the virtues of republicanism while distancing themselves from radical democratic ideals.

Historians have emphasized the Enlightenment (la Ilustración) in the early development of Spanish national consciousness, relegating the role of the clergy to the defense of a traditional Spain. For example, José Antonio Maravall and Juan Pablo Fusi highlight the works of Cadalso and Forner in arguing that "enlightened reformism articulated the Spanish nation."[27] Cadalso, writing in 1774, lamented that in Spain "now there is no patriotism, because now there is no patria." He relegated his beloved country to a premodern stage of historical development, in which the people embodied not a vital nation but rather a declining state. Cadalso focused on the concept of Spanish character, the indelible attributes of the Spanish people, arguing that "the Spanish character, in general, is composed of religion, valor and love for the sovereign on the one hand, and of vanity, contempt for industry (that foreigners refer to as laziness), and an overly developed propensity for love on the other." Cadalso clearly bound the idea of the Spanish character to religious devotion, but he did not praise religiosity as an admirable trait: "It appears, however, that such an ancient tradition, consecrated in Spain by the piety of our Spanish character, leads us to attribute to heaven the advantages won by our arms, thus they always appear extraordinary to us."[28] Forner also drew upon the idea of a distinct national character: "The love of the Country is the fundamental character of the Civil man; and this character almost always decides the destiny of Nations." While he frequently utilized terms such as *patria,* he did not equate the nation with its people. To the contrary, Forner completely dismissed the assertion that Spain could ever be governed by the people: "A large number of Philosophers, who have busied themselves inflaming human corruption in order to increase turmoil and the crimes of men, will say to you that there can only be love of the Country where the people are the artifice of their laws and their Politics. Moreover, I would like these ardent patrons of plebeian authority to tell me where a truly legislative people have ever existed. The people, Gentlemen, will always obey in reality, and will never lead except in appearance."[29] Cadalso and Forner articulated an elitist patriotism of enlightened absolutists, and they more often denigrated *la plebe* than eulogized the people. They did not advance the radical idea of the people as sovereign, the fundamental premise of nationalism. While laying the groundwork for nationalist discourses, Cadalso and Forner advocated a patriotic and traditional view of Spain and its cultural heritage.

Ecclesiastics such as the bishop of Salamanca, Antonio Tavira, and Miguel de Santander likewise preached from a patriotic template as they delivered sermons throughout Spain. For example, in 1775, Santander spoke to parishioners of the sanctity of "your patria" and glorified the history of "our nation, and . . . those men who are truly Spaniards."[30] In 1784, Tavira thanked almighty God for Spain's exceptional fortunes: "We come today in this sacred Temple to give thanks to our Lord for the great favors he has granted to the Spanish Nation." Tavira praised the historical grandeur of Spain and emphasized the idea of a strong national character: "I would like, Gentlemen, once again to inflame you with that true and legitimate love of our Country . . . of that love that has always been the distinctive character of our Nation, and was in our elders the fecund origin of so many virtues and strengths."[31] In a 1791 funeral oration, one prebendary in Mexico City honored the history of sacrifice among Spanish military leaders, "whose triumphs, victories and noble deeds will extol for all time the illustrious Nation that produced them."[32] Lauding Spanish expansion in the Old World and in the New, the missive celebrated the exploits of controversial figures such as the Duke of Alba, Fernando Álvarez de Toledo, Gonzalo Fernández de Córdoba, and the Velascos, viceroys of New Spain. He repeatedly invoked the allegory of the chosen people, with references to the "Christian people" and to Spain as "the City (Pueblo) of God."

Clerics narrated a complex tale of conquest and conversion, weaving together the unifying threads of Spanish history. While Cadalso and Forner played an important role in the articulation of Spanish identity, clergymen reached a wide audience, preaching patriotic homilies to a diverse array of parishioners across urban and rural Spain and Spanish America.

ENLIGHTENMENT IDEALS OF REASON, REFORM, AND RELIGION

Unlike the French absolutist monarchy, the Spanish government fostered Enlightenment ideals as key nobles, functionaries, and clerics embraced reform. European writers such as the Baron de Montesquieu and Adam Smith influenced the highest royal officials and penetrated Spain's notorious Inquisitorial regime. Spaniards largely rejected the anti-Catholicism of the philosophes and instead focused on scientific, educational, and economic reforms that epitomized the new currents of thought in the eighteenth century.[33]

A diversity of practice and instruction existed within the church.[34] As the Enlightenment flourished, however, traditional religious discourse continued to emphasize the obligations and duties of the subject. The often-used metaphor of the body politic symbolized the hierarchical state.[35] According to Joaquín Lorenzo Villanueva in his *Catecismo del estado* (Catechism of the State), "members [of the state], being unequal between themselves, and holding distinct positions, are subject to a single head."[36] Like-minded clerics proclaimed the inequality inherent in the natural world and projected similar notions onto the framework of the state. By exalting the harmony and order of nature, they sought to legitimize the absolutist monarchy. Spanish clerics often accentuated the ties between Catholic monarchs during the late eighteenth century. For example, sermons were given throughout Spain in the name of the French Bourbon Louis XV to honor him upon his death in 1774. In Seville, Francisco Nuñez began by stressing reverence to "Louis XV: the name sweetens the lips, and brings happiness to the heart." He referred to the king as "the Father of his peoples, beloved by his faithful Subjects."[37] Masses given at this time lavished praise on the French monarch and lacked any form of oppositional sentiment. Clerics grounded their discourse in the commonalities of the absolutist states, linking the Bourbon families ruling in France and Spain.

Old Regime authority centered upon relationships and bonds that mirrored the patriarchal structure of the family. Sermons such as those by Miguel de Santander commonly emphasized the central pillars of society—order and deference. Santander envisioned a paternal, functional world: "In all the kingdoms the Monarchs reigned like fathers: their vassals obeyed like sons for the love of their king and for the principles of their sacred religion."[38] The language used—*gente* rather than *pueblo, vasallo* rather than *ciudadano, estado* rather than *nación*—reinforced the idea of obligation and submission in contrast to the emotional ties of nationalism.

Jansenists, in line with Protestant dissenters of the time, had begun to renovate the Catholic faith during the course of the eighteenth century. What Pamela Voekel calls "reformed piety" advanced individualistic principles and undermined Old Regime church privileges.[39] Jansenists positioned themselves as quintessential Enlightenment reformers. Richard Herr argues that "an alliance . . . between partisans of enlightenment and those churchmen whom their enemies with little justification had labeled 'Jansenists'" came about precisely during the period of the French Revolution.[40] Although they were not directly linked to French Jansenists, Hispanic Jansenists were primarily concerned with similar ideals of "jurisdiction and authority, morality, spirituality, and education."[41] Herr puts primacy on the religious origins of Enlightenment thought and the role of clerics such as Benito Jerónimo Feijóo in advocating reform and skepticism within Spain. Conflict with the Jesuits also connected Spanish Jansenists to their French counterparts. According to Herr, "the first implication of the term 'Jansenist' as it appeared in Spain therefore was opposition to the theological and moral teachings of the Jesuit order. A second implication arose indirectly from the traditional mission of the Company of Jesus to be the right arm of the papacy."[42] And while Hispanic Jansenists allied themselves with a monarchy amenable to Enlightenment thought, their ideology and reforming bent can certainly be labeled as a form of dissent against the prevailing views of doctrinaire Catholic clerics.

Many Jansenists emphasized an interiority that complemented exterior manifestations of devotion.[43] According to Voekel, in her study of eighteenth- and nineteenth-century Mexico City and Veracruz, "because [reformers believed] God bestowed salvation through grace in the prepared heart and through that alone, and because the road to God was thus within, much of the Church's formerly necessary mediation between the individual soul and the Divine summarily evaporated."[44] Sermons such as those given by José Ruiz de Conejares epitomized this new conception of religion as an increasingly private concern. In a 1793 mass, Ruiz de Conejares urged his parishioners in Mexico City to look inward for sources of spiritual renewal: "We ourselves are temples of God. Yes, we are temples of God consecrated in baptism and we have inside of ourselves an altar, that is our heart, on which we must offer to the Lord pure, saintly, pleasing hosts and sacrifices consumed in the fire of the most tender and sincere love."[45] The new doctrine of faith, based upon interior forms of piety and moderation rather than exterior or performative displays, represented a rupture with baroque Catholic practices. While scholars continue to place a great deal of interpretive weight upon the Protestant Reformation's appeal to inner spirituality and the use of one's reason, similar dynamics emerged in the Hispanic Atlantic world during the Enlightenment.

Historians have viewed the use of vernacular language as representative of a fundamental divide between reformist Protestantism and supposedly static Catholic culture. David Zaret, for example, emphasizes the particularity of the English case, coupling his arguments on Protestant inner faith with descriptions of calls for individual Englishmen to read the sacred text of the Bible. Arguably, an analogous phenomenon occurred in the Hispanic world by the eighteenth century.[46] Officially sanctioned by the authorities, individual engagement with biblical passages contributed to breaking the clerical monopoly on religious discourse in Spain and in the Americas. Benedict Anderson claims that "Protestantism was always fundamentally on the offensive, precisely because it knew how to make use of the expanding vernacular print-market being created by capitalism, while the Counter-Reformation defended the citadel of Latin."[47] With the 1783 decision of the Inquisition giving the faithful permission to read the Bible in the vernacular, and the 1789 license to publish a Castilian translation of the Bible, reformers had altered the spiritual landscape of the Catholic world. Although Anderson's argument privileges Protestant Europe, the increasing use of the vernacular in Catholic states opened up new spaces in which to imagine the national community. As church leaders implemented these policies, clerics such as Joaquín Lorenzo Villanueva called for reading the Bible in the vernacular. He wrote a tract on the teaching of the scriptures in vernacular tongues in 1791, and adherents defended his position against opponents of reform: "Some years have passed since the translated holy Bible was in the hands of the people, and the treatment of its reading in vulgar languages was printed and well received by the public."[48] Not only did clerics such as Villanueva pave the way for the reading of the Bible in Spanish, but they justified their positions on the grounds that the public overwhelmingly approved of their actions. By appealing to the common good, clerics inoculated their arguments against criticism leveled by detractors and carried the debate into the public forum.

The basis of political authority in Old Regime European polities also came under attack at this time. Ideas expounding on the contractual (and consensual) nature of the relationship between subjects and the sovereign began to erode the theory of divine right and established the framework for a modern identity with its basis in national sovereignty. Zaret contends that, within a religiously oriented public sphere in England, Puritan covenant theology laid the foundations for a contractual relationship between people and God. He notes that the public's use of reason allowed them to contract with a heavenly being no longer shrouded in mystery by the keepers of sacred textual authority. This, in turn, opened up possibilities for radical political change in seventeenth-century England. Zaret does not posit a unidirectional relationship between religious reform and political change, but implies that the reverse may well have been true. Calls to open the political system may have affected religious practices and the church as well.[49]

Yet social contract theories had been in currency in the Hispanic world dating to sixteenth- and seventeenth-century thinkers such as the theologian Francisco Suárez and Fernando Vázquez de Menchaca.[50] These legal arguments became the basis of instruction in universities across the Spanish Monarchy. Joaquín Marín y Mendoza, installed by Carlos III as chair of law at San Isidro, published an influential work in 1776 on the theory of natural rights. Natural law, in the opinion of Marín y Mendoza, proceeded from the word of God, and as such could trump the rights of a monarch who abused power. Although he favored absolute monarchy, Marín y Mendoza argued that natural law dictated that kings owed their allegiance to the people vis-à-vis an original pact binding them together. Such works, serving as required reading for students of natural law, were central tools in advocating the contract theory of the origin of society.[51]

Under Carlos III, the government implemented a number of measures that undercut traditional practices characteristic of the Old Regime state. For example, royal instructions on teaching natural law—a subject required of all students of civil and canon law by 1786 in Valencia—included "subjecting always the lights of our human reason to those of the Catholic religion and showing above all the necessary union of religion, morality, and politics."[52] This view was consistent with European trends in Catholic and Protestant universities of the time. Their highlighting of reason as an instrumental aspect of faith shows that Enlightenment reformers perceived no inherent conflict between spiritual matters of the church and rational concerns of the state. Concomitantly, many clerics gave voice to the language of reason in pulpits across the Spanish Monarchy, emphasizing science and natural law among the other hallmarks of Enlightenment thought. Sermons upholding natural law as a manifestation of patriotism became increasingly common during the period. One cleric exhorted parishioners to embrace a love of the country and of the sovereign, indelibly linking such sentiment to "that love that authorizes all of our natural laws and our Religious laws."[53] Many such sermons highlighted the connections, rather than inherent contradictions, between law, patriotism, and religion. The Enlightenment in the Hispanic world, as a movement of reform that remained tied to the religious culture of the time, significantly diverged from the pronounced secularism of prominent French philosophes.

During the late eighteenth century and into the nineteenth century, currents of enlightened thought coursed through all levels of the church hierarchy in Spain and Spanish America. Influential voices within the Catholic church continued to emphasize reason in conjunction with faith. While many remained hostile to the new ideas, leading churchmen adhered to enlightened absolutism. For example, in a funeral oration for Carlos III in Seville, the cleric Manuel Gil lamented: "What part of the government has not been enlightened by Carlos? Natural and international law: public and particular law: relations between the Sovereign and his vassals: their obligations toward him . . . paternal authority . . . filial authority: forces for the defense of the State."[54] Gil outlined in great detail the enlightened reforms enacted by Carlos III, from agricultural improvements and scientific advancements to administrative and educational change. He maintained that "history does not offer in any Nation an example of the rapidity of progress that Spain has made in the reign of Carlos. . . . Through an admirable revolution, the science of religion has united solidity to subtlety: the science of laws has united the profundity of reason to erudition."[55] Due to the king's unflagging support of the natural sciences, poetry, oratory, manufacturing, and myriad other fields, Gil claimed, the reign of Carlos III represented a great revolution. He ended with a nod to the harmony between religion and justice: "I want to . . . show you the dignified origin of this love for justice—the soul of all enterprises—which is found in moderation, in kindness, in gentleness, and above all in religion, and, with more reason than Solomon to deserve such beautiful praise: for thy peace thou wast beloved."[56] This eulogy for a monarch that espoused both reason and faith symbolized the contingencies and possibilities of a reformed Catholicism that encompassed the philosophical premises of the Hispanic Enlightenment.

THE WAR AGAINST THE CONVENTION

The watershed moment of the late eighteenth century occurred shortly after Carlos III died in 1788, when violence and regicide became the symbols of a political revolution that had spiraled out of control, and the government of Carlos IV (1789–1808) turned its back on an Enlightenment legacy. Ministers such as the Conde de Floridablanca enacted a strict policy of censorship and marked off an ideological *cordon sanitaire* with France to prevent ideas of liberty and equality from entering Spanish territory.[57] While radical figures like José Marchena called for the convocation of the Cortes, the historic Spanish representative body, in 1794, the War against the Convention (1793–95) provoked reactionary sentiment directed toward revolutionary France. Ecclesiastics effectively mobilized the population in peninsular Spain against what they viewed as a heretical and godless enemy symbolized by the representatives of the French National Assembly and leaders such as Maximilien Robespierre.

The Spanish clergy became protagonists in the War against the Convention. Ecclesiastics preached a doctrine of holy war against the savage specter of anarchy and sacrilege and explicitly appealed to the faithful to defend themselves against the enemies of religion. Miguel de Santander gave a battle cry typical of the time: "It will be better to die gloriously in war than to see the formidable evils that menace our country and our sacred religion come to pass."[58] That Diego de Cádiz titled his pamphlet *El soldado-católico, en guerra de religión* (The Catholic Soldier, in a War of Religion) symbolized the way the clergy promoted the struggle against the French. Writing in 1793, Diego de Cádiz instructed the Catholic soldier, as "a good vassal," to fight against "the Assembly of France, that multitude, not now of Kings, nor of Sovereign Princes of the land, but of infamous, seditious and perverse men."[59] Although the people of France were not conceived of as the enemy, the war was understood as a sacred duty. Cries of "Long live the King and death to the Assembly!" rang through the streets rather than "Death to Napoleon, death to the French," which would echo from pulpits throughout Spain by 1808.[60] Less than three months after the war began with France in 1793, a sermon in Seville praised France as a generous nation while castigating the radical National Assembly: "No, it is not the generous Nation of the French that has lost its way: it is a cabal of blind, numb men, who are unjustly referred to as the National Assembly."[61] Spanish clerics presented the 1793 war as a religious war against the architects of the bloody revolution in France.

The polarizing effects of the 1790 Civil Constitution of the Clergy and the radical nature of de-Christianization campaigns caused many conservative French clerics to emigrate to other parts of Catholic Europe. Compounding the situation, the French National Assembly ordered all noncompliant religious to leave the country in August 1792. Exiled French priests residing in Spain contributed to the spread of a conservative patriotism in denouncing the violence of the revolution.[62] Sermons given by French ecclesiastics emphasized the tenets of deference and duty, yet often adopted the language of the revolution. Juan Carlos de Coucy, the bishop of La Rochelle, who had taken residence in Guadalajara, bitterly denounced the regicide of Louis XVI: "I favor with his Omnipotence the manifest desire to reedify the Church, protect the Country, avenge the State, liberate the French people from the cruelest tyrants, and save the Monarchy." Similarly, he vilified the French people: "Detestable people, unbridled people, you have in front of your eyes the body, divided from that Sacred Head, against whom you have conspired so much." Yet Coucy recognized the impact of the new political language even as he decried its excesses: "Oh, language that makes humanity wail, sentiments that degrade Nature." While he condemned the French for the regicide of Louis XVI, he tellingly referred to "the French people" rather than to the subjects or vassals of the king. Patriotic sentiment and references to the French as a people were interwoven into his antipathy toward the revolution and "the vile Populace" that brought down the monarch.[63] Clerics such as Coucy began to manipulate the idea of sovereignty and place it firmly within a traditionalist vision of emotional attachment. That references to the French people appeared in the rhetoric of reactionary clergy signaled an important break from the past, illustrating how ecclesiastics received and transformed revolutionary ideas. Sermons became a powerful weapon of propaganda against the French Revolution, while at the same time incorporating its new terminology. The War against the Convention brought the linguistic constructions of the French Revolution to like-minded absolutist clerics, who began to interpret revolutionary language in new ways.

The conservative bishop of Santander, Raphael Thomás Menéndez de Luarca, articulated a reactionary rhetoric clearly impacted by events in France. In propagating the war effort against the Convention, he wrote a series entitled *Opúsculos Christiano-Patrios* (Christian-Patriotic Opuscules) attacking the French campaigns against the church and the values of the revolution. He conceived of the war as a struggle against "the licentious French" rather than as against the entire nation, incorporating predominantly religious imagery and symbols within the treatise. Yet the discourse of Menéndez de Luarca encapsulated a period of instability as the language of the Old Regime became infused with revolutionary terminology and formed the basis of an incipient nationalism. He implored: "What people are the people that preach, the strong people, the valiant people, the courageous people, the people that in other times vanquished their enemies, greater than the French are today in number and strength; finally, what people are the Spanish people?" In addition, he composed a distinct version of the rallying cry: "Long live the King: Long live the Nation: Breathe, Spain: Courage, beloved people." In referring to the people as *el pueblo español* in numerous sermons, he rendered an emerging conception of national identity by asking: "Are the people of God today the Spanish people?" Thus he sanctified the nation and the people as chosen by God: "You will be called the Holy people; Nation that God sought."[64] Centering on the specificity of the Spanish people as an organic symbol of the nation not expressly linked to republican ideals of citizenship, Menéndez de Luarca began to form a dynamic vision of particularist Spanish nationalism.

Diego de Cádiz similarly fomented a religious vision of the struggle against France, claiming that "only obedience, piety, religion, zeal, charity, and justice have impelled you to take up arms." Duty obliged the Spanish soldier to fight against the enemies of religion, and priests were expected to recruit from the pulpit: "In the written Law was the charge of Priests to exhort Soldiers to the holy war of Religion." Diego de Cádiz portrayed the enemy as heretical, bent upon the destruction of the church. He argued that "with the pretext of liberty they convert the sinning against Gospel Law into unbridled license, and they deny that Jesus Christ is our sole Sovereign and Lord. . . . The liberty, which they foolishly boast of, and sustain with fear, has always been the root and origin of all heresies, and even of all sins."[65] A torrent of religious rhetoric from ecclesiastics throughout Spain condemned the French and the ideals of liberty and equality. For example, the enlightened cleric Manuel Gil denounced the ideology of "liberty, liberty, that extinguishes hierarchies, destroys the Clergy, ruins temples and altars, prohibits religion . . . and upon those it falls, and ends everything, foolish cry of this horrible war."[66] Miguel de Santander impugned the memory of French revolutionaries and their battle cries of equality: "The memory of *Egalité, Marat, Robespierre* and other monsters that have been at the helm of the memorable French revolution will be abhorrent through all the centuries."[67] To combat the advances of the philosophes and their sacrilegious attacks against the church, the clergy projected the ideal of the Catholic soldier. In a 1794 sermon dedicated to the king, Diego de Cádiz described the Spanish soldier as "full of the zeal of the honor of God and carrying the obedience owed to the holy mother Church and of the desire of the greater good of those who have put their armies in the field."[68] The word *patria* did not appear in the text at all, underscoring the war's fundamentally religious character.

Few ecclesiastics during the War against the Convention drew on the patriotic sentiment inherent within emerging conceptions of *patria* or *nación,* instead referring to *el reyno, la monarquía,* or *el estado.* The emotional connotations of *patria* had not supplanted the Old Regime conception of the state, in which the Catholic faith provided an outlet for devotion and attachment to a higher power. Villanueva's *Catecismo del estado* from 1793 represented the traditional view of the state and the centrality of religion within Spanish society. Writing at the height of the radical phase of the French Revolution, Villanueva firmly warned against all forms of unrest and disorder. He repeatedly downplayed the rights of the people in relation to those of a prince. In reacting to the French Revolution and the successful overthrow of the monarchy, he forcefully argued for the divine right of kings. In his introduction, Villanueva instructed, "He that has his eyes closed or blinded with the spirit of philosophism, open them to the light of the truth, and you can understand, as all good Catholics must, the intimate tie of the true Religion with all the ages and states and conditions of man; with paternal, domestic and political societies; with private and public order; with the offices of subjects and of Princes." He defined the state as "the civil society of a kingdom or of the many united under the same laws, and governed by one Prince." In contrast, Villanueva neither defined *nación* nor included it in the "index of notable themes" at the end of the text. *Patria* appeared with a warning: "He who attempts to shake off public authority does not serve the Country. Duties owed to the Country are inseparable from those owed to the Prince."[69] Thus, in denigrating philosophes and their libertine ideology, Villanueva posited hierarchy, obedience, and religion as counterweights to patriotic ideals, which had the potential to be disruptive and dangerous. He demanded that loyalty be sworn to the person of the sovereign king rather than to an abstract notion of a *patria*.

Villanueva worked throughout the text to combat the revolutionary idea of the sovereignty of the people. He demanded absolute subjection to legitimate authority, even in cases of the abuse of power. For example, he contended that "insubordination of vassals is not permitted even against bad Princes, because order must be preserved in everything and always." Linking the dangers of disobedience with French enlightened philosophy, he argued: "Libertine philosophers who say that man is born free, in what sense do they speak of liberty? [They speak] . . . of civil liberty that is opposed to subordination to legitimate authority, and is also called independence." By emphasizing the atrocities committed in the name of the French Revolution, Villanueva, along with many clerics of the time, in effect was fighting to contain revolutionary sentiment within Spanish borders. In constructing the religious foundations of the state, Villanueva denied the sovereignty of the people and insisted that "the authority and power of Princes emanates from God, who does not affirm even once that it comes from the people." He did not make reference to the Spanish people, and, similar to Diego de Cádiz, seldom utilized patriotic language.[70]

Other religious, who had not embraced the extremes of counterrevolutionary ideology, continued to foster patriotic sentiment after the War against the Convention. The complex case of the missionary Miguel de Santander shows how enlightened currents of thought impacted the church and constituted a fundamental challenge to Catholic dogma. Santander was as widely known as Diego de Cádiz and traveled throughout Spain preaching an unorthodox blend of Enlightenment rationality and accepted hierarchical doctrine.[71] Despite the tenor of his anti-French diatribes during the War against the Convention, his subsequent sermons portended the transition from the Old Regime to liberal government in Spain, combining traditional discourse with the language of patriotism. He tied the idea of *patria* to the Catholic religion, anticipating the way in which many clerics constructed the nation in the nineteenth century.[72] Similarly, Santander maintained that "the idea of God is evidently incompatible with a multiplicity of religions," espousing traditional ideas of the position of Catholicism within the state.[73]

In his 1798 *Carta de un religioso español, amante de su patria* (Letter from a Religious Spanish Patriot), Santander departed from convention in vehemently arguing for a system of representative government and limits on royal power. He praised the Cortes of Aragon as an early example of republicanism to be emulated: "In Aragon the form of government was monarchical as in Castile, but in some parts the spirit and the principles of their constitution were republican. The actual exercise of sovereignty pertained to the Cortes or to the Estates General. . . . This simple enumeration of privileges inherent to the Estates General of Aragon and to the rights enjoyed by Justice clearly shows that no more than a portion of very limited powers remained in the hands of the king." He grounded the new ideology of liberalism with references to the past assemblies of the Cortes, which represented the true republican spirit of Spain. He justified his position by claiming that "in Castile the king exercised a rather limited executive power, and legislative power resided in the Cortes. . . . These assemblies of our nation were ancient and their origin can be found in the first constitution of our civil state; that is to say in the most remote centuries."[74] By this time, Santander supported a form of constitutional monarchy increasingly at odds with the status quo. Such a model laid the foundation for liberal ideology and a civic Spanish nationalism.

Enlightenment ideology continued to resonate across the monarchy during the reign of Carlos IV. Santander delivered messages unequivocally influenced by the tenets of rationality and scientific inquiry during the last decade of the eighteenth century and the early nineteenth century. In a sermon published in 1802 entitled *Del carácter del christiano* (On the Character of the Christian), he emphatically urged men to embrace their "rational nature" and a "practical understanding of themselves" in order to achieve salvation. The ultimate measure of the Christian man was reason: "This is to be a man of goodness, to live in conformity to reason. . . . Live as rational men, then value being one: reason will be that which rules your thoughts, your words and your works."[75] These three tenets of man's rationality constituted the pillars of what emerged as Hispanic liberalism, endowing men with the right to free speech (*los pensamientos*), freedom of the press (*las palabras*), and the freedom to elect a representative government or rebel against a despotic state (*las obras*).

Prior to the War of Independence, clerics combined the language of patriotism with a fundamentally Old Regime discourse. Relationships between states were emphasized rather than antagonisms, and conflicts continued to be interpreted in terms of religion. In 1801, Antonio Tavira spoke of France as "a nation united with ours in a firm alliance and friendship through close ties." In addition, he noted that "in spite of the freedom of religion in the French Republic, and of the calamitous times that followed their Revolution . . . it has nonetheless been said in public tracts . . . that seven and a half of eight parts profess the Catholic religion." He emphasized "the mildness with which the actual government comports itself and [that it] turned to receive in the heart of the nation many that only fury and cruelty had obliged to emigrate."[76] Clerics did not view the French nation as the enemy and praised the moderation of the government. Spanish patriotic discourse focused on religion, and arguments in support of popular sovereignty remained muted. For example, in a sermon from 1805, Josef María de Miera Pacheco mirrored the rhetoric of Diego de Cádiz during the War against the Convention: "If the Country is invaded, religion wants all of us as soldiers." He advanced patriotic sentiments while maintaining traditional ideas of the body politic and the obligations inherent within a hierarchical society: "The rule of Christianity is that one must love with preference the body of which one is a member . . . and dedicate oneself entirely to the service and utility of their Country."[77] As clerics mixed the language of patriotism with a defense of privilege and hierarchy, the structures of the Old Regime persisted across the Spanish Monarchy, enduring until the French invasion in 1808.

THE LANGUAGE OF NATIONAL SOVEREIGNTY AND UNANIMITY OF FAITH

The sovereignty of the Spanish people was declared throughout all regions of the monarchy in the aftermath of French occupation, breaking with the language of absolutism and the idea that all power emanated from God. No longer did a king reign by divine right, but authority resided in the people of the nation. Liberals as well as absolutists exalted the virtues and heroic nature of the Spanish people. In order to legitimate the power of the provincial *juntas,* the Junta Central, and the Cortes of Cádiz, Spaniards proclaimed the sovereignty of the people in whose name they would govern.

While many pledged fidelity to King Fernando VII, held captive by Napoleon in France, the contractual theory of government dominated the thinking of those ruling in his name. In order to justify the provincial *juntas* and reestablish the rule of law, leaders claimed that sovereignty had reverted to the people in the absence of a king. The immediate ramifications of this principle took shape in declarations upholding the rights of the people as the voice of the nation. Rather than being subjects, obedient vassals of the king, Spaniards claimed an identity as integral components of the national community with the accompanying rights of the national citizen. According to the periodical *Semanario Patriótico* (Patriotic Weekly), "sovereignty resides, then, essentially in the Spanish nation, with the exclusion of Fernando VII, of his father and his grandfather, because it resided in the nation even before there were kings."[78] The idea that the sovereignty of the people preceded the establishment of monarchy was of crucial importance, demonstrating the basic premise of natural law theory. As early as September 1808, the bishop of León, Pedro Luis Blanco, argued that the people, as the original repository of sovereign power, had reclaimed their natural right to govern:

> The interest and the spirit that strengthen the valor of the solider are one, as are the anxieties of those who direct and lead, and the hardships of those who, driven by their zeal for religion, for the King and the country, are brought together as representatives of the people and as loyal repositories of their knowledge and their trust, to guard parts of the government until the fundamental laws regain their authority and vigor. . . . Now the Provincial Juntas, sending their commissioners to Court, deserve pure zeal and disinterest for the common good, returning to the center that part of authority that the people had conferred upon them temporarily.[79]

His sentiments echoed the statement issued on June 1, 1808, in León, one of the first regions to rise up against the French in the name of Fernando VII. Similar to dozens of decrees from 1808, the proclamation of León's Junta General de Gobierno asserted the right to represent the province as the legitimate local authority: "A Junta, composed of individuals from the Town Council and of other notables who wanted to join it . . . and others of the class of Deputies of the people themselves, in whom are deposited Sovereign authority . . . [,] dictates all the necessary measures to shake off the domination of the French."[80] The radical notions explicit in the language of national sovereignty became common currency after 1808 and changed the relationship between the king and the people of the newly defined nation.

The term *el pueblo español* became central to the new ideology of liberal nationalism. The Spanish people formed the nation, and representatives governed in their name and that of the captive King Fernando VII. The nation and the people were synonymous, and terms such as "monarchy," "kingdom," and "state" fell into disfavor among ardent liberals. Whereas prior to 1808, few clerics had utilized such revolutionary language, by the summer and fall of 1808 nationalist ecclesiastics all over Spain delivered their message of resistance to the sovereign people. Bishops such as Blanco argued that "your pained voices accelerated armament, ended the apparent apathy of your sons, who raced to pursue the enemy and drive them from your houses that they were infesting; and with the help of God the few will be taken from our Spain who have not died or been taken prisoner by our glorious armies, vanquishers of those judged invincible. Now, with experience, the loyal Spanish people have seen how laudable was their clamor for defense."[81] Similar to accounts appearing in the press and in pamphlets from the time, the oratory of the clergy underscored the idea that the Spanish people were the protagonists in the struggle against the French nation.

The story of the biblical guerrilla leader Judas Maccabaeus became a popular allegory in sermons that bridged past and present, providing an iconic image of a people's leader struggling against religious persecution and foreign military aggression. Judas was heralded as having "enhanced his people's glory" and as being "like a lion in his exploits." In the end, although he was killed, "he [had] rallied a people near to destruction."[82] The comparisons to Spain in 1808 were not lost upon priests on both sides of the Atlantic, and the religious invoked the ferocity of the Spanish lion to save the people and salvage their church.[83] The friar Manuel de la Virgen del Rosario, preaching in Antequera (outside of Málaga) in 1808, presented the story of Judas Maccabaeus as a contemporary morality tale. Tellingly, he recounted the advice of Judas and his brothers, "who said among themselves, 'Let us restore the shattered fortunes of our people; let us fight for our nation and for the holy place.'"[84] In quoting the Bible, however, he amended the original passage and inserted "Spain" as the signifier of the holy place. His interpretation read: "Let us restore the spirit of the people and the shattered nation . . . the success of this battle is dependent upon the conservation of our liberty, the sanctity of religion, and the happiness of all Spain."[85] Spaniards recognized their own struggle against Napoleonic tyranny and apostasy refracted through the lens of the biblical Book of the Maccabees. Accordingly, Judas waged war against Antiochus, the Syrian king, by enlisting the aid of the people as guerrilla leaders. Judas ultimately defeated a Syrian contingent and revived the temple, the symbol of the Jewish faith. His victories resonated with early Spanish successes and inspired hope that Napoleon, as the incarnation of a new and more terrible Antiochus, would be vanquished.

Sermons appropriating a discourse of victimization, of the sacred polluted by the (French) profane, were emblematic of the period. One priest maintained that "in light of these cruelties, of these horrors and blasphemies, we should assume in our hearts that our powerful warriors, and even all of the Spanish people, share the same greatness of faith, the same sense of piety, the same religious zeal."[86] The Spanish clergy constructed a national identity based on the idea of the people as the spirit of the nation and on their will to unanimously resist the French. Victories in early battles of the war, such as Bailén, were not attributed simply to God but to the heroic struggle of the Spanish people.

The clergy helped to create a mythological aura that defined and gave meaning to the war in Spain. In a sermon given in 1809, Ignacio Gutiérrez y Polop articulated a version of Spanish nationalism representative of the views of many ecclesiastics. Preaching in the Basque province of Biscay, he dedicated his address to the glorious people of Spain, regenerated after having suffered through the ministerial despotism of Manuel Godoy and the French invasion of 1808: "I am interested solely in the SPANISH NATION; in this part of the globe, that in spite of its size, should be renowned throughout all the world as the true people of God. Yes: as REGENERATED SPANIARDS. I will declare to you that they have proven, with true character, to be YOUR PEOPLE."[87] These emotional nationalist sentiments drew upon both liberal discourse and earlier forms of religious identification in Spain, allowing clerics to conflate the "people of God" with the "people of Spain." He venerated Spanish courage in the face of an implacable enemy and predicted that the war would be remembered forever by all nations: "THE SPANISH PEOPLE are made immortal in your cause, and their name will be respected in all nations as the UNRELENTING DEFENDER of the rights of their God." In addition, he argued for a religious interpretation of the people and the nation: "the SPANISH PEOPLE are the *loyal repository of the laws of their God.*" Just as liberal nationalists argued that the people were the original repository of sovereignty and the laws of the nation, traditionalists used similar language to claim the people had been entrusted with God's laws.

Priests such as Gutiérrez y Polop defined the war in terms of the initial spark of revolution in Madrid. When "the Tyrant presented his brother Joseph as King; when it heard the decreed extermination of the priesthood, and the profanation of the Temples; when he perceived the most sacred moral and religious laws to be reviled . . . the Lion [of Spain] arose furious, defying his enemy." Thus for Spanish nationalist clerics, el Dos de Mayo (the Second of May, 1808) became "the day of mourning, in which SPAIN saw with fear the overturning of their Cabinet, the horrible licentiousness of customs, cold assassination, the most cruel infanticide, the shooting of the Priesthood." Accordingly, vengeance for such atrocities came on the fields of Bailén, and with cries of "*Long live Spain,* [the soldiers] assaulted the sacrilegious Dupont, and obliged him to surrender his army."[88] This interpretation of the war contrasted greatly with the rhetoric generated during the War against the Convention. By 1808, the people had become the focus of the discourse, replacing God as protagonist, and references to divine intervention dwindled. While clerics continued to highlight religion and the importance of faith, they used the language of liberal nationalism to glorify *el pueblo español.*

From the outset of the war, ecclesiastics called men to arms against the invading French forces. Clergy all over Spain explicitly exhorted Spaniards to attack the armies of Napoleon. D. F. J. Molle, an ecclesiastic from Málaga, implored men to take up arms: "Now, Spaniards, we must deploy all the means of our most pure patriotism: multiply donations, enlist all those capable of taking up arms, hear the noise of the cannon and of the hammer throughout all of the Kingdom: open, form arms factories: build cannons: there is no other occupation than war, this holy war, just, necessary and useful to all living; and finally arm the Nation in mass in an extraordinary way."[89] Similarly, the archbishop of Toledo, Luis de Borbón, proclaimed that "that which is now important for you to know is, even though the enemy fled hastily from our Province, you should not therefore squander a moment in *rising up as a body* like the people of Israel, and all the provinces of Spain, taking up arms and training to fight with them."[90] The archbishop of Mexico City also beseeched his congregation to support the war effort in peninsular Spain, reacting to news of the conflict in 1808.[91] The friar Ramón Casaus Torres y Lasplazas, speaking from Oaxaca the same year, pleaded with "the good sons" of "our Madre patria" to reach out and save the beleaguered peninsula. He ended by appealing to the people of "both Spains" with the cry: "Long live my beloved people . . . now and in eternity."[92]

The clergy called upon their own to inspire as many men as possible to join the ranks of the soldier. Villanueva supported the premise that all ecclesiastics were obliged to arm themselves and defend the free exercise of their faith, although the American deputy Blas Ostolaza demurred. As members of the nation, the religious were enjoined to fight. The periodical *El Conciso* (The Brief) maintained that the public, during the first sessions of the Cortes of Cádiz, expressed great satisfaction that the congress had sanctioned all citizens, including clerics, to take up arms and defend the country. The battle was not portrayed as an offensive war prosecuted by a government disconnected from its subjects, but rather as an epic struggle "of all the nation, whose liberty, lives and religion were in danger."[93]

Nationalist clergy predicated their campaign against Napoleon upon anti-French propaganda. While clerics targeted the French National Assembly as the symbolic enemy during the War against the Convention, the entire French nation became demonized during the War of Independence. The Spanish clergy portrayed the French as capable of all forms of evil: "Those unnatural men have made, make at present and will make without doubt in the future all manner of evil, perfidy and treason."[94] Tomás de Salas, preaching in Seville, argued that "all Spaniards abhor the French."[95] Reducing the enemy to subhuman status, one priest denounced France as a nation "moving in a few years from Christian to Atheist, from civil to barbarous, from human to fierce and bloodthirsty."[96] A prebendary from Málaga warned his flock that Napoleon might indeed be the biblical "beast with seven heads and ten horns."[97] In Oaxaca, a prominent friar repudiated the French effort to reduce Spaniards to the status of "miserable slaves of Angola." Using language replete with apocalyptic imagery, he also drew upon extreme anti-French rhetoric in support of the war against Napoleon.[98]

The effect of the new ideology of nationalism on the war against the French was recognized by clergy of the time. For example, the ecclesiastic and historian Salmón, writing in 1812, discerned that "the present war is a struggle of all the Nation," as a fundamental shift in the dynamics of warfare had taken place.[99] The impact of nationalism had dramatically changed conflict between states. An entire people fought against an enemy nation and dehumanized the other through a discourse that denigrated all members of their national community.

Uniformity of sentiment, however, rested upon the idea of the Spanish people as inherently Catholic. Prior to a procession in the center of Mexico City in 1809, one friar promised the faithful that "the war against France is one of the most just that mortals have seen. Our cause is intimately united with that of God."[100] Ecclesiastics such as Simón López and Villanueva constructed the Spanish nation on the basis of its religion. By comparison, clerics viewed France as a fractured nation, divided by a sacrilegious and heretical ideology. According to López, "this uniformity of sentiment, fidelity and Christian patriotism could not have been hoped for in the France of the time of their revolution and change of government in 1790. Why? Because they did not have the unity of the Catholic religion." Furthermore, he asserted that the unity of the Spanish nation, bound through the Catholic church, was self-evident and plain to see: "Now Napoleon and all of his partisans have seen . . . the single voice of the Spanish people, animated by Religion, by trust in God, and devotion to the Virgin and love for their legitimate Sovereign." Yet the supposed unanimity of the Spanish people and nation rested upon an unstable political foundation. López argued that the Spanish people ardently supported the traditional basis of the Old Regime state: "In effect, to whom, but to the spirit of religion, dominant in the mass of the Spanish people, should one attribute the uniformity of sentiments, and the shout of the nation that at one time resonated through all parts, saying: Long live Religion, long live the Church, long live the Virgin, long live God, long live FERNANDO VII?"[101] López's absolutist framework stood in stark contrast to the views articulated by Villanueva. By 1812, Villanueva had become one of the leading proponents of liberalism at Cádiz and an outspoken advocate of the sovereignty of the people. He argued that "civil law is the expression of the general will of the people, that is, a constitution made by the people."[102] He struggled to promote a theological interpretation of liberalism under the auspices of constitutional government, and looked to unite the Spanish church: "As Catholics, as theologians, and as Spaniards we should all live animated by the same spirit."[103] As a deputy in the Cortes, Villanueva articulated a civic-minded nationalism during the War of Independence.

The people as the nation became the subject of intense debate during the War of Independence. During the sessions of the Cortes in December 1810, the American deputy Ostolaza continued to insist that "*nation* is not the same as *people* [pueblo]."[104] Ostolaza struggled to preserve the notion that authority and legitimacy resided within the monarchy and did not emanate from below. Yet as the term *el pueblo* became a part of common political parlance, its many advocates clamored to brand the people as their own. All sides proclaimed that the "true" Spanish people were partisans of their distinct political cause. Clerics such as the absolutist Manuel Traggia began to question the faith of the people in the wake of the proclamation of the Constitution of 1812 and the beginnings of the debate over the Inquisition: "Now then, my Spanish people, permit me a question: Are you still Catholic, Christian, apostolic, Roman; or have you abandoned this gem, crown and inheritance that was the greatest glory of your parents?"[105] Menéndez de Luarca, who had glorified the heroic character of the Spanish people in 1794, questioned the true spirit of *el pueblo español* by 1812, as hidden enemies had destroyed the unity of the state. He claimed that "the actual Spanish people, and the Spanish people of the years that came before, maintain, and maintained within their midst, many declared, and other more hidden enemies of the Sacred State; therefore they are unable to consider themselves now as that people."[106] With the restoration of Fernando VII in 1814, absolutist invective flourished, and clerics attacked liberals for espousing popular sovereignty. In December 1814, one American priest professed his continued adherence to the Old Regime because "the scriptures . . . speak of the power of the King, not of the authority of the people."[107] The 1814 *Catecismo natural* (Natural Catechism) portrayed the Spanish national community as one of common consent, declaring that those not professing Catholicism "would be obliged to leave Spanish territory."[108] Conservatives discursively circumscribed the boundaries of national identity as a corollary of the Catholic faith and continued to shape a particularist Spanish nationalism.

Miguel de Santander followed a distinct path during the War of Independence, working with the French and advocating the Napoleonic system of moderate liberal government. He chose to cooperate rather than fight and was decried by Spanish nationalists as a traitor and an *afrancesado.* A sermon given in Cádiz in 1810 quoted Santander as having ended a mass by instructing the faithful to submit and defer to the government of José I. He urged parishioners "to maintain the principles of tranquility and obedience, lamenting the pernicious conduct of those, who in spite of the repeated blows experienced by the *insurrectionary* party, always continue to err and to resist in vain."[109] Along with many elites and enlightened reformers, Santander firmly believed in the Enlightenment project and had decided to work within the French system rather than wage war against it.[110] As an early proponent of civic nationalism, he defended his iconoclastic views as consistent with the ideals of liberalism as well as with being a Spaniard.[111]

Spanish nationalist discourses during the French occupation epitomize the tensions between older notions of power and government and the new ideology of the sovereignty of the people. Impacted by the French Revolution while simultaneously relying upon Hispanic juridical precedents, Spanish patriotism transitioned from an essentially traditional hierarchical conception, infused with religious imagery and language, into a nationalist discourse that served as a mobilizing populist rhetoric. Competing political forces drew upon a common linguistic template, essentially merging notions of civic and particularist identity by 1810. Popular sovereignty ultimately became enshrined in the Constitution of 1812, which predicated an inclusive citizenship for all Spaniards upon the exclusivity of the Catholic faith as the crux of the Spanish nation. Ecclesiastics attempted to raise battlefield morale and encourage enlistment through the ostensibly unifying language of Spanish nationalism. They directed their sermons and instruction to the people of Spain, referring to the faithful in religious, but more importantly, in national, terms. The prominence of Spanish nationalist discourses during the war does not imply an interpretation of unanimous resistance—an entire nation mobilized to fight against the enemy. Yet it attests to the importance of the fact that nationalists shared a rhetorical commitment to *el pueblo español* as the embodiment of the nation united through the bonds of the Catholic church.

2

URBAN REVOLT, NATIONALIST REVOLUTIONS

Valencia and Seville, 1808–1814

During the wars of independence, the clergy increasingly directed their sermons and religious instruction to a nation-in-arms in addition to their parishioners, celebrating the people of Spain as the people of God. In Seville in 1808, the priest Manuel María Rodríguez y Romero proudly proclaimed: "This was the happy moment in which the voice of the people was the voice of God, the voice of great virtue and power, that moved all of the citizens of Seville" to action against the French.[1] Likewise, a new spirit of inclusivity suffused the politics of the time. In Valencia, a manifesto issued in 1808 boldly affirmed that "America and Spain form a single body, and their sentiments should be uniform. An American is a true Spaniard."[2] Accordingly, the people on both sides of the Atlantic had united under the banner of Spanish nationalism and rallied in support of religion and their dispossessed monarch.

Presiding over a predominantly rural and illiterate population, clergymen interpreted political and cultural values, facilitating communication among the people of the Spanish Monarchy. By May 1808, the press, local notables, and clerics began to appropriate nationalist discourses and sought to mobilize the populace by appealing to their attachment to the Spanish nation. While these discourses remained fundamentally tied to Old Regime notions of tradition and Catholicism as well as to regional loyalties, a distinct nationalist language, cutting across lines of class and regional difference, emerged during the war as Spaniards struggled to define themselves in opposition to the French.[3]

The cities of Valencia and Seville represent important variations from the dominant narratives of the War of Independence in Spain.[4] Seville resisted French incursions until February 1810, and Valencia held out for four years after most population centers had been occupied, an anomalous case in the Iberian Peninsula.[5] Valencians had defeated invading French forces under Marshall Moncey in 1808, and the city was one of the last to fall to Napoleonic troops, succumbing in January 1812. Contemporary accounts rendered the local revolts that began in 1808 as a "revolution." The Augustinian friar Salmón, in his 1812 *Resumen histórico de la Revolución de España* (*Historical Summary of the Revolution in Spain*), argued that the founding of a liberal state to supplant the corrupt, torpid institutions of the Old Regime was the greatest accomplishment of the era: "Convoking the Cortes, in the midst of the ruins and desolation of such incredible tyranny was the greatest, most admirable and illustrious work of this glorious revolution."[6] In many ways, the fact that elected deputies wrote a constitution and created the institutional apparatus of a working government points to the unique successes of Spanish resistance to the French imperium years before similar battles took shape in central Europe. Yet the combined efforts of local actors and municipal bodies established a revolutionary template upon which a concerted and increasingly centralized organization consolidated the artifice of a new liberal regime by 1812. Across the provinces of Spain and Spanish America, regionally based *juntas* had seized power in 1808 to stave off the French threat to Spanish sovereignty. Thus, the "revolution" that transformed the Spanish Monarchy must be analyzed first and foremost at the local level.

The Franciscan monk Juan Rico recounted his experiences of localized rebellion in Valencia in 1808 in a retrospective text. Written three years after the initial uprising, his *Memorias históricas sobre la revolución de Valencia* (Historical Memories of the Valencian Revolution) echoed a central pillar of José Cadalso's *Cartas marruecas* (Moroccan Letters). Like Cadalso, Rico bitterly denounced the lack of patriotic sentiment prior to the revolution: "Under the old regime . . . there was no patria . . . Spanish soil was sapped by its passions, and the infamies of a despotic government."[7] Yet his account documented the dramatic ascendancy of a nationalist discourse forged in the crucible of urban revolt: "As the general revolution in Spain has coalesced around a group of partisans in each province that by distinct means . . . fought for the same end and almost at the same time, their object being to throw off the yoke of slavery and avenge the insults committed against the Spanish people and their Kings, there was space left to write about the particulars of Valencia, that was the kingdom where the people rose up with the most energy and enthusiasm exalting in the first cries of independence, and of the war against the tyrant [Napoleon]."[8] In May and June 1808, political revolutions transformed the stratified structures of multiple Old Regime municipalities. These processes reveal the fundamentally analogous dynamics that played out in the regions of Spanish America and the Iberian Peninsula during this time. In Valencia and Seville, revolutionary regimes led by liberal and moderate figures, including clerics such as Rico, sought to fortify the city while at the same time enacting reformist legislation to alter local governance and engage in the political process begun in May 1808 and culminating with the promulgation of the Hispanic Constitution of 1812. While Spaniards prided themselves upon distinctive regional identifications, "localist energies" coalesced ideologically.[9] In the provinces of Valencia and Andalusia, regionalism, although remaining a powerful force of affiliation, did not challenge the rise of nationalist discourses in the immediate aftermath of the Napoleonic invasion.

CITY, REGION, AND NATION: COMPONENTS OF THE SPANISH MONARCHY

Examining both urban and rural dynamics, this chapter traces the plurality of regional and national identities that came to be advanced during the War of Independence through the lens of popular religion in Valencia and Andalusia. According to Xosé Núñez Seixas, regions can be considered "economic entities, historical territories, frontier areas and geographical units bounded by natural features. But they are also a form of collective identity."[10] Whether plotted in terms of concentric circles or through complex webs of relationships, different identities can be called upon depending upon specific circumstances. Peter Sahlins interprets the ways in which nationalism came to be fostered through localism in the case of the frontier borderland of Cerdaña in Catalonia during two centuries marked by war and disputes over boundaries. Catalan identity provided an important counterpart to national identity in Spanish Catalonia whereas French Catalans tended to regard regional culture as folklore by the mid-nineteenth century.[11] Sahlins gives agency to villagers in demonstrating that they were able to build a national identity that "drew strength from . . . enduring expressions of local identity."[12]

Other works have similarly engaged with the idea that local and regional identifications were not necessarily constructed in opposition to other forms of loyalty.[13] Ferran Archilés and Manuel Martí, in their research on Valencian identity, argue that the distinctiveness of language and history, as the basis of an ethnic identity, "could not come into conflict with the new Spanish national identity" as liberals struggled to transform the Spanish state during the period 1808–40. They emphasize the nonconflictive nature of regional identity that emerged during the War of Independence in Valencia.[14]

The outgrowth of regionalism has generated a great deal of literature on the supposed exceptionalism of the modern Spanish state. Whether studying society, the economy, or politics, historians have found myriad examples of supposedly retrograde policies and structures from nineteenth-century economic development to the institutions of Francoism. Accordingly, Spanish backwardness proceeded directly from the failure of policies of centralization by the nineteenth century: "The result was long stagnation and political and economic backwardness, reinforced then by the loss of empire and its revenues. Nationalism not having been consolidated by religious fervor and mass exclusion neither unified or engaged the populace in its secular authority nor inflamed revolutionary or liberal efforts to cut itself loose from absolutism. Instead, popular identification with regions remained often stronger than loyalty to the whole."[15] Implicit or explicit comparisons with Britain and France tend to serve as proof of Spain's status as a "failed state." This has been carried over into studies of nationalism and identity in Spain, where the prominence of peripheral nationalisms and regional movements in the twentieth century has demanded historical exegesis and close analysis of center-periphery relations. Thus much of the literature on nationalism in Spain begins with the second half of the nineteenth century and the rise of Basque and Catalan nationalism rather than with the War of Independence or the Enlightenment. Even works emphasizing the failure of the liberal state to invent national traditions often start with the liberal ascendancy of the 1830s.[16]

By the 1980s, few historians had worked on issues of Spanish nationalism in spite of the growing body of literature on national identity from a wide range of perspectives. Spanish nationalism was equated with Francoist ideology, National-Catholicism, and the brutality of authoritarian rule. Few wanted to explore the roots of an extreme conservative vision of the nation as Spain transitioned to democracy after Franco's death. Studies remained limited and incomplete, according to Núñez Seixas, and often focused on the advent of separatist nationalisms. Methodologically, most scholars emphasized political and ideological factors at the expense of social or cultural history. Many contemporary historians working on questions of nationalism continue to conflate state formation and identity production.[17] For example, Javier Varela claims that "it is the State, and not the culture or character, neither the market nor the 'bourgeoisie,' that is the creator of the nation."[18] In order to fill the historiographical gaps, Núñez Seixas points to the shift away from purely structural methodologies and "the need for deeper research into the Spanish national question . . . and the supposed tension between region and nation."[19]

Regional identity in Valencia and Andalusia—two of the last regions to hold out against the French onslaught during the War of Independence—came to be subsumed under national identities throughout the course of the campaign against France. Clerics across the Spanish Monarchy conceived of and imagined national identities in terms that intersected with and built upon extant local and regional allegiances. Citizens of the monarchy began to conceive of themselves as a distinctively Spanish people while not entirely shedding historic regional loyalties. Eighteenth-century enlightened writers who had found little cause to celebrate Spanish patriotism, such as Cadalso, had accentuated regional differences. Cadalso definitively declared: "A Catalan is totally distinct from a Galician, and the same can be said of a Valencian and a Montañés [resident of Cantabria]."[20] Whether previous identification had been at the village or regional level, however, identities came to be shaped around the nation during the War of Independence.

Expressions of Spanish national identity, grounded in a Catholic religiosity and the ambit of the church, centered on the development of the idea of the people as the nation. As discussed in chapter 1, Spain was depicted in essentialist language as a Catholic state with a Catholic people. The seamless transition from the term *el pueblo de dios* to *el pueblo español* provided a religious foundation for discourses of national identity. Accordingly, clerics could speak of the people in unitary terms under the banner of religion. For example, Felipe Scio, a priest from Valencia, referenced both the nation and the faithful, blending the two together in a sermon from 1809. As his audience consisted of "the Catholic people, that bring glory in being so," he addressed his parishioners as "Spaniards" first and foremost.[21] The formulation of the Spanish people as inherently Catholic did not stem solely from religious tropes, however, and regional identity remained a compelling signifier during the early nineteenth century. Regional identification with *el pueblo valenciano,* for example, referred not only to the people of a city (*pueblo*), but also to inhabitants of the province as a whole, the *patria chica.* Ecclesiastics propounded a national identity interwoven with religious referents and the language of popular sovereignty and contributed to the successes of military and ideological mobilization at the local level during the course of the war.

THE REVOLUTIONS OF 1808

Throughout the first months of 1808, as French troops marched south and began to occupy Spanish military posts, royal authorities avoided inflammatory rhetoric and confrontation. A royal decree issued in March by King Carlos IV had downplayed the threat posed by Napoleonic France: "My beloved vassals. . . . Breathe freely: you know that the Army of my dear Ally the Emperor of the French crosses my Kingdom with ideas of peace and friendship. . . . What do I have to fear?"[22] Within weeks, Napoleon's troops occupied Madrid and held the king and his son—the heir to the throne—hostage in France. Yet a decree in April continued to emphasize fraternity, declaring that the Spanish monarch avidly wished to consolidate the bonds of friendship and the intimate alliance between Spain and the emperor of France in the names of their respective peoples and nations.[23] The uprising of May 2 in the streets of Madrid ended the delusion of a Franco-Spanish alliance. Renegade military officers, defying orders to avoid confrontation, were killed in the fighting, thus becoming, according to Álvaro Flórez Estrada's contemporary account, the first "martyrs to the liberty of the country."[24] On May 2 and May 3, the French massacred approximately four hundred Spaniards, including fifty-seven women, in Madrid.[25] In spite of the atrocities, the royal press as well as the influential Council of Castile, called for order and obedience.[26] Across the Spanish Monarchy, the Old Regime fell to forces promising to defend Spain and raise armies to end military occupation and political subservience to Napoleon.

After Napoleon forced both Fernando and Carlos IV to renounce the throne on May 6, local authorities were toppled across Spain. While many reacted with horror to news of the brutal suppression of the riots in Madrid, the abdications of the throne and the passivity displayed by Spanish authorities such as the Council of Castile sparked widespread outrage. The first concrete declaration of war against France, made by the Junta of Asturias on May 24, was replicated across the monarchy. In Valencia at the end of May, an upheaval occurred that displaced the municipal government and established a *junta* by May 25. Such committees often included prominent figures within the community such as bishops and canons. Significantly, the provincial *juntas,* as newly created representative bodies for regions throughout Spain, declared that the sovereignty of the nation resided with its people.[27] On May 30, 1808, the Junta of Cádiz issued a proclamation specifically addressed to the nation as a whole, "*el Pueblo Español.*"[28] A newspaper from 1808 encapsulated the nascent nationalist sentiment of the time, describing the *juntas* as spontaneously generated by the people: "It is said, unfortunately, that the populace has done it, as if the dignified Spaniards who were the first to express their allegiance should be referred to with this name: the people, properly said; only the people could have done it; only the general collaboration of all made it possible to fight for the advantages we have achieved; and only their well-directed force and energy can complete our triumph."[29] On September 25, 1808, the Supreme Central Governing Junta of the Kingdom, a centralized committee convened at Aranjuez, began to coordinate the actions of the provincial organizations and to integrate the regular and irregular troops fighting the French occupation. Ultimately driven to the southern port city of Cádiz, the government worked to prosecute the war, hold elections across all the territories of the monarchy, and write a constitution.[30]

The Junta Central, composed of members of each of the provincial *juntas,* made similar claims to speak for the nation. The Cortes likewise opened with the declaration that "sovereignty resides essentially in the nation."[31] In justifying such a radical statement, a decree explained that "the general Cortes . . . declares null, of no value or effect, the renunciation of the Crown in favor of Napoleon, not only because of the violence that intervened in those unjust and illegal acts, *but principally due to the lack of consent by the nation.*"[32] Authority had to be grounded in the consent of the nation, or, in other words, in the will of the people. Thus state power could no longer be arbitrary and required consensus before action could be taken. Formally legislated and reified in the Constitution of 1812, the original claims of the regional *juntas* were transposed into powerful statements of national identity, defining the nation as "the union of all Spaniards from both hemispheres" and affirming that sovereignty resided "essentially in the Nation."[33] Nationalist discourses originally articulated on a local level fundamentally altered the political structure and political struggles of nineteenth-century Spain. By linking a primordial Spanish "nation" struggling to assert its rights with the defense of the municipal privileges of *los pueblos* (the towns), representatives reinforced the equation of the nation with the people (*el pueblo*).[34]

Priests such as Rico played important roles in the revolutionary *juntas* that rapidly undermined the Old Regime authorities.[35] As other local notables had maintained the voluntary nature of the abdications of Carlos IV and Fernando VII at Bayonne, Rico fervently opposed accommodation with the French. On May 20, the Franciscan friar Juan Martí, accompanying Rico, read aloud the recent news from Madrid, which had reached Valencia only that day. Public pressure mounted to speak out against France and denounce Napoleon's treachery, and clerics such as Rico agitated for military mobilization to begin. A vendor of straw for mattresses, Vicente Domenech, is said to have issued the first battle cry of the war, shouting: "Death to the traitors!"[36]

City leaders soon resolved to establish a new governing *junta*.[37] Although at first hesitant to take his place in its ranks, Rico became one of two representatives of "the people," speaking for the classes that previously had been disenfranchised in municipal government.[38] Members represented the three estates, and served in the church hierarchy and the military as well as the state bureaucracy. Others were titled aristocrats, lawyers, merchants, and artisans. Clerics at all levels, from the archbishop to four parish priests and four regular ecclesiastics, comprised over 40 percent of the *junta*'s representatives.[39] Rico recalled: "The junta was installed immediately; and everyone swore the most solemn oath to defend the rights of the nation, liberty and the independence of the people, and to continue the war against France until our King and our national honor have been avenged."[40] Working in concert with Rico, Vicente González Moreno, the captain of the army, explained the events as a concrete manifestation of the principle of equality: "We will combine ideas and proceed . . . to create a supreme governing junta, composed of all classes of the people."[41] He issued a declaration two days later, arguing that "our only object is the salvation of the country." Moreno signed the decree "Commander of the Sovereign people," boldly declaring adherence to the liberal tenet of national sovereignty.[42] By the end of May 1808, leaders such as Rico and González Moreno were celebrated publicly as champions of the Spanish cause, and, according to Rico's own testimony, "everyone clamored in unison: *Long live Spain, long live Religion, long live Fernando.*"[43] In a letter sent to Valencia's *ayuntamiento* in October 1808, Rico clarified his motivations in sparking the "revolution" as a representative of the people. He lauded "el Pueblo Valenciano," the people who admirably displayed their civic pride in remaining loyal to the Crown. Writing with humility, he claimed to have simply "compl[ied] with the duties of my class, estate, and birth in the famous events of May 23 until the present day."[44] In the aftermath of such successes, May 23 was celebrated as the day on which the revolution began and the heroic defense of occupied Spain was first mounted.

On the same day, enlistment began of resident males between the ages of sixteen and forty. A proclamation was read aloud to the public, but bystanders clamored for a stronger statement. Rico observed: "In spite of this [decree], the people did not remain satisfied, because the proclamation did not express in whose name or to what end the enlistment was ordered; and everyone cried out in unison, that the general enlistment should have been in the name of Fernando 7.° as the legitimate King of Spain and the Indies; and with the clear declaration that it was to raise an army to oppose the tyrant on Spanish soil, and to defend the liberty and independence of Spain."[45] By the end of the day, Rico had secured an agreement that reflected the "will of the people."[46] Recruitment quickly took place in the convents of Santo Domingo and San José and in the churches of the Virgin of the Forsaken and Salvador. On May 26, even the regular and secular clergy were implored to join in the defense the city.[47] By May 27, the *junta* had enlisted more than eight thousand men.[48] Firmly establishing the war as a nationalist struggle against French tyranny, Rico saw the Spanish nation as the primary embodiment of the authority of the king. By declaring the de facto sovereignty of the people while maintaining loyalty to the throne, Rico presaged the legitimating rhetoric of constitutional monarchy and successfully mobilized a militia.

In order to pay the expenses of the newly consecrated armed force, Rico, as the people's representative, intimidated the notables and played off of their fears of disorder and anarchy. Letters circulated with pleas for contributions from the church as well as from individuals, who had "a grave obligation as all good Vassals, interested in the defense of the Sovereign, the Nation and the Country."[49] Rico issued a statement that concluded: "The people of Valencia desire tranquility. In order to achieve this, residents of all classes must understand and suggest to all the plebeians the precautions that they should take to evade the common enemy, which can only succeed . . .with members, or individuals, admitted into the Junta Suprema, each having a vote and a voice, supporting the plans proposed by the people in defense of the Kingdom."[50] In effect, Rico pleaded for the representatives of "the people" to take the lead and influence the affairs of the reconstituted municipal government. Rico served the interests of a constituency that historically had been marginalized in local affairs. He alluded to the potential for violence if the people's voice was not heard, although he insisted that the populace desired peace and harmony.

Similarly, in working with the *junta,* Rico made plain that "the distrust . . . in the old authorities, common in times of revolution, could have divided opinions and paralyzed [our] great success: following upon that would have been anarchy and disorder and as a consequence the ruin of the state."[51] He threatened and cajoled those he associated with the Old Regime and did not hesitate to leverage the power of the people in arms to ensure political victories. He converted the local representative from Madrid, a potential *afrancesado,* to the nationalist cause and warned of the dangers of a spontaneous uprising. Rico insisted that he would be able to mollify the townspeople, who had questioned the patriotism of the intendant, if he remained loyal to the *patria:* "Extremely intimidated and disheartened, the intendant was introduced in the company of Rico, and he told the people to renounce the suspicions that they had harbored against his conduct, as the present situation would convince him to cherish the same patriotic sentiments held by the rest of the Spaniards."[52]

Similar dynamics shaped the uprising that began in Seville three days after the "revolution" in Valencia first unfolded, with priests such as the archbishop of Laodicea, Juan Acisclo de Vera y Delgado, Manuel Gil, and Mariano de Sevilla spearheading the movement to establish a *junta.*[53] After violence marred the first calls to arms and Francisco Solano, the Marqués del Socorro, was killed, priests galvanized residents with a civic nationalism that coexisted with traditional articles of faith. For example, the friar Mariano de Sevilla began a procession through the streets carrying a crucifix, rallying citizens with a plea to return to order and publicly swearing allegiance to Fernando VII. He convinced the people who had gathered to name a new city leader and requested that all arms be turned in to the Capuchins. As the threat of violence receded and a revolutionary *junta* was formed, including Mariano among its members, war was declared against France on May 27.[54] Little has been written about Seville between May 1808 and February 1, 1810, when the city fell.[55] But the decision of the Junta Central, comprised of members of thirty-five of the provincial *juntas,* to move its base of operations from Aranjuez to Seville in December 1808 testifies to its importance as the center of early efforts to stave off French occupation.

At the end of May 1808, the Junta of Seville immediately decreed the mass levy of all men between sixteen and forty-five. As eight thousand men had responded to the nationalist call of Rico and the Junta of Valencia and registered within days of the enlistment order, more than twenty thousand men swore their allegiance to Fernando VII on May 26 in Seville.[56] The proclamation of the *junta*, published on May 29, emphasized "the sacred obligations that we have contracted before as Spaniards, as Vassals, as Christians, as Men free and independent of all foreign authority."[57] The *junta* castigated the weakness and indecision of the Council of Castile, which had endorsed the renunciation of the throne in favor of a foreign prince, and insisted that the men of Seville remain united against the French threat. The authors praised the efforts of citizens and claimed that "the people will soon take up arms, invite the Learned of all the Provinces to preserve public opinion, and refute those insolent libels full of atrocious falsehoods [that had been spread by a foreign Prince]."[58] As the authorities quickly recognized the strength of the resistance against the marauding armies of Napoleon, the *junta* proclaimed the fidelity of the people. In doing so, they built upon a historical narrative focused upon *el pueblo* as the protagonist in an epic struggle against the French.

Even contemporaries sympathetic to the nationalist cause were hesitant to exalt the lower classes, however, noting "the dangers that could have followed from [rule by] a people who regularly judge by first impressions."[59] Others impugned the ignorance of "the plebeians" and decried the "revolution."[60] The friar Martínez Colomer, in a narrative of the uprising in Valencia, vividly portrayed the atmosphere surrounding the enlistment of local men. Fears of the lower classes pervaded Valencia and pointed to the tensions and volatile class structure within its walls.[61]

Class anxieties were exacerbated in the aftermath of two bloody incidents that took place in Valencia at the end of May.[62] Enraged residents demanded the head of the Baron de Albalat, Miguel Saavedra, accused of being a traitor and working on behalf of Napoleon. Popular violence was channeled against those associated with the French, and Saavedra was beheaded in the Plaza de Santo Domingo. Rioters ripped apart his corpse and paraded through the city with his head on a pike. Subsequently, the *junta* took measures to eliminate the potential for any further harm to be caused by those who might have been sympathetic to a French regime. Incriminating evidence pointed to several members of the government who harbored pro-French sentiment, including the intendant, and Rico took various steps to bring them into the nationalist fold.[63]

The following week, the city faced an even larger disturbance when opposition to French occupation and the atrocities committed in Madrid boiled over within the city walls. Baltasar Calvo, a canon who had just arrived from Madrid, led attacks propelled by a virulent nationalism with roots in violence that had taken place during War against the Convention in 1793–95. More than two hundred French residents of Valencia, imprisoned in the wake of the May 23 uprising, were slaughtered in the initial onslaught. Calvo, originally from Valencia, conspired with local farmers and took over an important military garrison on the night of June 5. He then manipulated the situation to precipitate violence, enjoining the French to break out of the fortress to avoid a supposed threat against them. Finally, Calvo spread the rumor that the prisoners were going to escape, and armed men killed them as they fled. As the massacre took place, according to witnesses such as Rico, people were screaming: "Death to all; Junta, get out."[64] Many believed that conspirators and traitors, such as Saavedra, had infiltrated the *junta* to subvert their work. Rico and all others were powerless to stop the bloodshed. The following day, Calvo and his supporters slaughtered another 143 prisoners at the Quart Towers. Close to four hundred were killed in total, and only twelve people survived. By the night of June 6, Calvo had entrenched himself in la Ciudadela, the garrison he had first attacked, and, seizing the cannons, continued to fight. He issued a declaration, mimicking the notion that Rico represented the city's people, which concluded: "6 of June of 1808 and the first year of the reign of our august monarch Fernando the seventh. In his name, and as the representative of the people."[65] The killing only stopped due to the sustained efforts of the local notable Vicente Bertrán de Lis, Rico, and other city officials.[66] Rico and the *junta* finally arrested Calvo on June 7. Prior to his deportation to Mallorca and subsequent execution on July 4, Calvo was garroted publicly for four hours with a placard dangling below him which read: "traitor to the country, leader of assassinations."[67]

For the time being, the *junta* remained wary of the presence of large numbers of farmers and rural laborers, in addition to those whose occupation and status could not be identified, within the city limits. A handwritten letter to the president of the *junta* on June 6 indicated an overriding preoccupation with commoners and favored placing armed guards composed of "honorable farmers" and patrols of clerics and the nobility around the local military barracks to "maintain the peace."[68] Concerns over the presumed impetuous and fiery nature of the people, however, were smoothed over by appearance of the ordered and disciplined men of the militia. And by August 1808, the Junta of Valencia had focused its recruiting efforts on heads of families, with rhetoric emphasizing defense of property rather than nationalistic ideals. Day laborers were discouraged to join the ranks of these "honorable guards" serving as the bulwarks of legitimate authority and the common good.[69] Nationalist language remained fraught, as usage of the term *el pueblo* fluctuated between its older connotations and ardent assertions of national identity.

Beginning on June 21, although urban unrest had subsided, the city faced an invading army. The French had fought their way toward Valencia with a series of victories over unprepared Spanish forces, including the defeat of Rico and others on June 24. On June 25, 26, and 28, the French Marshall Moncey sent letters demanding an immediate surrender. The *junta* refused, and the French continued to march toward the city walls. Rico believed that the Conde de la Conquista, a French sympathizer, along with other *afrancesados*, likely would have worked under a collaborationist administration, but nationalists carried on the struggle.[70] The pivotal battle was fought on June 28, and Moncey retreated after an ineffectual campaign. The *Gazeta de Valencia* (Gazette of Valencia) heralded the valor of the city residents and specifically mentioned the zeal and ardor of clerics and the religious, who not only animated the spirits of the soldiers but fired on the enemy themselves as dignified representatives of the Spanish nation.[71]

Although Valencia had triumphed, the fear of unrest and anarchy was manifest in sermons from the time. Preaching on July 22, the archbishop of Valencia, Joaquín Company, excoriated the actions of the people and ordered all residents to "blindly obey your legitimate Sovereign to whom you have sworn allegiance, and to those who represent him and exercise his powers. In this way, you will be good citizens, loyal vassals of your legitimate King, [and] good soldiers."[72] The bishop of Orihuela, Francisco Antonio Cebrián y Valda, expressed his immense gratitude to the Junta of Valencia for suppressing the violence unleashed by Calvo in his pastoral letter of August 3, 1808, addressed to all of the clergy within his diocese. He did not mention the war or Napoleon explicitly, adhering to a strict interpretation of events as divine retribution for the sins of the people. He called upon all ecclesiastics to perform services each and every Sunday as well as on holy days, emphasizing the obligations of the Christian to obey and uphold order. Cebrián y Valda exhorted the clergy to remember "the obligations they have, and impose divine Law and the sacred Religion we profess in giving the most dignified example of obedience to God's holy Law and to the legitimate, established power, and of Christian moderation in all actions."[73] An absolutist cleric concerned above all with Old Regime ideals of order and deference, Cebrián y Valda conveyed antagonism toward the unpredictable "people." The discourse of these bishops exposed the challenges to an emerging consensus that government must be grounded in popular sovereignty.

Sermons from the time attempted to reconcile possible tensions between nation, region, and religion. In September 1808, Vicente Facundo Labaig y Lassala paid tribute to the defense of Valencia in June of that year. An enlightened absolutist, he used patriotic tropes to sanctify the victory of Spanish arms but fundamentally remained committed to the values of the Old Regime. He glorified the heroic soldiers of Valencia and their sacrifices but began by addressing the entire nation: "Nation of heroes, terror of the world, generous Spaniards, and especially, loyal Valencians: In this way, I will speak of faithful and just posterity, when the great book of history has recorded the noble and glorious memory of our valor, of our patriotism, and of our love and fidelity to the King."[74] Labaig y Lassala did not clearly differentiate the regional from the national and did not demarcate the boundaries of the *patria* he celebrated in the term *patriotismo.* He eulogized Spanish and Valencian patriotism as overlapping forms of identification. In addition, Labaig y Lassala highlighted the religious dimensions of the struggle, maintaining that "the war which we discuss can be considered a war of Religion." Yet he placed God and country side by side in claiming that "a single voice and a single desire armed the men and moved the tongue of all good citizens to shout out loud: *War, war, we die for God and for the King: long live the faith, long live the country.*"[75] Such battle cries, reminiscent of countless others, bound together religious, regional, and national identifications.

Religious devotion, regionalism, and nationalism converged in many sermons from Andalusia. For example, Rodríguez y Romero propounded: "One hears in all the streets and plazas: *Long live holy religion: Long live Fernando VII.*"[76] In the cities of Spain, from Seville to Valencia, clergymen pictured their parishioners, the people of God, as locked in a millenarian struggle to uphold the values of a besieged Christian faith. The Valencian Labaig y Lassala asked rhetorically: "Will we say, Catholic listeners, that Valencia was on that occasion the city of God, which faced the terror and panic unleashed by the Moabites and Ammonites?"[77] Just as clerics began to conflate the religious nation and the Spanish nation, they continued to refer to the local faithful as the people of God. Both Rodríguez y Romero and Labaig y Lassala argued that the citizens of Seville and Valencia, respectively, constituted God's chosen flock, a rhetoric ideally suited to a nationalism grounded in Catholic particularism.

The war featured prominently in sermons from 1808. Key cities such as Tudela had fallen, and the French, under General Lefebvre-Desnouettes, continued their march southward. On June 12, 1808, French troops attacked Zaragoza and began a siege that would last two months. Residents mounted a heroic defense under General José Palafox, symbolized by the efforts of Agustina de Aragón.[78] But the first great victory of Spanish arms came on the battlefield in Andalusia, with a significant contingent sent by the Junta of Seville. In order to immortalize the moment, clerics dedicated a week of services and processions to General Xavier Castaños and his soldiers, who had fought so valiantly in vanquishing the French on July 18, 1808, at Bailén. From Sunday through Friday, from August 7 through August 12, sermons preached throughout the parishes of the city venerated the success of the Spanish forces. Calls to arms followed in the wake of continued warfare against the French. In a proclamation issued to all the citizens of Seville, Gil juxtaposed the death and glory of heroic fallen Spanish soldiers with the infamy of the coward: "It is worth more to die on the battlefield with honor, than to live in the Patria with dishonor. Death and infamy to the indolent and the coward, praise and honor to the brave and valiant."[79]

On August 3, 1808, the Junta of Seville issued a statement advocating a national government. In order to justify their position, the *junta* built upon the firmly established notion that the people had been the driving force behind the resistance. Thus, due to the absence of the king, power legally reverted back to the people of the nation. The *junta* posited that, in accordance with the laws and the history of the kingdom: "The people legally reassumed the power to create a Government, and the various Juntas Supremas have openly attested to this truth. . . . The legitimate power, then, has remained with the Juntas Supremas, and through this power they have governed and govern with true authority. . . . The situation has not changed: the danger remains: no new Authority has come in their place: thus legitimate authority resides in the Juntas created by the people."[80] The Cortes, reopened in 1810, utilized the same language of liberalism in arguing that the sovereignty of the nation resided in its representatives in Cádiz. The localized struggles in both Valencia and Andalusia against collaborators and the French invasion sparked ideals of national resistance, and language borrowed from the original proclamations issued throughout the peninsula became reified in the Constitution of 1812.

In public proclamations as well as in sermons delivered from pulpits

EL VENERABLE CLERO,
É ILUSTRE ARCHICOFRADIA
DEL SANTISIMO SACRAMENTO,
DE LA IGLESIA PARROQUIAL
DEL APOSTOL SAN ANDRES
DE ESTA CIUDAD,
QUE ANIMADOS DE UN ZELO RELIGIOSO HABIAN ROGADO Á DIOS NUESTRO SEÑOR,
Y SU SANTISIMA MADRE CON EL TITULO DEL ROSARIO,
POR EL FELIZ EXÎTO DE LAS ARMAS ESPAÑOLAS;
AHORA QUE VEN LA FAMOSA VICTORIA QUE HAN CONSEGUIDO EN LOS CAMPOS
DE ANDUJAR, Y BAYLEN,
CON LA QUE SE HA EXÂLTADO LA RELIGION CATÓLICA
LIBRADO LA ANDALUCÍA DE LOS MALES QUE LA AMENASABAN,
Y EL EXÉRCITO ESPAÑOL LOGRADO UN TRIUNFO DE VICTORIA ETERNA;
HAN DETERMINADO DAR GRACIAS Á NUESTRO DIOS SACRAMENTADO,
Y Á MARIA SANTISIMA NUESTRA MADRE Y SEÑORA POR TAN GRANDES BENEFICIOS,
DESAGRAVIANDOLOS DE LOS ULTRAGES Y SACRILEGIOS QUE HÁN COMETIDO LOS ENEMIGOS
DE SU SANTO NOMBRE, Y ROGANDOLES POR LA CONTINUACION DE LA FELICIDAD DE NUESTRAS ARMAS,
COLOCACION EN EL TRONO ESPAÑOL DE NUESTRO CATOLICO MONARCA.
EL SEÑOR DON FERNANDO VII.
Y EL FELIZ ACIERTO EN LAS DISPOSICIONES
DE LA JUNTA SUPREMA DE GOBIERNO DE ESPAÑA É INDIAS
ESTABLECIDA EN ESTA CIUDAD.
PARA ELLO SE CELEBRARÁN LAS FUNCIONES SIGUIENTES
QUE PRINCIPIARÁN Á LAS NUEVE DE LA MAÑANA.

Domingo 7. de Agosto; habrá Procesion de Tercia, en la que se cantará el *Te Deum*, y seguidamente la Fiesta que hace el Clero, y Hermandad, y predica el M. R. P. Fr. Antonio Vega de la Concepcion, Prior en su Convento de nuestra Señora del Populo, y Exâminador Sinodal de este Arzobispado.

Lunes 8. hace la Fiesta una devota, y predica el M. R. P. Fr. Francisco de Paula Pacheco, Maestro de Teología en el Colegio de San Buenaventura.

Martes 9. hace la Fiesta una devota, y predica el M. R. P. Fr. Joseph del Castillo, Lector de Sagrada Teología en el Convento Casa Grande de San Francisco.

Miercoles 10. hace la Fiesta una devota, y predica el P. D. Juan Nieto, Lector de Sagrada Teologia en el Colegio de San Basilio.

Jueves 11. hace la Fiesta una devota, y predica el M. R. P. Fr. Felipe Sanchez Pasqual, Lector de Sagrada Teologia en el Convento Casa Grande de nuestra Señora del Carmen, y Calificador del Santo Oficio.

Viernes 12. se celebran por el Clero, y Hermandad Honras por las Almas de los Españoles muertos en las Batallas, y predica el M. R. P. Fr. Pasqual Rodriguez, Lector de Sagrada Teología en el Colegio de Santo Tomas.

SEVILLA: EN LA IMPRENTA MAYOR. AÑO DE 1808.

"The venerable clergy, and the illustrious confraternity of the Blessed Sacrament...animated by religious zeal, have prayed to the Lord Our Father, and the Holy Mother...for the opportune success of Spanish arms; now that you see the famous victory that has been achieved on the fields of Andujar and Baylen ..." (Seville, 1808). From the Colección Documental del Fraile.

across the south, the people were represented as a unitary force possessing a single will to defeat the enemy. On January 1, 1809, the Junta Central issued a manifesto to all Europeans decrying the tyranny of Napoleon and lauding Spanish resistance: "Only a fool can fail to recognize the will of the entire nation in this universal and magnanimous movement that aspires to defend their honor and their independence. How can we explain it but as an admirable and yet singular political phenomenon of many different Provinces, without preparation, and without communication between themselves, that has moved in almost a single day with the same spirit, on the same path, and under the same form of government?"[81] A sermon delivered in Antequera by the friar Manuel de la Virgen del Rosario portrayed a defiant people animated by a unifying national spirit as well as their faith: "The Catholic Religion, far from abating spirits . . . makes them more addicted to the Sovereign and to the country; and a people on the battlefield have always been invincible when moved by religious zeal, animated by the hope for an afterlife, putting all their trust in the justice of their cause and in God's protection of their armies."[82] Partisans of enlightened absolutism, clerics such as Rosario argued that a unified Spanish nation could not be defeated. Led by the invincible people and shielded by divine protection, Spanish armies would ultimately prevail.

With the armies of Napoleon advancing south once again in 1809, D. F. J. Molle, a cleric in Málaga, attempted to redress Spain's military failures and inspire the people to unanimously rise up and resist. The French had won decisive battles against Spanish and allied British armies, forcing them to retreat and sail from La Coruña in northwestern Galicia. They had taken besieged towns and appeared poised to conquer the Iberian Peninsula. José I reentered Madrid in January, Zaragoza fell to Marshal Lannes in February, and the French pushed back fifty thousand Spanish troops in the strategically important Castilian town of Ocaña in November. A path southward into Andalusia had been opened by the Spanish defeat. Yet much of Spain remained unoccupied, and calls to arms continued to resonate throughout Andalusia. Molle envisioned the entire peninsula as "an encampment and a factory for arms. Before the men go to war they should be disciplined, armed and dressed, and then provided with provisions. This is the sacred obligation of all Spaniards; in their plazas they listen to the din of the hammer, of iron and of bronze: all of the young men between 16 and 40 years of age leave for the campaign: married men manufacture arms and bring them to the armies together with the provisions: the women make tents and clothing for the troops. . . . [Clerics] preach about the defense of and love of the Country in all public spaces: they promote the values of the warrior, and in this way they will sustain the sacred cause that the Spaniards defend."[83] The archbishop, acting as both the president of the Junta Central and the spiritual head of the church within his ecclesiastical jurisdiction, urged all of the clergy to inspire soldiers to fight on in the name of God: "Again I exhort, in the name of God, my venerable brothers the secular and regular ecclesiastics from all across the nation, to inspire them in many ways with zeal, to continue contributing to the enlistment of troops, and the formation of Cruzados and of guerrilla parties, stirring religious loyalty to the country against the perfidy of the invader."[84] Similar appeals were sounded overseas, as the archbishop of Mexico City issued an impassioned manifesto exhorting Americans to aid the war effort against France.[85]

THE STRUGGLE IN RURAL SPAIN

Many of the battles fought during the War of Independence took place in rural Spain, pitting French forces against the guerrilla parties that had formed throughout the peninsula by 1809.[86] The factors propelling events in urban Valencia and Seville did not necessarily conform to the socioeconomic geography of the countryside, where the majority of the population lived. Yet the case of the most important guerrilla leader operating in the Valencian countryside suggests that liberal ideas and constitutionalism resonated clearly among many of the peasants in the Levant. Fray Ascencio Nebot recruited four thousand combatants during his campaigns against the French, during which he disrupted communications, captured arms, and defeated French deployments. Helping to drive the French out in the spring of 1813, Nebot played a decisive role in resisting the occupation and fracturing supply lines. Manuel Ardit argues that Nebot capitalized on the wartime deprivations suffered by the peasants and successfully appealed to men who were otherwise unable to subsist.[87] Other historians have noted that a local *junta* ruled over areas liberated by his forces, and that Nebot established a manufacturing zone to produce and maintain war materials and armaments.[88] The economic crisis and dislocation caused by the war certainly contributed to effective recruitment. Yet such structural conditions do not account for the radical liberal ideology propagated by Nebot and his followers. Detailed reports sent to the *Gazeta del Reyno de Valencia* (Gazette of the Kingdom of Valencia) extolled the campaigns of Nebot. One article described an offensive action led by Nebot in the town of Morella and emphasized the soldiers' valor and courage in the heat of battle, a telltale sign of Spanish "national character": "The first sergeant Tomás Galindo raised the ladder again, and in true Spanish fashion said this: *captain, the two of us have to die today, but let death touch me first.* This valiant Valencian climbed, following the captain and all the company, and after various skirmishes, and blows from sabers, they seized the wall. Again the cry rang out: *Long live Spain, long live the Constitution,* and we began to pour through the streets. It is not easy to describe the men's amazement, nor the speed and valor of our Valencians."[89] Accordingly, Nebot's troops fought and died in the name of both Valencia and the Spanish nation as a whole, demonstrating the importance of liberal nationalism to his band of guerrilla fighters. Composed largely of landless peasants and smallholders, Nebot's army was mobilized behind the causes first articulated by nationalists in the provincial *juntas* and later consecrated in the Constitution of 1812. Nebot continued to fight for the ideals of constitutionalism in March 1820, censuring the persecution and tyranny of Fernando's despotic regime and hailing the return of "our Sacred Constitution."[90]

CONSTITUTIONAL SPAIN

Valencia remained outside the zone of French occupation for close to four years while almost all other major Spanish cities fell. Political developments in Valencia followed those of many urban areas of Spanish America, as local leaders harnessed liberal ideals and calls for a reconstituted Cortes resounded. In February 1810, elections were held for a national assembly. The governing *junta* celebrated "the illustrious Representatives of the Spanish people" who "declare the sessions of Bayonne null and void, uphold their fidelity to Fernando, proclaim the imprescriptible rights of man, unify the fraternal accord between the European Spaniard, the African Spaniard and the Asian Spaniard, and between the inhabitant of the Americas; forming a family of integral parts of the Spanish Monarchy, without regard for the difference of climates, colors or of fortunes. . . . Valencians, Castilians, Andalusians, Spaniards . . . now you will have a country."[91] This rhetoric expressed the ideals of inclusivity encoded within burgeoning liberal nationalist discourses. Despite Spain's regional variation, the nation-as-family incorporated the distinct peoples and territories of the monarchy within a universalist model of the liberal state. Catholicism represented the remaining tie to a Hispanic cultural patrimony. As the *junta* proclaimed its allegiance to the Cortes and vowed to live in freedom or die, they simultaneously swore to "sustain with our blood the holy Religion of Jesus Christ."[92]

Significant figures, such as Archbishop Company, steadfastly opposed the new political landscape, arguing that the deputies of the Cortes must place religion above all else. Bluntly stating that "religion is the only support of government," Company rejected the principle of popular sovereignty in spite of the advent of representative government in the city and upheld the notion that "the Lord gives us sovereignty. . . . The social compact opens the door to rebellion."[93] Internecine conflicts threatened the viability of the liberal project. Although French forces took the city prior to March 1812, city leaders proclaimed the Constitution on July 25, 1813, after combined English and Spanish armies had ousted French troops earlier that month.[94] Elaborate festivities were held to celebrate the sacred articles of liberal, constitutional government.[95]

By 1813, the French had been driven from Andalusia, and city leaders celebrated the great Spanish victories of the preceding years. The sieges of Zaragoza and Gerona were presented as the tragic preludes to the victories at Bailén, Ciudad Rodrigo, and Salamanca. Proclamations in Seville also memorialized the first days of the uprising against Carlos IV in March 1808 as the spark of liberal revolution. On March 18, 1813, five years after the struggle against the French began, an edict posted in Seville publicized the following day's military parade to honor the heroic Spanish troops: "This day is doubly memorable in the glorious annals of our sacred revolution. The nineteenth of March of 1808, the Spanish people threw off the yoke of ministerial despotism . . . and on the nineteenth day of the same month of 1812 the representatives of the Nation affirmed the rational and political liberty off all Spaniards by way of the Constitution. . . . Soldiers: we repeat with voices emanating from the heart, Long live the Nation, the Constitution that assures our happiness, and our beloved Monarch Sr. D. FERNANDO THE VII."[96] With military campaigns no longer being waged, political leaders venerated the war as having ended both French occupation and decades of ministerial despotism in Spain. Soldiers, glorified as heroes of the *patria,* recited liberal nationalist slogans and paid homage to the Constitution of 1812. Such edicts displayed few vestiges of regionalist sentiment, instead upholding "Spanish valor" as the defining trait of "heroic Spain."[97]

The end of Spain's first liberal government came swiftly, however, as men such as Company supported Fernando VII in abrogating the Constitution in May 1814. Yet significantly, the new regime appropriated the symbols of nationalism and the language of popular sovereignty in the years following the reinstatement of absolutism. During festivities held to welcome Fernando VII, cities hearkened back to the final days of May

1808 and the movements to resist the French invasion. The ceremonies in his honor deployed the imagery of national insurgency, featuring royalist regalia amidst paintings that glorified those who had first called on their fellow citizens to rise up against the French. Fernando entered Valencia on Saturday, April 16, 1814. In the royal chapel, artists had erected transparent pyramids with two oversized medallions in between, adorned with images of Fernando VII and King George III of England. Reminders of the combined efforts of Spain and Britain during the war, the symbols evoked traditional conceptions of the Old Regime Spanish Monarchy. A female figure representing the city of Valencia prayed before the altar of the Virgin Mary for the health and well-being of the king. A separate portrait of the monarch appeared with the words "Viva Fernando" underneath it. There were other symbolic displays as well, such as the coats of arms of Spain and England. Another installation featured images of Fernando and George III next to a rendering of Joseph Bonaparte, bottle in one hand and cup in the other, with a flask of liquor placed in between. The crown falls from his head as dogs and a leopard—representations of the enduring strength of the provinces of Spain and their allies from England—pounce on him and overtake the inebriated tyrant. An additional transparency showed a French general pursued by bats, the iconic symbol of Valencia. All of the transparencies were illuminated at night so that they could be seen by the public.[98]

Not all of the elaborate artwork commissioned for the king conjured up royalist sentiment alone. At the Royal Academy of Art, paintings depicted the work of men like Rico and their participation in the "noble and loyal movements of May 23, the most glorious day of Valencia's glorious and heroic revolution, an example which started the general revolution throughout the Nation."[99] In sanctifying the anti-French resistance in cities such as Valencia, artists and their patrons tacitly paid tribute to liberal nationalists such as Rico. Similarly, a number of prominent clerics continued to call for representative government and to pay homage to the Constitution of 1812. In 1814, Joaquín Sanchis Albella applauded the intimate alliance between the Spanish, Portuguese, and British. He argued that liberty and Spanish independence emanated from the rule of law and necessitated protection under the benevolence of a constitutional regime. An image in the text, with a medallion pictured in the center, mirrored those that had been designed to honor Fernando VII upon his triumphant return to Spain. In it, Lord Wellington points approvingly to the engravings of both the English and Spanish kings and the flags flying in the background. Beneath the legs of two generals embracing one another, a lion avenges Spanish honor, attacking an eagle symbolizing Napoleon's hubris and ambition.[100]

The caption underneath the image begins: "Spain and England, allied against France and their Caudillo Napoleon Bonaparte. Lord Wellington fortunately directs the alliance of both Nations, signified by the friendly embrace of the Generals and the union of the Flags, so that the Spanish live free and independent, as their inimitable patriotism merits" (Valencia, 1814). From the Biblioteca Valenciana.

The disjuncture between the liberal nationalism espoused by those who would maintain representative institutions and the revived absolutism advocated by reactionary leaders was manifest during commemorations of el Dos de Mayo in 1814.[101] Describing Fernando's return to Spain after his years of captivity in France, the Valencian friar Facundo Sidro Vilarroig celebrated the restoration of Old Regime values, symbolized by the rechristening of Constitution Plaza, in the city's historic center, as the Royal Plaza of Fernando VII. Occurring on May 2, the event did not take place without controversy. The engraved stones were placed as armed militia members looked on, "zealously guarding the rights of the king, no longer able to tolerate the insults and lack of respect shown in the presence of the Sovereign." According to Sidro Vilarroig, the regiment diffused the tension in the crowd, a mixed gathering of all the classes within the city, and prevented "dissidents" from spreading discord among the populace.[102] The fact that witnesses mentioned the political divisions within the city attests to the difficulties faced by Fernando as he undermined the work of the Cortes and attempted to purge liberalism from his kingdom.

CONCLUSION

Clerics within Spain understood that the War of Independence represented a break with the past and with the language of the Old Regime. The war was no longer solely sustained by hierarchical ties of vassals to their lords and lords to kings—the people owed their fidelity to the nation of Spain above all else. The people had become the protagonists of the narrative and had successfully broken their ties to a feudal society. According to Antonio Alcalá Galiano, "the people passed from obeying to commanding, and from not looking after the public cause to taking charge of it with ardent zeal [and] with vigilance."[103] Molle, writing in 1809, discerned the fundamental changes that had taken place: "The war in which the Nation is engaged is not one of those we are accustomed to seeing ordinarily between Princes. They have their struggles without for the most part consulting the interest of the people, and they are guided by obscure politics and cannot count on more troops or auxiliaries than their strength allows them. The luck of these wars is delivered by fortune and by the good or bad calculations of the Cabinet. But at present that which the Peninsula is enduring is national war; the nation will persevere in mass as long as is necessary until the destruction of the monster it detests."[104] He perceived the struggle in terms of an entire people mobilized against another, requiring a national undertaking to prosecute and secure victory. No longer did princes and cabinet ministers face off against one another in battles decided by the whims of fortune. Only collective actions could stem the advance of a modern armed force reinforced by mass levies and supplied by an entire nation mobilized for war.

Emile Durkheim maintained that "language, and consequently the system of concepts which it translates, is the product of a collective elaboration. What it expresses is the manner in which society as a whole represents the facts of experience. The ideas which correspond to the diverse elements of language are thus collective representations."[105] Although Durkheim interpreted the evolution of linguistic forms over the *longue durée,* certain periods of history mark watershed moments of flux and transition. During the wars of independence in the Spanish Monarchy, the idiom of nationalism began to represent a changing and fluid reality in which loyalty to the nation was superimposed over local identities and came to represent the struggle of a Catholic people against the French. Ostensibly erasing class divisions and often tying together rural and urban communities, discourses of Spanish nationalism resounded from pulpits and on the battlefields. The experiences of those living through the revolutions of the late eighteenth and early nineteenth centuries inspired a new political vocabulary that meshed collective identities with emerging conceptions of the nation in Spain.

The localized, collective actions of 1808 stamped the war as a national conflict. The familial metaphor of regions as loyal brothers fighting on behalf of their *madre patria* resonated powerfully as municipalities organized *juntas* to resist the French invasion. According to an anonymous account, Valencians, without prior knowledge of the events in Asturias of May 24, openly resisted "the unjust pretensions of the perfidious enemy, proclaiming martial law, and the youth, in mass, and without class distinctions, intrepidly ran to arm themselves." The war, fought initially at the local level, was inscribed indelibly as a national struggle. Tens of thousands of soldiers came together and volunteered in the war effort as a concrete manifestation of the vibrancy of Spanish nationalism. In conclusion, the pamphlet's author effused: "Impartial posterity will enthusiastically praise the inexpressible valor of the Spanish people."[106]

3

THE EMERGENCE OF THE CATHOLIC PUBLIC SPHERE

In spite of early recruitment successes in Valencia and Andalusia, the war dragged on for years. French armies took to the offensive, and clerics openly debated strategy through the medium of print and actively engaged in politics. Juan Constans, a Catholic priest from Catalonia, wrote an impassioned appeal to the Junta Central in June 1809 asking the government to sanction the formation of armed bands, called *cruzados*, led by priests engaged in guerrilla warfare against the French. He painted himself as a tireless defender of the *patria* who wanted to contribute more to the nationalist cause: "Since the Nation took up arms against our most vile enemies, animated by great patriotism, I have not ceased to demand that everyone come together in the defense of the Country by all means possible, now in the pulpit, now in the confessional, now in private conversations, and now finally in Schools. But even this did not satisfy my ardent desires for the public good."[1] A prelate preaching at the same time in Málaga proclaimed that clerics and the religious should conform to their traditional roles in shaping public opinion rather than fight on the battlefield. In an effort to instigate a war of public opinion against an allegedly traitorous and French-aligned print media, the prelate urged clerics to "foment public opinion, rejecting the pernicious writings of that throng of miserable Francophile journalists."[2] From private conversations and published tracts to the public spaces of the pulpit and the plaza, churchmen diffused conflicting political ideologies to their parishioners during the wars of independence. The fight over whether or not ecclesiastics would join the ranks of the soldier offers but one illustration of a larger pattern of debate and dispute within the Hispanic public sphere. Despite disagreements over their proper place in a war-torn society, clerics took center stage in the arena of public opinion during this time of crisis and had a profound impact upon emerging conceptions of national identity.

Yet who constituted the public? And was public opinion an amalgamation of popular beliefs or the result of reasoned debate and critical thinking? Furthermore, were conservative clerics or the agents of liberalism more powerful in shaping the forces of public opinion? Many secular critics defined public opinion in terms that excluded the church. They viewed the public realm of politics and ideology as the font of rational discourse articulated through individual free speech, political representation, and freedom of the press. In the periodical *El Robespierre Español,* one editorial argued that "public opinion, or the general will of the citizens," was expressed "with speech, with works, and with a free press."[3] Premised upon a Rousseauian conception of the general will and a liberal vision of individual freedoms, this view of public opinion echoed Miguel de Santander's enlightened manifesto *Del character del christiano.*[4] Yet the treatise remained silent on the subject of religious contributions to an emerging political sphere carved out of the remains of Bourbon absolutism.

Keith Michael Baker defines public opinion as "a political invention appearing in the context of a crisis of absolute authority in which actors within an absolutist political system appealed to a 'public' beyond as a way of reformulating institutional claims that could no longer be negotiated within traditional political language."[5] This definition clearly applies to the case of the Spanish Monarchy during the first decades of the nineteenth century. The Old Regime state faced a dual crisis of political legitimacy and liberal revolution during the War of Independence, which had ramifications in all of the Spanish dominions. Uprisings against royal authorities spread across Spanish America after 1810, further complicating questions of legitimacy and identity. As warring factions looked for support in the name of God, King, and Country, notions of sovereignty became increasingly contested. For a brief period, liberalism took hold from the church to the halls of government, and subjects were anointed citizens. As traditional political language began to break down, new actors across the social and political spectrum, from the pulpits to ad hoc assemblies and the print media, engaged each other within an emergent Catholic public sphere.[6]

THE CATHOLIC PUBLIC SPHERE IN THE HISPANIC ATLANTIC WORLD

The foundations of national identities were discursively constructed within an emerging public sphere. Historians such as Geoff Eley note that, across Old Regime Europe, a public sphere "took clearest shape where the overall context of social communication was being institutionally reformed." As a corollary, he maintains that "the emergence of nationality (that is, the growth of a public for nationalist discourse) was simultaneously the emergence of a public sphere."[7] Therefore, nationality and the public sphere were mutually constitutive in that both required the reordering of the political and cultural spaces that had opened up during the crisis of the Old Regime.

Some scholars insist that public opinion and modern politics, products of the advanced Protestant states of northwestern Europe, had limited effects in southern and eastern Europe. Countries like Spain, they claim, were "largely cut off from Europe's Enlightenment by the unchallenged Catholic Church." Max Weber posited a clear distinction between a Catholic worldview and the progressive spirit of Puritanism: "The supposed conflict between other-worldliness, asceticism, and ecclesiastical piety on the one side, and participation in capitalistic acquisition on the other, might actually turn out to be an intimate relationship." Otherworldliness corresponded unmistakably to a Catholic propensity to eschew risky ventures and new ideas, according to Weber, while Puritan Protestants characteristically pursued more materialistic goals in the increasingly secularized world.[8] Yet this dichotomy between the Protestant Atlantic and the Catholic world, posited explicitly by Max Weber and tacitly by historians such as David Zaret, presents a simplistic and deterministic model of the early modern Atlantic world and the fundamental religious changes that swept across borders and continents.[9] Many recent works raise questions about such conclusions, persuasively demonstrating that a Hispanic Enlightenment culture, emphasizing science and rational reform, developed parallel to the new ideas articulated in France, Scotland, and England.[10]

In the Spanish Monarchy, however, religious tropes infused the new political ideologies of the early nineteenth century. Ideas crossed secular and religious lines, and religion helped to regenerate the political culture of the constitutional Spanish state by 1812. Even salon society, as a medium for rational-critical thought, included members of the clergy within its ranks. Antonio Alcalá Galiano emphasized the fact that he first embraced the new political and literary philosophies with zeal in Manuel Quintana's *tertulia* (salon). The clerical deputy Juan Nicasio Gallego, the theologian and writer José María Blanco White, and the Catalan Antonio Capmany, among many others, frequented the poet's gatherings both before and after the French occupation in 1808.[11] In his historical memoir of the period, Alcalá Galiano referred to enlightened salon society as "España intelectual," a font of polemics and poetry that did not necessarily coalesce around unanimous opinion and often ignited rancor and discord.[12]

But on what grounds can sermons, the principal vehicle of the clergy, be considered an essential component of the public sphere? Could these discourses, delivered without an obvious forum for response, have functioned as an integral part of rational-critical debate? This chapter argues that just as political monologues and editorial pages stimulated response and rebuttal, sermons contributed to, rather than detracted from, political sociability. Furthermore, published sermons appeared alongside newspapers and broadsheets in the marketplace of ideas. In Habermasian terms, sermons came to serve as one of the mediums for "people's public use of their reason" that would fundamentally challenge the order of the Old Regime monarchy.[13] In turn, the construction of national identities in these discursive spaces came to be grounded in both revolutionary political rhetoric as well as traditional religious tropes.

With roots in Enlightenment culture and Jansenist theology, discourses of Spanish national identity merged secular and religious culture and language. Clerics across the Spanish Monarchy—many of whom were among the class of educated elites serving as newly elected political representatives—propounded Enlightenment tenets of reason and rationality in the context of a distinctly Catholic public sphere.[14] José María Portillo Valdés and Brian Connaughton suggest useful terminology such as "Catholic citizen" and "the citizen parish" to reinterpret this period.[15] Indicative of the convergence between secular and religious spaces, parish churches became theaters of political deliberation as sessions of the Cortes and elections were held inside their halls. Clerics participated both as ideologues and as elected officials in local and national politics, and representatives promulgated the Constitution as a fundamentally religious document. Ideas preached from pulpits across the Spanish Monarchy during the wars of independence cannot be separated categorically from simultaneous debates concerning politics and the Constitution.

Ironically, the lack of debate over state support of the church and the legal limits placed upon freedom of speech in regard to religious matters distinguished what I term the "Catholic public sphere" from its counterparts elsewhere in Europe and the Atlantic world. Few *letrados* advocated religious tolerance for the Spanish Monarchy or questioned the primacy of the Catholic faith. During some of the first sessions of the Cortes of Cádiz, representatives equated public opinion with freedom of speech. According to Evaristo Pérez de Castro, a peninsular deputy from Valladolid, one could not exist without the other.[16] Yet little support was generated to extend the freedom to discuss politics and the state to matters of religious orthodoxy. This was not seen as a contradiction in terms, in spite of the fact that religiosity imbued the spaces of the Catholic public sphere and influenced its partisan struggles. Religion remained the one subject closed to debate, and the Hispanic public sphere was in no uncertain terms a Catholic domain.

THE PUBLIC, THE PRESS, AND THE REVOLUTION OF 1808

The wars of independence were, in many ways, a call to revolution, reflecting attempts across the Atlantic world to convene representative assemblies, promulgate constitutions, and grant individual rights and freedoms. The economist Álvaro Flórez Estrada, author of the 1810 *Introducción para la historia de la Revolución de España* (Introduction to the History of the Revolution in Spain), argued that the transition to liberalism in Spain was the most important event of its time and would alter Europe's political landscape. Although Spaniards had suffered through the "deplorable" reign of Carlos IV and the machinations of his minister Manuel Godoy, Spain would not stand idly as its religion was insulted and its independence threatened.[17] Bartolomé Gallardo, librarian of the Spanish Cortes, endowed the word "liberal" itself with tremendous significance, associating it with the struggle against the oppressive French occupation begun in 1808: "Now that we have shed our blood liberally fighting to ensure our liberty against all vestiges of tyranny, we should give all our latitude to the word *liberales,* establishing its legitimate meanings, impressing them deeply in our soul, to not have a thought, deed nor word that becomes unworthy of a SPANIARD, that is to say, of a strong man, constant, free, and *liberal.* And a man that screams and shouts against the mob of antiliberals."[18] Gallardo portrayed liberal freedom fighters waging a war to break from the shackles of tyranny symbolized by both Napoleon and reactionary absolutists. Thus, a restored polity would resemble the virtuous republics of classical Greece and Rome. Conversely, Quintana—poet, writer, editor of the influential periodical *Semanario Patriótico,* and political activist during Spain's War of Independence—explicitly modeled the liberal experiment upon revolutionary France, arguing that "the French revolution is for us like the remains of ships destroyed on the shoals; they teach the sailor to avoid the dangerous reefs, but do not distract him from his path."[19] Yet above all, Spanish liberals aspired to build a state upon the ideals of liberty and equality, shorn of the vestiges of the feudal past.

In circumscribing the boundaries of Spanish liberalism, liberals such as Gallardo and Quintana declared that constitutional government would guarantee freedom, especially freedom of expression. Gallardo emphasized the ideal of press freedom as a central element in the struggle against the remnants of the Old Regime. Just as enlightened Spaniards called for rational governance and fostered scientific investigation during the reign of Carlos III, Gallardo asserted that the political edifice of liberalism rested upon the foundation of reason:

> *Liberty* is the right of all rational creatures to order their lives *conforming to reason and justice.* There are three types: natural, civil, and political: or in other words, liberty of men, liberty of the citizen, and liberty of the nation. Natural liberty is the right that men enjoy regarding their own free will, conforming ultimately to the way in which they were raised. Civil liberty is the right which society guarantees to all citizens so that they can act in any way they please as long as it is not contrary to established laws. And ultimately, political or national liberty is the right of all nations to work for themselves, free from dependence on another nation, whether servile subjection or any form of tyranny.[20]

Political freedom demanded the freedom to write and publish with impunity. Armed with a writer's tools, Gallardo contended that "paper and words would save us!" He decried the censorship characteristic of absolutist monarchy, stressing the positive impact of print culture upon the structures of modern society.[21]

Periodicals instantly provided a public eager for news with coverage of local, national, and international politics. The *Gazeta de Valencia* began publishing on June 7, 1808, and with its first issue argued that the struggle for "national liberty" was a "new phenomenon in the history of Nations." Lamenting the lack of communication among Spaniards, the *Gazeta* focused on the campaigns of allied forces in the peninsula, the successes of the Spanish army, local decrees, and the proceedings of the Junta Suprema of Valencia. Editorials offered an engaging forum for "a people that are more noble than others on the continent and are so interested in public deliberations." Imagining the press as an eternal monument to public virtue, the editor promised to avenge Napoleon's invasion and inaugurate a new era of peace and prosperity for the world.[22]

Both clerics and the press fostered ideals of rationality and reform underscored by appeals to public interest during the wars of independence. The periodical press, a central conduit of public opinion, issued innumerable calls for representative government—within a framework of constitutional monarchy—from the disparate reaches of the monarchy.[23] Of the liberal newspapers from the period in peninsular Spain, Quintana's weekly *Semanario Patriótico* was the most influential. Beginning publication in Madrid on September 1, 1808, in the wake of José I's flight from the city, the newspaper initially grew out of Quintana's salon, a quintessential Enlightenment forum for the discussion of new ideas. It started off with extraordinary success, netting three thousand subscribers in the first several days.[24] Liberal newspapers epitomized a Habermasian conception of the public sphere and often relegated religion to the margins of their discursive imaginings of the nation. Writing in 1808, Quintana summed up the popular response to French occupation and the rise of a new mass political force: "Public opinion is much stronger than alien authority and armed forces. This is what has been born under the extraordinary circumstances in which Spaniards find themselves: public opinion took down the insolent Favorite [Godoy] who for twenty years had insulted the Nation; public opinion put on the throne an idolized Prince of the people who saw in them a companion of his oppression, and the tree of his hope. . . . Opinion will crown our forces with independence and the sovereignty we were going to lose, and opinion finally will consolidate our fortune with an interior organization that we will protect for a long time from the evils we have suffered."[25] Quintana identified public opinion as the decisive factor in the overthrow of Godoy and the ascendancy of Fernando VII in March 1808. Others repeated the idea and heralded the emergence of an enlightened public more powerful than the force of arms: "[Public instruction] unifies the nation's way of thinking and the inclinations of its individuals, and thereby establishes a general will that has a force equivalent to that of many armies."[26] Newspapers such as *Semanario Patriótico* were a vibrant expression of a public sphere in civil society, with roots in the enlightened currents of Spanish salon society.

Quintana, in his third issue, mapped out the liberal conception of *patria* in an article titled "Reflections about Patriotism." He described patriotism as "an eternal source of heroism and of political prodigies."[27]

Accordingly, the people were "ardent in their most pure and heroic sentiments of loyalty and patriotism."[28] Quintana argued that "La Patria . . . is a power as ancient as society, founded on nature and order. . . . Patriotism, similar to the light, to the fire and the rest of the great agents of nature, is the same for all men, and in the same manner . . . inspires the Chiefs of the Republic as well as its very last members."[29] He asserted the following week that "in that happy instant that the people recover their rights and make use of them, to castigate tyranny, defend innocence, or extol virtue, the sacred fire that burns in their chest receives new nourishment from each new event."[30] Quintana presented constitutional government and patriotism as elemental, symbiotic components of the natural world; one could not exist without the other. He juxtaposed love of country with the unnatural oppression of tyrants, which pitted patriots against absolutists in a Manichean struggle of good against evil. Quintana demonized the exclusive privileges enjoyed by the wealthy few under the Old Regime: "The fundamental principle of this power so repugnant to nature, so contrary to the general interest of the Nation, in particular to individuals, consists of ignorance. Ignorance makes people irrational, and makes them see the usurpation as right, and their servitude as a duty: their oppressors appear as natural superiors, created to give orders and enjoy their comforts, while they were born to obey and suffer."[31] The inverse of the Old Regime, which was epitomized by an ideology of difference and inequality, *patria* was a just and benevolent entity, governed with an overriding concern for equality: "La Patria is a tender mother who equally loves all her children; and only distinguishes between them when they distinguish themselves through their actions. She suffers if there has been opulence and mediocrity; inequality necessarily produced by industry and fortune; but she does not want there to have been indigents in her bosom; she does not permit the oppression of one by another; and reestablishes equilibrium between them by making all equal under the law, and facilitates the path toward principal employment."[32] Quintana developed a narrative of the people and the nation as the inheritors of an ancient natural order, while absolutism and the usurper king thrived on ignorance, despotism, and privilege based solely on birthright. Linking words such as *patria, nación,* and *pueblo,* liberals constructed a discourse simultaneously vilifying the invasion of the French and the Old Regime of Carlos IV and his minister Godoy.[33]

In hailing the advent of a centralized administration to fight the forces of Napoleon, outspoken liberals and nationalists vehemently pilloried two decades of unfettered absolutist authority as "twenty years of despotism."[34] In New Spain, the bishop of Michoacán condemned the venality of Carlos IV's minister Godoy while upholding the people as the archetype of steadfast loyalty: "The Spanish people, always devoted and loyal to their kings, suffered with resignation the disorders of the disorganized government of the favorite Godoy: and also suffered the attacks of Bonaparte, while they were well disguised (or poorly disguised) with the appearance of friendship."[35] Others emphasized the possibilities of a novel transatlantic relationship no longer bound by the language of colony and metropole: "You see all of these considerations fulfilled in the deliberations of the Junta Central gubernativa, abolishing the name of colonies for the Americas and declaring them an essential and integral part of that Kingdom."[36] Creoles eagerly anticipated a new era and an end to policies pursued at the expense of Spanish America.

Some prominent clerics interpreted the period of Godoy's ministry within a longer epoch rife with the abuse of power and epitomized by a culture of decadence. This discourse of "decline" idealized an earlier age of supposed ancient liberties. The bishop of Michoacán, writing in 1813, argued that "Spain has been decadent almost without interruption for three centuries due to the ambition, ineptitude or apathy of some of its Kings, and because of the despotism of its Ministers."[37] He hearkened back to a time when limits on royal authority gave local representative institutions political power to maneuver within their own circumscribed territories. Many critics of the monarchy blamed the rise of the Habsburg Empire, and their suppression of the Comunero revolt of 1521, for the end of medieval freedoms. This distinctly liberal reading of history clashed with a conservative vision of a decline in Spanish power attributed to the ascension of the Bourbon monarchs, who, beginning in 1700, had deviated from Habsburg imperial grandeur and had modeled Spain upon the French state. The term *afrancesado,* or Francophile, came to resonate with derisive connotations of effeminacy and foreignness.[38]

Quintana and many like-minded liberals appealed for the Cortes to be reestablished as a representation of the national will. Quintana claimed that "the Cortes was, in a different time, the bulwark of our liberty and independence: it formed an essential part of our primitive constitution: the people desired it, and the prosperity the people deserve due to the long suffering and incalculable sacrifices that the rescue of the country has cost awaits their deliberations."[39] His pleas reverberated with countless others, including calls from clerics for a reformed government. As early as 1798, for example, Miguel de Santander had advanced a similar agenda for political representation that hearkened back to the medieval representative institutions that had flourished across the peninsula.[40]

When the Junta Central issued a call on May 22, 1809, to convene the Cortes, Spaniards faced the twin tasks of sending deputies across oceans as well as through war zones. Despite these great obstacles, debates over electoral procedures often centered on more mundane matters such as class. One liberal periodical published in Seville, *El Voto de la Nación Española* (The Vote of the Spanish Nation), pushed for a representative system that would allow for all heads of families, regardless of status and wealth, to vote. This would have provided a counterweight to the pretensions of the clergy and the nobility, as all males twenty-five and older could have voted for deputies. On January 10, 1810, the paper advocated for individual clerics to serve as representatives of the third estate: "We judge that far from being prejudicial, it will be very useful that the same individuals of the clergy are called to the service of representation which the towns desire."[41] Ultimately, many ecclesiastics were elected to local and provincial offices, and a third of the deputies who served in the Cortes of Cádiz, which assembled without regard to estate, were clerics. In addition, clerics had been charged with conducting the elections across the Spanish Monarchy, and certain stages of the indirect electoral process took place within parish churches.[42] According to the Constitution, mass was to follow the selection of parish electors, bestowing solemnity on the electoral system. In New Spain in 1813, a priest involved with elections in Guadalajara urged parishioners to use their rational faculties in voting: "Your vote has to be entirely free, entirely yours. But at the same time it should be rational, dispassionate and honest for the sake of your reputation, for your own good and for the benefit of all."[43]

Not only did clerics serve as national representatives, but they also mediated between the sacred language of the church and the rhetoric of partisan politics. Proclaiming the Constitution of Cádiz in the cathedral of Valladolid in 1812, the friar Manuel Martínez addressed this issue in his sermon: "I will speak: in a ceremony or political assembly I would speak only as a political philosopher; but at this site, in this sacred temple, in a ceremony that while political is perhaps the most religious ever seen in this land, I would be guilty of lèse-majesté, if I disdained speaking the idiom of religion, that harmonizes so well with the language of healthy politics."[44] Demonstrating the interplay between politics and religion during the era, Martínez emphasized the harmonious blend of a religious idiom with the political language of constitutionalism. Participation by the clergy in the realm of politics demonstrated that a Catholic public sphere incorporated political and religious spaces in the Hispanic world. Parishioners could also read this participation as evidence of a politico-religious public sphere in which they were engaged in their daily lives as members of a parish.

Representation of all the territories of the Spanish Monarchy occurred for the first time in Cádiz beginning in September 1810. The assembly of the Cortes first took place in the cathedral hall of San Felipe Neri, thus establishing the church itself as the locus of rational and critical debate. The integration of the functions of church and state symbolized the ways in which a public sphere was constructed within a religious framework and a Catholic language of spirituality and legalism. Religion was infused into the liberal political system. On the first day of the national assembly, September 24, 1810, following three days of public prayer, the archbishop of Toledo gave a mass and received an oath of loyalty from deputies who swore in defense of religion, the integrity of the Spanish nation, and their king, Fernando VII. Mass continued to be celebrated daily by a deputy of the Cortes in the halls of the church prior to the often vitriolic disputes over how best to conceive of the functions of the state in the absence of the king.[45]

DISSENTING VOICES ACROSS THE ATLANTIC

Although the Cortes had given a voice to those who not only called for liberal reform but rebuked the monarchy for its failure to integrate the political structures of its vast territories, civil war had engulfed the Bajío region of New Spain just weeks before its inauguration. Competing pamphlets and broadsides expressed conflicting opinions on the strife that began with Miguel Hidalgo's 1810 call to arms in the town of Dolores. Significantly, Hidalgo never publicly contested royal authority. He claimed to be fighting against *mal gobierno,* bad government, rather than against the rule of Fernando VII. Likewise, prominent public figures in urban municipalities, while promoting an agenda similar to that of the insurgents, called for autonomy within the auspices of the Spanish Monarchy. They printed propaganda advocating the insurgent cause and engaged in correspondence with rebel leaders. They even smuggled printing presses out of the city to enable insurgents to distribute their political manifestos.[46] In Michoacán, governing officials prohibited the publication and distribution of insurgent propaganda, fearing that the free circulation of ideas represented a threat to public security in times of war.[47] Even periodicals such as Blanco White's *El Español* were banned.[48] Yet the convocation of the Cortes, with elections held for representatives from all territories of the Spanish Monarchy, offered the possibility of realigning political power and fundamentally altering notions of sovereignty. In contrast to the fiery rhetoric of anti-*gachupín* sentiment, autonomists remained open to the possibilities of an inclusive Spanish Monarchy and pushed for equal representation and a greater voice in the Catholic public sphere.[49]

Writers entered into transatlantic dialogues and disputes, citing influential articles from peninsular Spain as well as the Americas and engaging in protracted polemics. A letter published in *Ilustrador Americano,* for example, referred to Quintana as a wise and impartial voice in Cádiz, while bitterly denouncing the royalist platitudes of ecclesiastics such as the Poblano José Mariano Beristáin de Sousa.[50] Many clerics, writers, and members of the political class drew upon Enlightenment ideals of reason and reform in order to substantiate their claims. The canon Manuel de la Bárcena argued that reason demonstrated the viability and legitimacy of monarchy. Reacting to the Napoleonic invasion of Spain and the spread of revolutionary ideas in New Spain, he maintained that "ultimately, example, reason and experience show us that the best government is Monarchical."[51] Other clerics, like Beristáin de Sousa, echoed such sentiments in supporting the king: "The Kings of Spain took you from nothingness to life, from the shadows to the light, from ignorance to the understanding of the Sciences, from misery to happiness, from poverty to abundance, from vulgarity of customs to the finesse and delights of rational life."[52] Beristáin de Sousa emphasized rationality as the key to replacing ignorance and tradition with scientific knowledge and modern ideas. By 1811, however, a growing number of publications in New Spain decried peninsular liberals and the Catholic public sphere as unrepresentative of an American viewpoint. In *Ilustrador Americano,* the priest and insurgent leader José María Cos asserted that "absent the sovereign[,] the inhabitants of the Peninsula have no right whatsoever to appropriate supreme power themselves and represent the king in these dominions."[53]

Creole autonomists urged moderation in the wake of growing violence and warfare. In an editorial in *Ilustrador Americano,* Cos argued that "the two belligerent parties recognize Fernando VII; the Americans have given ample evidence of this, swearing and proclaiming oaths of loyalty in all parts . . . and stamping it on their money and coins: the enthusiasm of everyone depends upon this fact, and the insurrectionary party has always been grounded on this assumption as well." Cos insisted that "Spain and America are integral parts of the monarchy, subjects of the king, but equal among themselves and without dependence or subordination with respect to each other." In essence, he bridged the gulf between factions by highlighting their common ties to the Bourbon monarchy. Cos further opined: "Loyal America has more right to convoke a parliament and call representatives than the few patriots of Spain infected with disloyalty."[54] Criticism of the political process in Cádiz did not imply a rejection of parliamentary government. Instead, American autonomists continued to voice their objections to political subordination. Figures such as Cos advanced notions of an American identity within an inclusive Spanish constitutional system and demanded equality as Americans and as Spaniards.

The inauguration of a liberal political system, embracing the entirety of the Spanish dominions, faced tremendous challenges from the outset. A rational voting public, constituted by an aggregate of individual members of the state, voiced myriad opinions on the formation of the new government, conceived in the midst of war against a foreign aggressor. Andrés Quintana Roo, in *Semanario Patriótico Americano,* the influential insurgent periodical published in Michoacán, devoted a great deal of attention to the beginnings of liberal government. In the introductory "plan" of the paper, Quintana Roo dedicated his work to the nation, "for the enlightenment of the public."[55] Justifying his positions on the inalienable rights of nations, he pushed for justice and equality. The first issue, titled "Clamors for Reason," indicated that the viceroyalty no longer served the common good. According to the editorial, reason dictated that, under French occupation, a legitimate representative government should have been convened on American soil. Quintana Roo offered unbridled criticism of the Junta Central, the Regency, and the establishment of the Cortes, a body he designated as a forum for disagreement and conflict among the deputies from both hemispheres. *Semanario Patriótico Americano* viewed the various incarnations of Spanish authority between 1808 and 1810 as illegitimate and unrepresentative of the larger Hispanic public.[56]

THE PRESS IN CÁDIZ

After the fall of Seville and the convocation of the Cortes in Cádiz in September 1810, the newspapers of Cádiz became the most important sources of information on government activities during the years 1810–14. According to Ramón Solís, "the newspaper was the one point of contact between the people and the Congress."[57] Dozens of periodicals were published, many with competing political agendas. Some contemporary observers decried the seemingly unlimited number of publications available and their unmitigated defense of liberalism. One satirical paper, written by "Dr. Pedro the Strong," ridiculed the flourishing print media with the title *Diarrhea of the Press: Memory of This Epidemic Which Actually Struck Cádiz.* The publication offered a description of the epidemic's origins and symptoms and suggested a possible cure.[58] With so many publications available, one popular daily, *El Redactor General* (The General Editor), chose to excerpt the "most interesting" news and correspondence from national and foreign sources, with an emphasis on politics, literature, art, and the sciences.[59] Those involved with the publication included figures from Quintana's salon such as Alcalá Galiano, Capmany, and Gallego.[60]

Yet consumers in Cádiz displayed a seemingly inexhaustible appetite for the written word. *El Conciso,* for example, became one of the most influential papers in the city and carried detailed transcripts of the debates in the Cortes. It had a press run of close to two thousand, the largest of any periodical in Cádiz during the war.[61] Unlike Quintana's weekly newspaper, *El Conciso* initially came out every other day and became a daily by 1812. Gaspar María de Ogirando, in collaboration with writers and poets such as José Robles, a friend of Alcalá Galiano, began publishing in Cádiz in August 1810.[62] Providing detailed reporting on the proceedings of the Cortes, Ogirando covered the opening day of the sessions and praised the elected representatives that had gathered: "Spanish people! Now your sovereignty is represented with dignity in the Deputies that your election and propitious luck have brought to the sanctuary of the Country!"[63] The paper continually referred to the Cortes as the expression of the will of the people.[64] Ogirando quoted a speech by the deputy Agustín Argüelles in which he "declared the Spanish people incapable of disobeying the mandates of a body which they have so desired, which they have formed, in whom they deposited their rights, and to whom they will defend and sustain against the power of tyranny."[65] A subsequent issue posited that "all these kinds of propositions, born of justice and rectitude, produce such an effect on the people that they become enraptured in pleasure and penetrated with love toward the august congress where they resoundingly give consolation to the innocent and oppressed, and infuse the others with terror."[66]

The Cortes tackled divisive issues that had implications beyond the confines of politics and institutional restructuring. Debates over the limits of monarchical power and the inquisitorial regime touched upon the meaning of Spanish identity in an increasingly secular world. For instance, in sessions that elicited a great deal of attention from the public, representatives in the Cortes pushed for the consecration of liberal ideals such as free speech and the elimination of state censorship. According to *El Conciso,* "the people decidedly patronized [the debates over freedom of the press]."[67] Deputies such as the cleric Diego Muñoz Torrero urged the Cortes to stand up for individual rights of expression as a guarantor against arbitrary and despotic government: "The Nation has the right to fulfill its duties and to examine the conduct of all its officials and Deputies, as the only judge that must know if they complete their obligations, a right which it cannot relinquish as a Nation . . . it is necessary as a safeguard to restrain the will of the Cortes and of the executive power, in case they want to separate themselves from the will of the Nation: this safeguard cannot be anything else but the peaceful tribunal of public opinion; that is to say, the ability to speak and to write."[68] This polemical statement drew criticism from conservative members of the Cortes because the freedom to speak and write outside of the authority of royal censors signified a radical break with established norms. Yet liberals fought back, with one deputy arguing that the right to express one's thoughts came directly from God: "Sr. Morales proves that the ability to express one's thoughts comes from heaven, being the auxiliary to the spoken word and to the invention of written language, that is, to deprive a man of such a precious prerogative, would be to usurp tyrannically from him a gift that the same God granted to him."[69] No longer did the monarchy wield absolute authority, but the representable populace, the people of the nation, mediated political power through the periodical press and the voices of their elected officials.

Liberals at Cádiz, including prominent ecclesiastics such as Muñoz Torrero, put restraints on freedom of expression and separated ideas concerning politics from those that impinged upon Catholic doctrine. Yet the Constitution had enshrined Catholicism as a fundamental part of the liberal state. This produced the paradoxical effect of stifling religious dissent while encouraging political debate. In *El Robespierre Español,* an 1811 editorial argued that legal limits be placed upon freedom of speech but did not specify where to draw the line.[70] While some deputies, such as José Mexía, "asked to extend freedom of the press even to religious works," the majority of representatives rejected such a radical proposal.[71] The Constitution ultimately retained censorship of all matters pertaining to religion and deferred to the rulings set down by the Council of Trent. The right to express political ideas was protected by law; religious matters were not covered by the legislation. Deputies claimed that this would prevent the abuse of the newly established right to free speech. Ogirando highlighted the importance of public opinion in relation to freedom of the press: "The opinion of the people is that they should be consulted in order to prevent mistakes. And how do we know the general opinion, if we deny freedom of the press?"[72] Accordingly, elected representatives were subject to the general will of the people, and freedom of the press was critical. Without the right to publish, Ogirando stated, the people would not be able to express themselves.

Other periodicals similarly hailed public opinion as the overarching symbol of a society in which representative government and liberal values had taken root. Pedro Pascasio Fernández Sardino, a medic and former officer in the military, published *El Robespierre Español, amigo de las leyes* (The Spanish Robespierre, Friend of the Laws) with his wife in Cádiz from 1811 to 1812. While the publication did not enjoy the commercial success of Quintana's *Semanario Patriótico, El Robespierre Español* represented a more radical and populist liberalism that had taken hold in many circles. Fernández Sardino openly quarreled with liberals and conservatives alike in the pursuit of liberties such as freedom of speech. After attacking two generals and the minister of war in issue number seven, he faced tremendous pressure from the Cortes. On July 6, 1811, debate largely focused on the issue of press freedom, and deputies disputed whether or not the established procedures would prevent the abuse of the law, with *El Robespierre Español* being cited as the case in point. "The name itself is seditious," one representative asserted, wondering aloud how the editor had been able to avoid prosecution. Complaining that "Robespierre and friend of the laws are ideas which are entirely opposed to one another," he roundly condemned the embrace of revolution, terror, and anarchy.[73] In the aftermath of such polemics centering on Fernández Sardino's publication, the government detained him and confiscated his papers; yet the enterprise carried on under the auspices of his wife, María del Carmen Silva.[74]

In spite of these difficulties, *El Robespierre Español* described public opinion as founded upon prudent judgment and rational debate. The paper praised the effects of public opinion, "which the representatives of the people should incessantly consult. . . . This is the touchstone, where the purities of the law are tested, to ascertain if it is true: this is the crucible, where the fire of true reason cleans, purifies, and refines."[75] Like Quintana Roo, Fernández Sardino considered the formation of public opinion a process grounded in reason rather than emotion or sentiment. In a stylized manner that paralleled religious catechisms from the time, he composed a dialogue of rhetorical questions followed by detailed responses to drive home his argument: "Q. I am impatient to know what public opinion is. A. It is public judgment that the majority of citizens form around an interesting subject for the common good of the country."[76] Significantly, he did not claim that all citizens shared a common opinion, but rather that public opinion formed from the majority position. This pointed to an interpretation of public opinion as a process that involved discussion and debate among a plurality of views, ultimately leading to public judgment. While he may have glossed over contradictions between pluralism and unanimity, Fernández Sardino advanced the notion of a sphere of dialogue and rational-critical thinking rather than a unitary conception of the general will. Although the majority of citizens' judgments formed public opinion, minorities did have their voices heard. Jean Jacques Rousseau similarly had noted that "for a will to be general, it need not always be unanimous," a statement he qualified by emphasizing that it was indeed necessary "for all the votes to be counted."[77] This vision of the public sphere encouraged rather than stifled a wide range of opinions and ideological dispositions.

The public sphere, as described by Fernández Sardino in *El Robespierre Español,* emerged along with constitutional debates over free speech and freedom of the press. As noted, Fernández Sardino outlined a paradigm of public space in which public opinion was expressed through "speech, with works, and with a free press." In a follow-up issue, he further explained the three categories that were essential to the rights of the Spanish citizen and to the existence of public opinion. He asked: "How does one manifest speech? A. Each citizen speaking with their friends secretly in their house, and publicly in the streets, plazas, cafes, salons, theaters, etc." Freedom of speech correlated with the responsibilities of elected officials to represent faithfully the views of the public. He qualified this point by noting that not all free speech constituted the manifestation of public opinion, as elected officials could not always discern the plurality of opinions on a political issue: "But that public opinion, as is plain to see, is insufficient; because Deputies cannot go gathering opinions in private and public spaces, to calculate exactly the plurality, and thereby arrive at a knowledge of the general will."[78] Fernández Sardino invested the power of all citizens "to print freely and frankly their opinion, without violating the rights of the society, nor of any citizen in particular," with a great deal of significance.[79] Citizens could articulate their views on public matters most effectively through the outlet of print media. Freedom of speech, accordingly, had to be complemented by freedom of action and of the press.

Fernández Sardino decried arbitrary and despotic rule as antithetical to liberal government. He defined freedom of action in terms of the right to revolt against unjust and illegitimate authority: "In modern States this idea of public opinion as action, when it is verified, is properly called revolution. These revolutions succeed, almost always, because despotic Governments do not consult nor do they respect public opinion."[80] As absolutist regimes were not concerned with the rights and opinions of the people, they did not retain legitimate recourse to state power in the liberal age.

Within this model of the public sphere, Fernández Sardino claimed that ideas that reflected all social classes circulated in a vibrant print culture. In a rhetorical dialogue from 1811, he wrote:

> How can the free press verify the manifestation of public opinion, being that in a nation not all citizens have the talent necessary to print their opinion, but only journalists, the lettered and the wise, and some writer or another with limited abilities, scarcely more than the common mass of the people? A. The general opinion of journalists, the lettered and the wise is enough to express and represent public opinion; just as two hundred Deputies are enough, for example, to represent all of a nation, composed of many million citizens. . . The people competitively buy their writings to read with ardent desire, joyously seeing in them their own opinions.[81]

Comparing political representation with the process of producing and distributing the periodical press, *El Robespierre Español* argued for a democratic vision of liberal society. Just as elected representatives calculated public opinion and governed accordingly, the press responded to the spectrum of public opinion. Due to the market forces of competition as well as to the critical faculties of readers and their lettered correspondence with editors, Fernández Sardino claimed, the public sphere accurately conveyed the voices of all Spanish citizens.

Conservatives, including prominent clerics, also published newspapers and pamphlets, benefiting from the opening of a public space for dialogue during wartime. Simultaneously, a liberal political revolution and brutal warfare engulfing the peninsula offered opportunities for expression across the political spectrum. Manuel Traggia, for example, offered a contrasting view of the rise of the periodical press, highlighting the continued importance and relevance of traditional Catholic dogma to the

Spanish public. In his periodical, Traggia advocated the print media as an extension of the ephemera of the spoken word: "I believe that something more is needed to imprint upon the heart certain religious truths that are of the utmost importance. A pious periodical is the most simple and effective medium. The doctrine of sermons is nothing more than a voice that passes, and is forgotten with ease. . . . Not so the periodical, that is brief, simple, and pleasing to hear with a variety of issues, ideas and doctrines. The newspaper passes through the streets and plazas; it is read in crowds, and in the homes of families. It passes hand to hand, it is repeated at all hours, it is contemplated and conserved."[82] Traggia captured well the burgeoning of political sociability and the ways in which information was transmitted. Rather than focus on the pulpit, he urged the faithful to embrace the press and to serve as conduits of news for the illiterate. While espousing conservative views, Traggia, along with many other opponents of liberalism, began to play a part in the public debates between competing ideological forces.

Despite fundamental differences, religious referents often bridged the gap between oppositional political factions. A comparison between the insurgent periodical *El Despertador Americano* (The American Awakener), edited by the priest Francisco Severo Maldonado, and a royalist sermon illustrates the discursive convergence between competing forces of identification in New Spain. In the second issue, Maldonado painted the insurgency as acting according to the will of God: "*Americans.* Heaven has declared for you, the will of God manifests itself each day with unequivocal indications of the most decided and celebrated approval of our Cause."[83] One week later, in January 1811, he implored his compatriots to join the cause: "Why do you fight on the side of the Europeans? Are you perhaps moved to the defense of Religion, the defense of our Sacrosanct Faith? But this is exactly our cause, on this matter our feeling is the same as theirs."[84] In invective leveled against the rebellion led by Hidalgo, the royalist priest Miguel Santos Villa exclaimed: "Your God and Lord is inside of you, and you will fight with your gifts to liberate yourselves from the danger of the rebellion."[85] Santos Villa portrayed God as a central figure within an individualized struggle, invoking the image of a soldier fighting in the name of religion. Significantly, both factions fought in the name of the Catholic faith and ardently believed God was on their side.

Even the most liberal periodicals such as *Semanario Patriótico* often fell back on religious paradigms in characterizing the War of Independence in peninsular Spain. In an editorial devoted to the subject of patriotism,

Quintana identified countries privileged by God as the most patriotic: "Only in those countries favored by heaven can one find the passion that we know by the name of *Patriotism*." In the same issue, he noted that divine retribution would befall the enemies of Spain, contrasting "the horrible calamity of an avenging God going to inspire terror in our enemies, and pursuing them in their flight" with "the love of the country, and recent Spanish triumphs, with jubilation and happiness overflowing in all Spaniards."[86] Quintana ultimately maintained that religion had been a prominent factor animating the defense of the nation: "The war we have endured is against a foreign aggressor, against an outside tyrant who has neither the right nor any reason to rule over the Spaniards, and whose domination and government we resist for justice, religion, honor, vengeance and for all types of obligations and political and moral incitements."[87] Along similar lines, in an article on the rights of societies, *El Robespierre Español* asked: "What are the privileges of a nation, or the social rights that must be respected?" The response listed: "Their religion, their constitution, their laws, their government, their institutions, their habits and customs, and the integrity of their territory."[88] Notably, religion appeared first, followed by devotion to constitutionalism and observation of the law. Even for a radical publication, religion was not an object of denigration. While religion did not suffuse the editorials of these periodicals, Hispanic liberals did not rail against Catholicism or espouse a purely materialist agenda.

Other *letrados,* such as Gallardo, although ridiculing friars and monastic life, manifested a continued attachment to Catholic spirituality.[89] Unlike revolutionaries involved in the de-Christianization campaigns undertaken during the French Revolution, notable Hispanic radicals decried the extravagance and hypocrisy of ecclesiastics while adhering to the tenets of Catholic faith. Gallardo introduced his satire of conservative views in Spain with a disclaimer: "My aim has never been (nor would God permit it!) to upbraid the ecclesiastical estate in general, nor in the least the individuals that through virtue and exemplary doctrine are the edification of strong souls, the alimentation of the weak, and the support of just liberty. I only take aim against the dissolute members of the various hierarchies of the Church."[90] Gallardo separated his anticlerical position, disparaging representatives of the church, from an overarching attack on religion itself. As liberals pushed forward an agenda of reform, in part aimed at restructuring the finances of the Old Regime church, they began to face growing opposition among conservatives, whom they pejoratively labeled *serviles.*[91]

Despite resistance from the right, the Constitution, promulgated in March 1812, enacted the core principles of nineteenth-century European liberalism. On March 19, 1812, the day the new Constitution was proclaimed, *El Conciso* declared, "Today starts the great epoch in which justice rises above the ruins of despotism on her liberal throne."[92] Editorials in *El Conciso* imagined the people as the symbolic embodiment of the promise of liberalism. Throughout 1812, for example, Ogirando printed a nationalist call to arms under the date of each issue: "Year V of the glorious struggle fought by the Spanish people against tyranny." Increasingly, the idea of the people was all-encompassing—they served as the defenders of the country and as champions of the liberal cause.

The cleric Bárcena came to be a fierce proponent of the Constitution of 1812 in New Spain. Preaching in 1813 on the sanctity and inviolability of the compact between all Spaniards, both European and American, and their king, he proclaimed: "These radical laws, this fundamental pact made between the individuals of a state, is that which we call the Constitution."[93] Although Enlightenment intellectuals had grounded this idea of a social compact in their firm adherence to absolute monarchy, the political crisis that engulfed the Hispanic world in the aftermath of 1808 had precipitated new justifications for national sovereignty, based on an original accord between the king and the people. The Constitution of 1812, as the liberal interpretation of natural law epistemology, was presented as the logical extension of contract theories dating to the sixteenth and seventeenth centuries.

The Constitution also enshrined the basis of state authority and national identity in religion. The text begins: "In the name of God almighty, Father, Son and Holy Ghost, author and supreme legislator of Society."[94] Quintana praised the compromise legislators achieved in the wording of the introduction, as traditionalist deputies had advocated a lengthier passage devoting the work of the Cortes to the Virgin Mary: "Some deputies wanted a more extensive invocation, that embraced the mysteries and the Virgin, so that even children could learn Christian doctrine from the constitution; but like all of this, however good it may be, it didn't come to pass, and certainly did not give the political constitution the air of an ecclesiastical constitution with an inopportune or formal exposition that our enemies might make use of to censure the assembly of the council and ridicule them: the article was approved as it was."[95] According to Joaquín Lorenzo Villanueva, deputy of the Cortes from Valencia, representatives in Cádiz had divinely sanctioned the Constitution and its laws as being based upon Catholic principles and as an expression of the sentiments and faith of the Spanish people: "In it [the Cortes], first as the most solid foundation of this great edifice, we proclaim the holy apostolic Roman Catholic religion, as the true and sole religion of the state, establishing that the nation protects it as it will always protect it following the example of our elders, with wise and just laws. To this incomparable and most solid good, without which it is not possible to move forward on the path toward happiness, and that manifests the true piety and religious sentiments of the deputy representatives that have sanctioned it, we add the august and solemn declaration that sovereignty resides essentially in the nation."[96] Spaniards, accordingly, formed a national community on the basis of their common Catholicism, which provided the most solid foundation for the construction of the nation. Villanueva exhorted priests and the religious at all levels to preach the new political doctrines of liberal nationalism to their parishioners in the name of God: "This is the fortunate occasion on which respectable prelates, the venerable parish priests and the rest of the ecclesiastics of all classes, will be able to and even should teach the people, as the holy religion of Jesus Christ commands, proper submission and obedience to the powers, that is, to our legitimate actual government and their decrees."[97] Thus a public sphere had emerged that encompassed the church and placed clerics squarely within the parameters of debates over state formation and national identity.

Moreover, the clergy did diffuse the ideology of constitutionalism and representation in the name of religion and monarchy.[98] On May 2, 1812, the Cortes sent out detailed instructions on how to observe and properly honor the new constitutional code. The end of the text specified: "In all the Cathedrals, Colleges, Universities, and Religious Communities a Mass will be held [followed by recital of] *Te Deum* after the respective Town Councils and Communities have sworn loyalty to the Constitution. . . . In the Armies and Navy . . . after receiving the Constitution . . . and reading all of it in a loud voice, the Chief, Officials and Troops will swear loyalty immediately in front of the flags."[99] Municipalities across the monarchy received and implemented these orders exactingly. Edicts printed and posted by local governments decreed specific days on which to swear loyalty to the Constitution in all parochial churches and in city cathedrals. For example, a proclamation issued in Seville on September 10, 1812, read: "All the residents of each town must come together during the holiday in their respective parish church . . . the Constitution will be read before the offertory; it will be done by the Parish Priest . . . and after the Mass concludes all the residents and the Clergy will swear an oath to defend the Constitution, and to be loyal to the King, under the profession of faith contained within the same decree; they will end by singing the *Te Deum*."[100] By law, the clergy were charged with organizing the consecration of the Constitution, and the decree listed the ceremonies to be held in each church the following Saturday and Sunday.

In the Americas, clerics openly espoused the benefits of the electoral process to their parishioners. Manuel Abad Queipo, an Asturian who had come to New Spain in 1786, preached the doctrines of liberalism as bishop of Michoacán: "The same Spanish Nation, legitimately represented in the august and majestic Congress of the general and extraordinary Cortes, has just finished swearing before all to defend to the death the purity of the apostolic, Roman Catholic Religion, the freedom of the King, the independence of the Nation and the integrity of all its territory, to whose most sincere exposition, the most solemn and sacred that a people can make, all formally concur by way of the National Representatives."[101] Significantly, clerics such as Abad Queipo supported ideals of negotiation and contestation in the realm of politics. They celebrated the displacement of absolute authority and hierarchy by political representation and power allocated to individual voters charged with an elective capacity. Many clerics in Spanish America ardently deployed liberal ideals to voice displeasure over what they viewed as the arbitrary rule that had been exercised in the overseas provinces of the monarchy since the era of the Bourbon reforms. The idea of the representable individual as a national citizen fundamentally altered conceptions of political relationships and sovereignty in the Americas and in peninsular Spain. With citizens no longer bonded to the monarch by the duties of a subject as the legal ties of seignorialism were abolished, conceptions of identity also changed.

Abad Queipo also pointed to the just treatment of the Indians as a hallmark of the new constitutional system. Although he noted that "if the Indians have not advanced more it is because they are very backward in their civilization," he praised the extension of legal rights to their communities. In contrast to the treatment of the indigenous meted out by other imperial powers such as the French and English, Abad Queipo argued, Indians in Spanish America received the same legal rights and protections as Spaniards: "The Spanish Nation brought together since the beginning these conquests of the Crown of Castile, making them integral parts of the Monarchy, and communicating to the conquered natives all the rights the Conquistadors enjoyed, making all the parts one and the same Monarchy, one and the same Nation and one single family, as the general Cortes explains in their sanction of the Laws proceeding from last October fifteenth."[102] The Constitution, while excluding those of African ancestry, did bestow individual rights to Indian males in a conception of citizenship and identity more inclusive than any offered by other European states of the time.

CONCLUSION: THE OVERLAPPING SPACES OF THE PUBLIC SPHERE

Public opinion grew out of the overlapping spaces of religious culture, print media, salons, and politics. Just as many priests joined the struggle and took up arms as soldiers in Spain and Spanish America in the wars sparked by peninsular turmoil, clerics acted as citizens, writers, deputies, and representatives of the church in opening up the Catholic public sphere across the Spanish Monarchy.[103] The clergy participated alongside actors from a variety of classes and occupations in establishing the parameters of the new national government. Drawing from ideological roots in Jansenism, Hispanic Enlightenment culture, and European liberalism of the early nineteenth century, clerics circulated new conceptions of state authority and national sovereignty in the Catholic public sphere. They published newspapers, wrote editorials, and spoke from pulpits and town plazas, encouraging rational-critical debate and the use of the vernacular in secular and sacred spaces. They used a language common to all public figures by 1808 that was steeped in both liberal thought and religious tradition. With the sacred domain of the church serving as a legislative chamber for the secular state, the roles of cleric and elected official became blurred. By preaching the doctrines of natural law and the contractual theory of government, clerics had succeeded, by the late eighteenth century, in establishing a connection between patriotism, rationality, and religion. Reason and religion coexisted harmoniously within the boundaries set out by reformist clerics and enlightened officials. Instituting the radical ideology of national sovereignty in place of royal absolutism and creating citizens in place of subjects changed the political landscape by 1812, while Article 12 of the Constitution maintained the traditional role of religion in a confessional state. The public became endowed with considerable power over elected officials charged with the functions of national government in the name of the people.

Rational-critical debates involved not only the creation of a new state but altered definitions of identity in the new age of nationalism. Citizenship incorporated the great majority of the inhabitants of the territories of the Spanish Monarchy, including Indians in the New World, and established the basis of a new nation stretching across the Atlantic. Yet religion and the mantle of monarchy provided a common thread of identification for all Spaniards, transcending ideology and nationalist identification. A common culture of Catholicism, constitutionalism, and fidelity to the monarch tied together the far-flung Spanish territories. Nationalists imagined Spanish identity in discourses structured around religious imagery and liberal symbolism in the variety of spaces of the Catholic public sphere in the Hispanic Atlantic world.

4

MAKING THE SPANISH CATHOLIC CITIZEN

Inquisition, Race, and Gender

After the success of writing a constitution for the war-torn provinces of the Spanish Monarchy at the height of the conflict with France, the elected deputies of the Cortes engaged in a protracted struggle over the nature and meaning of the Inquisition, one of the most enduring symbols of the Old Regime. The cleric and deputy of the Cortes, Diego Muñoz Torrero, declared in 1812: "The Inquisition is incompatible with the Constitution, because it is opposed to the sovereignty and independence of the Nation and of the civil liberty of Spaniards, which the Cortes wanted to assure and consolidate in the law." "The inquisitor," Muñoz Torrero insisted, "is a sovereign within a sovereign Nation, or at the side of a sovereign prince; because he dictates laws, applies them to particular cases, and oversees their implementation."[1] The early-nineteenth-century liberal vision of a sovereign, national people, freed from the shackles of an Inquisitorial regime, contrasted greatly with opposing invective launched by defenders of the Inquisition and the Old Regime state. In a Catholic nation, from the point of view of conservatives, the defense of religion must be an ongoing struggle: "As princes, in times of peace, maintain their armed forces to keep their enemies abroad at bay, the same model should remain for the internal enemies of a Catholic Nation to preserve it from the insult of heresies."[2] Accordingly, the Inquisition was the internal bulwark against heresy just as loyal soldiers defended the faith against foreign aggressors. The battle over whether to maintain Inquisitorial courts was part of the larger debate over the definition of the new transatlantic Spanish polity of 1812 and exactly what it meant to be a member of the national community.

Was religion—and the Inquisition as its most potent symbol—central to an imagined Spanish national character, as subsequent writers would claim? William Prescott, writing in 1855, understood nineteenth-century Spain as a country "folded under the dark wing of the Inquisition . . . shut out from the light which in the sixteenth century broke over the rest of Europe, stimulating nations to greater enterprise in every department of knowledge."[3] Yet enlightened clerics, among many prominent critics, decried the Inquisitorial process and sanctioned a centralized constitutional government with the power of judicial oversight. As the generation of 1812, the *doceañistas,* proffered civil liberties and the idea of national citizenship to replace the arbitrary rule of a monarch over its subjects, how did the politics and culture of revolutionary Cádiz affect the looming confrontation between church and state? Did a majority of the people prefer the Inquisition and the preservation of traditional forms of order and hierarchy to a liberal program of political freedom and cultural change? The fate of the Inquisitorial courts was not decided in 1812, and within a year, vitriolic debates ensued over the rights and privileges of Inquisitors and the church in a liberal state. Encoding Spanish citizenship with religious overtones in the Constitution of 1812 prior to a definitive ruling on the status of the Inquisition destabilized an otherwise inclusive national identity across the Spanish Monarchy.

In contrast to the heated public discussions over religious tribunals, issues of race, class, and gender in relation to citizenship did not generate great controversy. The concepts of lineage and descent tied such conversations together, linking anti-Judaic sentiment to ideologies of ethnic difference and inferiority. Similarly, women's exclusion from the political spectrum was premised upon a gendered rhetoric that ascribed weakness and sin to femininity. The language deployed during debates over the Inquisition mirrored the broader discussion over the nature and meaning of the nation and the national citizen in the newly consecrated transatlantic Spanish Monarchy. In turn, church-state conflict proved far more divisive than did drawing distinctions between Indians and those of African descent, between active and passive citizens, and between the public political sphere and the private sphere of female domesticity.

MODELS OF NATIONAL CITIZENSHIP

As one contemporary historian notes, "The spread of citizenship arose from the equation of civil and political rights in the new principle of popular sovereignty."[4] In comparison to other cases in Europe, however, the Spanish Monarchy does not conform to the models of citizenship and nationality that have been put forward by scholars. Charles Tilly argues that "religious solidarities . . . generally lost their legal standing as bases of civic distinctions in Europe during the broadening of citizenship. . . . What became rare was the official incorporation of religious distinctions into definitions of citizenship."[5] Rogers Brubaker proposes two "distinctive understandings of nationhood . . . embodied and expressed in sharply differing definitions of citizenship." Thus he contrasts "the expansive, assimilationist citizenship law of France" with "the German definition of citizenry as a community of descent." Other scholars make similar claims that revolutionary France "brought into being one of the most participatory and democratic national communities in the world."[6] The dichotomy between the inclusiveness of French citizenship, based upon ideals of assimilation, and exclusive German citizenship, corresponding to Romantic conceptions of the *volk* and a community of ethnic descent, does not correspond to the transatlantic community of national citizens envisioned for the Spanish Monarchy in 1812.[7] Spanish legislators drew upon a confluence of competing discourses of nationalism that merged notions of civic and particularist identity. Defenders of the Old Regime, to the contrary, upheld a particularist notion of national identity as an outgrowth of Catholic faith.[8] Yet both civic and particularist aspects of Spanish national identity ultimately became enshrined in the Constitution of 1812, which mandated inclusive citizenship requirements while maintaining Catholicism as the true measure of a Spaniard.

The Constitution of 1812 definitively declared Spain a confessional nation as it abrogated seignorialism and a divine right monarchy, and built the framework of liberal government. Liberalism coexisted with traditional conceptions of a state that privileged the church and retained the figure of the monarch. The Spanish national citizen was by definition Catholic and resident in the dominions of the Spanish Monarchy. Tamar Herzog posits a thesis of continuity between early modern forms of citizenship, *vecindad*, and those put into practice in 1812. She argues that local processes and Old Regime terminology profoundly influenced the construction of the national citizen and notions of inclusion and exclusion.[9] Broadly inclusive elements of the Constitution, such as the establishment of legal standing and civil rights for Indians of the Americas, stood in stark contrast to the exclusion of those considered outside of a community of descent, such as those of African ancestry. Paradoxically, Spanish citizenship incorporated both a discourse of inclusivity, marked by consensual rights for male residents, as well as of exclusivity, which emphasized ethnic descent and religious uniformity.

During the debates of the Cortes of Cádiz, deputies positioned race, class, and gender at the center of definitions of the citizen. Indians in the Americas received rights accorded to all Spaniards, while those of African descent were denied political and civic privileges. Issues of class became especially salient regarding the status and representation of Creoles, Indians, and the *castas,* those of mixed ancestry, in the Americas. Representatives deliberated over whether rights would be conferred upon citizens regardless of property qualifications or whether different levels of citizenship corresponded to one's class. Women were excluded definitively from political participation, as only "hombres libres" (free men), "avecindados" (residents) in the Spanish dominions, fell under the definition of *españoles* according to Article 5 of the Constitution. As liberal politics created the gendered domains of public and private, women were increasingly marginalized. In addition, citizenship certainly was not considered for those outside of the Catholic faith. The history of church-state relations, along with the confessional clause contained in Article 12 of the Constitution, nonetheless complicated debates over nationalization and citizenship.

SPANISH CITIZENSHIP AND THE INQUISITION

The Inquisition played a central role in defining not only political affiliations but the nation and the citizen. Conservatives equated liberals with the godless French and their collaborators, the *afrancesados,* who, they claimed, were determined to infect Spanish culture with French values and undermine Catholic tradition. The French quickly put an end to the Spanish Inquisition in occupied territory with the Constitution of Bayonne, signed in 1808. In addition, in the wake of revolutionary France's admittance of Jews as national citizens and Napoleon's edicts of tolerance toward the Jewish population, anti-French sentiment came to be associated with anti-Judaism in popular wartime rhetoric, establishing a connection between atheistic French revolutionaries and heretical Jews. For example, Antonio de Capmany even titled his famous pamphlet *Centinela contra franceses* (Sentinel against the French), playing off of a seventeenth-century diatribe entitled *Centinela contra judíos* (Sentinel against Jews).[10]

Such associations cemented a connection between the dangers posed by French occupation and the threats to religious purity symbolized by Judaizing *conversos* (the converted, or New Christians).

As discussed in earlier chapters, nationalist rhetoric conflated the virtues of Catholicism with the qualities of essential Spanishness. To staunch defenders of the Inquisition, only the sacrilegious, who by definition were not members of the Spanish national community, would seek abolition. In the brief period between the much-anticipated return of Fernando VII to Spain in March 1814 and the annulment of the Constitution in May 1814, reactionary priests increased their attacks on the legislative agenda implemented by the Cortes of Cádiz. One friar explicitly distinguished between ideals supposedly imported from France and the religious convictions of Catholic Spain: "Is it necessary to discuss prematurely those points that are, in some ways, walls that divide the Spaniards and the French? Is there, by fortune, an Inquisition in France? Are there Clerics and Friars? Are there Nobles? Do they maintain decorum and moderation in the Military? Do they prohibit heresy and blasphemy? All to the contrary. And is this a fundamental contrast between both nations? So it is. Why then is there such a rush in wanting to make them the same?"[11] He represented Spain as the antithesis of an imagined French enemy, in which all inhabitants lived as equals in an atmosphere of unmitigated profligacy. All social rank, religious practice, and legal restraint had been abolished. Priests, in drawing such a stark contrast between supposed national traits, fostered the notion that a separate Spanish identity, guarded by Inquisitorial courts, had to be immunized against the French contagion. The tone and content of indictments leveled against the constitutional government served as the basis of an oppositional, conservative discourse on Spanish nationalism.

This line of reasoning clearly constructed a particularist, exclusionary notion of Spanish national identity, based upon a traditional reading of Spanish history. Conservative bishops insisted, "We know very well that all of the Spanish people are solidly Christian, and want to be so." Furthermore, they argued that "the general insurrection in all of Spain, and its admirable perseverance in the war against a decidedly impious enemy; [and] the energetic and multiple representations in favor of the Inquisition" demonstrated both the people's will to sustain a religious war and their support for the Inquisitorial tribunals, drawing parallels between the two sacred causes.[12] Being Spanish, being Christian, fighting the impious French, and defending the Inquisition were inextricably linked in such rhetorical flourishes. The anonymous author of *Apología de la Inquis-*

ición (Defense of the Inquisition) railed against a popular press described as unrepresentative of the authentic voice of the people: "The opinion of the Spanish people is not that of four authors or editors of public papers; the opinion of the people, or of a corporation, is not that of everyone: *the good Spaniards* detest the abuses and the infractions against wise laws that should govern us. . . . The largest part of the kingdom, invaded by enemies, cannot manifest to us their desires and opinions."[13] Accordingly, true Spaniards—*los buenos españoles*—could not vote in favor of abolishing the venerable and historic institution of the Inquisition, and as Catholics and deputies, representatives in Cádiz could not overturn centuries of clerical privilege.

Such rhetoric spilled over into the Catholic public sphere, as often virulent newspaper editorials and sermons advocated controversial and polemical positions. Conservatives waged a war of words against those who would claim to speak for the Spanish people. The author of *Apología de la Inquisición* claimed to legitimately reflect public opinion in the Spanish Monarchy. He asserted that he understood the desires of the Spanish people: "I do not judge myself authorized to be the organ or the interpreter of public opinion; but I believe that, without temerity, I can put forward the following proposition: THE SPANISH PEOPLE WOULD VIEW WITH GREAT DISGUST THAT THE INQUISITION HAS BEEN ABOLISHED IN SPAIN."[14] Yet liberals also claimed to represent the national will, and a decisive majority of the Cortes voted to abolish the Inquisition, in the name of Catholic principles and state support for the church, on January 22, 1813. Writing as president of the constitutional commission charged with reviewing the record of the Spanish Inquisition, Muñoz Torrero maintained: "There is no doubt that it is the general will of the Nation to conserve the purity of the Catholic religion; that it be protected by wise and just laws, and that the profession of another faith not be permitted. The universal joy that the Constitution has received, and the eulogized article XII, is convincing proof of it."[15] Ratification of Article 12 of the Constitution demonstrated continuity with Spain's historical legacy of defending the Catholic faith. Liberal legislators fundamentally agreed with the principle of state-sponsored religion and did not seek to tolerate other faiths. Despite agreeing with conservatives on the importance of preserving Catholic hegemony in Spain, however, many liberal clerics serving in the Cortes, such as Muñoz Torrero, voted to end the Inquisition, and traditionalists, known derisively as *serviles*, avidly sought to maintain it. The Inquisition became a measure of Spanish national heritage, a cultural patrimony of sorts, pitting those defending order, tradition, and hierarchy against advocates of representative government, popular sovereignty, and greater civil liberties for individuals endowed with natural rights.

To staunch liberals such as Muñoz Torrero, the history of the Inquisition proved that Spaniards of all classes never unequivocally supported the tremendous powers wielded by Inquisitors. He argued that the church in Spain had flourished prior to the Inquisition and that the faith was preserved through the strict administration of civil laws. He recounted the history of the establishment of the Inquisition as a process rife with conflict and contestation: "The Inquisition was established against the will of the towns and the complaints of the Cortes. . . . The towns recognized then their privileges (*fueros*), liberties and rights were opposed to its establishment . . . and there was not a single province in the kingdom of Aragon that did not oppose it and even openly resist it."[16] Seen through the optic of jurisdictional law, the rights of the people, equated with those of the towns (*los pueblos*), had been trampled by a disinterested centralizing authority.[17] In reference to the Cortes of 1518 that gathered at Valladolid, Muñoz Torrero claimed that a reawakened Spanish nation had spoken with unanimity against the abuses of an unrepresentative court:

> This is the first time that the Nation, through its representatives, manifested its way of thinking about the Inquisitorial court that had been established without a hearing. Their words radiated the zeal that always distinguished Spaniards, through their faith and justice, their adhesion to the old customs and the Canons that established them, their love of the laws and the vigilant observation of them; and their desire and requests of prosecutors that wrongdoers be punished, but that the innocent do not suffer; and to achieve this they ask that the courts that hear this class of crimes return to their old status; that ordinary judges take up issues of faith and justice, which does not give them a subordinate position as under the Inquisition, but a principal role, because they are the judges born of the faithful of their bishopric and judge, not by new ways and tortured paths, but on the basis of the holy Canons and common law.[18]

This exemplified the way in which liberals viewed the "decline" of Spain, a nation that had atrophied since the accession of the despotic Habsburgs. In order to regenerate Spanish vitality and return to a supposedly ancient spirit of liberty, representative councils had to be reconvened and deputies once again given a voice in policy matters. Accordingly, Spanish history during the Habsburg dynasty had been knocked off its true course by royal absolutism and the diminished powers allocated to local and regional authorities, thereby severing Spain's historical tradition of civic representation.

The Inquisition, therefore, did not serve the general will, and in fact deviated from the consensus of the overwhelming majority. Muñoz Torrero purported to have evidence of ecclesiastical infighting: "The Inquisition was always in a perpetual fight against the bishops, courts and royal councils that were the authorities, which offers another way of understanding the people's way of thinking."[19] Even in the first years of its operation, Muñoz Torrero pointed out, the Inquisition had been resisted openly: "Read, if you want, all the collections of the Cortes that exist, and you will never find in them, nor in the historians of the time, one single document that proves that the Inquisition was the will of the Nation. At the 1480 Toledo Cortes, the prosecutors contented themselves with resolving that the Moors and the Jews separate themselves from the Christians and live and reside in different neighborhoods. . . . What is more, not only did the Cortes not consent in the establishment of the Inquisition, but as one can see, almost all the provinces openly resisted it, causing commotions and disturbances."[20] This type of argument is sustained by many contemporary historians, who have documented efforts to rein in the excesses of the Inquisitors and to challenge the secretive nature of the trial process. From the fifteenth through the nineteenth centuries, critics worked to curtail the powers of the Inquisition. As Henry Kamen notes: "Quite obviously a persistent stream of opposition was in continuous existence, dedicated not so much to the suppression of the Inquisition as to the cure of abuses."[21] Advocates of reform called for prisoners to be allocated a number of rights such as legal counsel, access to the accusation and to names of witnesses, and visitation privileges.

Other nineteenth-century liberals cited the exaggerated figures of deaths reportedly caused by the Inquisition and attributed the decline and degeneration of the national body to its excesses. Celebrating the Constitution in 1812, a radical cleric from León, Juan Antonio Posse, attacked the Inquisition: "This odious court has depopulated Spain, has destroyed moral health among us . . . has caused the death of millions of men, including seventy thousand in one city alone, and seven thousand of these in a church." He denounced fanatical devotion to superstition and the hypocrites he alleged to be defending the Inquisition.[22] Posse's numbers were inflated dramatically, as Kamen argues that at the height of its activity, the Inquisition put to death no more than two thousand people in Spain.[23] After 1530, Kamen contends, the Inquisition executed few in the entire Spanish Monarchy, "certainly a lower rate than in any provincial court of justice in Spain or anywhere else in Europe."[24] Posse, although a parish priest, advanced the type of sentiment that would come to characterize Spanish anticlericalism in subsequent decades. Posse's accusations against a court he believed to possess almost unlimited power reflected a growing sense among liberals that reason and law had to replace religious dogmatism as the legitimizing tradition of the nation.

Drawing on the history of the Inquisition to support their case, the commission appointed by the Cortes unwaveringly designated the Inquisition as an illegal body, ineffective in its religious oversight and a threat to the newly proclaimed sovereignty of the Spanish people. The commission could not recommend state support of the tribunals and strongly urged deputies to abolish the Inquisition: "Is there any institution more illegal, more useless to religion, more contrary to all civil and ecclesiastical authorities, more opposed to the rights of Spaniards, that threatens our Sovereignty more?"[25] Evidence from the period suggests that such political pronouncements also reflected popular indignation at the continued existence of the tribunals. The Inquisition had openly supported submission to the French invasion and occupation and demanded order in the face of the uprising of May 2 in Madrid.[26] In New Spain, an anonymous article in *Semanario Patriótico Americano* titled "Letter from an American" roundly condemned the Inquisitors of Mexico City who had declared the idea of the sovereignty of the people to be heresy.[27] Influential figures from the United States such as Benjamin Franklin also had spoken out against the Inquisition. Antonio José Ruíz de Padrón, a cleric and representative from the Canary Islands, cited Franklin's opinion, along with those of others he had met in Philadelphia, in a public session of the Cortes in January 1813.[28] In addition, letters petitioning the Cortes to act on the question of the Inquisition in peninsular Spain displayed hostility toward maintaining an Inquisitorial regime. An overwhelming majority of the laity who had petitioned their legislators favored abolition, although a significant number of clerics lobbied to keep the tribunals.[29]

Yet many vehemently protested that the Inquisition represented continuity with Spain's historical legacy of religious purity. In order to maintain traditional ties between the church and the state, they insisted, the Inquisition must be defended at all costs. Otherwise, the identity of Spain would be jeopardized. One bishop, forced from his diocese by French occupation, beseeched the Cortes to revive the Inquisition in Segovia in order to fulfill their religious duties to the nation: "I speak to an august Congress, that wants to protect, and should protect, the apostolic, Roman Catholic Religion without permitting any other faith or the propagation of errors that could pollute its purity. The holy Tribunal of the Faith has been of the greatest utility in this effort. . . . The reestablishment of the supreme Inquisition would be, then, the complement of such a great work, that all of the Spanish people, not only the Pastors, ardently desire."[30] The symbolism of religious purity infused many such appeals, tacitly invoking the specter of heresy and religious pluralism. Blas Ostolaza, the conservative American deputy to the Cortes, categorically inveighed against the prospect of renewed heretical activity within the territories of the Spanish Monarchy: "Our fundamental laws prevent kings from taking the throne without first swearing to maintain the religion of our fathers, and to prohibit the introduction of heresies into Spanish territory." Explicitly drawing upon historical references, he insisted that Spaniards distance themselves from the false ideas of the French philosophes: "No civilized republic ever permitted philosophes to insult with impunity religion and morality, the laws and the legitimate government."[31] In addition, conservatives rhetorically positioned themselves as partisans of reform, although they saw no reason to abolish the divinely sanctioned tribunals: "If the Inquisition in Spain has as its object the conservation of the purity of the Catholic faith, there can never be a reason to destroy it, and if in that institution abuses are found, prudence dictates that it be reformed."[32] If abuses occurred, according to staunch defenders, they must be corrected, but the Inquisition as a historic institution had to be preserved to ensure the purity of the faith.

The vote on January 22, 1813, to abolish the Inquisition has generally been treated as a divisive and partisan watershed in the historiography of nineteenth-century Spain. For example, William Callahan argues that "the achievements of the Cortes of Cádiz in ecclesiastical affairs were essentially negative," and that deputies left "a legacy of bitterness toward the liberal State among many clerics."[33] Thus, despite the commission's recommendations, the vote did not reflect growing consensus on constitutional monarchy, but instead showed that the government faced strong opposition to policies that impinged upon the sphere of the sacred and the terrain of cultural identity. Ninety deputies voted for abolition, including prominent clerics, and sixty representatives cast votes in favor of maintaining the Inquisition. A pronounced majority of clerics voted for a continuation of the Inquisition's historic role as arbiter of religious practice, yet the figures given by scholars have varied. Raul Morodo and Elías Díaz, subsequently cited by William Callahan, list thirty-two clerics voting to uphold the Inquisition and eleven voting for its elimination.[34] Emilio La Parra López writes that thirty-six clerics voted against abolition and thirteen voted for an end to the tribunals.[35] Yet the January 24, 1813, issue of *El Procurador General de la Nación y del Rey* (The Solicitor General of the Nation and the King) provides the names of fourteen ecclesiastics supporting abolition, and cross-referencing these figures with those of Morodo and Díaz produces a total of nineteen members of the clergy voting to end the Inquisition, with thirty-four against closure.[36] This figure suggests that 36 percent of clerics voted against the Inquisition, representing a sizeable minority of clerical deputies and a much larger proportion than is generally recognized in the historiography. On February 22, the Cortes issued a decree definitively abolishing the Inquisition.

ANTI-JUDAISM AND SPANISH IDENTITY

The debates over the Inquisition and its history as a body charged with rooting out heresy and false converts to Catholicism betray an important legacy of anti-Judaism in Spain. The Inquisition has been treated by most contemporary scholars as an institution primarily concerned with *conversos* and Judaizers residing in peninsular Spain. Kamen argues that in 1480, the Catholic monarchs Fernando and Isabel "set in motion a body whose entire concern was the judaizers: the Inquisition." With large numbers of conversions occurring in the wake of the 1492 decree expelling Jews, persecution of *conversos* increased in the first quarter of the sixteenth century. Over 90 percent of those tried by the Inquisition in its early years were *conversos* of Jewish origin, according to Kamen.[37]

Anti-Judaism, as distinguished from anti-Semitism, refers to a predominantly religious worldview in which the Jewish faith represents an inverse image of Christianity, symbolized by the trope of Jews as murdering not only Christ himself but young Christian children in rites of blood libel. Lineage and communities of faith defined by blood purity laws (*limpieza de sangre*) provided an exclusionary, particularist language with which to connote the religious kingdom.[38] During a time in which religion provided the context for understanding both the natural and spiritual realms, anti-Judaism was an especially virulent ideology, although one that was tempered by the idea of conversion. While the notion of the wandering Jew prevailed, suggesting a rootless community exiled from its homeland, conversion held out the opportunity for Jews to become Christian and embrace the "true" faith. Converts, accordingly, could embody the ideal of the Christian Spaniard, and the passage of time could lessen the stain of Jewish descent. With the onset of scientific racist knowledge and the articulation of essentialist visions of the "Other" in European thinking, however, Jews came to signify not only the practitioners of a religion but a people and a race.[39] María Elena Martínez argues that the term *raza* (race) had its roots in religion and lineage as "to have raza essentially meant to have Jewish, Muslim, and, in some cases, even Protestant antecedents."[40] According to Robert Miles and Malcolm Brown, "due to the growth of secularisation and nationalism, associated *inter alia* with the French Revolution, religious anti-Judaism gave way to an antisemitism articulated in terms of 'race.'"[41] Central to this discourse was not only the idea that Jews constituted a national people, but also that they lived in isolated and dispersed lands not tied to a historically delineated national territory. While the Spanish Inquisition can thus be considered as an example of anti-Judaism in early modern Europe, concerned as it was with the purely religious issue of Jewish deviance from Christian practice, the Inquisition in early-nineteenth-century Spain displayed tensions between older forms of state-sanctioned religious exclusion and the rise of nationalist ideology.[42]

Spanish nationalists disparaged the enemies of Catholicism in part by deploying anti-French rhetoric tinged with anti-Judaic sentiment. During sessions devoted to the provisions of Article 21 conferring citizenship upon the legitimate children of foreigners residing in Spanish dominions, the conservative cleric Simón López insisted that an exception be made for those of French lineage:

> In this article [21] it appears to me very expedient that a particular exception be made to the general quality of Spanish citizenship with respect to the French, because now Your Majesty sees the difference that there is between this Nation and the rest. As the French border the Spanish, and have the ability to interfere and mix families with others, this would cause grave harm for the foreseeable future. . . . It appears to me that we should prevent them from establishing themselves so easily among us, and that also could be a just vindication for all of the injuries we are suffering. Just as the Jews are worthy of all the world's antipathy, the French, for having been traitors to all Governments and

> contrary to all religions, deserve to have some difference established with respect to them in this article.[43]

Comparing the sacrilegious French with Jews allowed López to make the argument that a great difference separated the French from all other nationalities. Accordingly, the stain upon its Catholic heritage marked France as a uniquely transgressive nation, a traitor to the rest of Christian Europe. In a separate session concerning nationality requirements for members of the Regency, the Valencian deputy José Castelló posited a fundamental divide between the Spanish and French national character: "I know the French character, having lived for so much time among them: and I can verify that a Frenchman will never forget what he is: and it is necessary to understand that these men are the greatest enemies of the human species, especially those from Spain."[44] In a publication from 1809, López conflated Frenchness with a long list of so-called false philosophies undermining the true Catholic faith: "Half of their inhabitants, that is, twelve or fourteen million were Protestants, Lutherans, Calvinists, Anabaptists, Socinians, Jansenists, Jews, Atheists, Unbelievers or Freemason Philosophes, which are the same."[45] Popular culture from the time similarly ascribed the supposed traits of Jews to stereotypical renditions of the French. For example, a character in a play written about the Constitution of Bayonne decried French attacks on churches and monasteries in the city of Cuenca, impugning "those men that are inevitably Jews."[46] Many Spaniards rhetorically positioned Spanish national identity in opposition to that of the French, which was characterized by a radical denial of the Catholic church.[47] In turn, the rejection of the true faith, for many Spaniards, signified an embrace of heresy, regardless of the form it took. Jews, Protestants, and atheists, among many others, were by definition excluded from this emerging conception of Spanish national identity, premised upon the religious community and bound together by a common national lineage. And conservatives deployed each of these derogatory labels as convenient epithets for the French and their sympathizers.[48]

During the debates over the Inquisition, deputies presented the idea of the citizen-resident as a Catholic Spaniard first and foremost. The construction of this category facilitated a contrast with its opposite—that of the nonresident Jew. For example, in recounting his debates with the French theologian Gregoire, Joaquín Lorenzo Villanueva declared: "In Spain, religion was now dominant in a very special sense, because it did not allow residency for Jews as did Rome and other Catholic States; as this is one of the fundamental laws of the Kingdom, I convinced Gregoire that the Sovereign had sworn an oath to uphold it." Similar to Muñoz Torrero, Villanueva firmly believed the Inquisition to be incompatible with the Constitution, and asserted that "all of the Catholic people speak out against the establishment of this Tribunal as it is opposed to Christian liberty."[49] Villanueva premised his case by arguing that religion played a unique role in the history of Spain, justifying the exclusion of Jews from rights accorded to other legal residents. Ironically, Villanueva castigated Gregoire not for impugning the Inquisition but for advocating tolerance toward other faiths in Spain and calling for legislation to protect religious minorities. Deputies such as Villanueva were able to vote against the Inquisition while maintaining steadfast opposition to any form of civil rights for Jews.

DISCOURSES OF ETHNIC DIFFERENCE

The understandings of ethnic difference as based upon lineage during the early nineteenth century in the Spanish Monarchy displayed an uneasy tension between liberal conceptions of individual citizens as the beneficiaries of natural rights and discourses denigrating ethnic and religious difference. In the context of the British Atlantic, Joyce Chaplin writes that "perhaps more than any other set of ideas, race was Atlantic." She foregrounds the fact that "settlers' insistence that race dictated political identity crossed the Atlantic eastward, making English law complicit with colonial policy."[50] Put simply, ideas of ethnic and "racial" difference were formed in large part through colonial encounters between Europeans, Indians, and enslaved Africans in the Atlantic world, which were then exported back to the metropole. From the perspective of the Spanish Monarchy, however, ideas of difference had a longer history and were linked inextricably to older discourses of lineage and *limpieza de sangre*.[51]

Many historians have focused on the fluidity of conceptions of caste and race in Spanish America. Magali Carrera, in a study of eighteenth-century New Spain, argues that Spanish "identity was not fixed or defined by a specific or definitive set of physical characteristics."[52] Differences could be diminished by "passing" as a higher caste, whether by way of dress, physical appearance, or even through the purchase of papers conferring the rights of a Spaniard. If those of mixed birth or of a lower caste adopted European fashions and did not appear to be descended from blacks (and so tainted by slavery) or Indians, they could effectively pass into Spanish colonial society. For example, *pardos* were light-skinned mulattos who could pass for Spanish. Wealthy elites could even purchase official papers, known as *cédulas de gracias al sacar,* conferring legitimacy and thus higher status if doubts existed concerning their lineage.[53] Unlike in English America, where a person's ethnic identity was more clearly delineated, in Spanish America one's lineage was much more complex. For example, in Spanish America free blacks, in addition to mulattos, although occupying marginal social positions, did have access to legal protections through the court system. Even the term *negro,* which could connote the status of slave and commercial commodity, did not necessarily refer to a person in bondage. While caste hierarchies in Spanish America clearly denigrated blackness and European ancestry was a privileged commodity, the vocabulary and elaborate system of classification contained a number of in-between categories.[54]

The ideological foundations of anti-Judaism, with an emphasis on *limpieza de sangre* and a community of descent based upon bloodlines, corresponded closely to discursive renderings of ethnic difference during the Enlightenment and the early nineteenth century. Religion and lineage had often been discursively intertwined, as Jewishness had been legally defined in terms of descent rather than simply religious belief.[55] As the religious community across the Spanish Monarchy was understood as a community of descent (*linaje*), pure and uncontaminated by religious difference, conceptions of Spanishness hinged upon lineage. Article 18 of the Constitution of 1812 stipulated: "Those Spaniards that through both lines trace their origin to the Spanish dominions of both hemispheres are citizens."[56] Those tracing their lineage to Africa remained outside the definition of the national citizen, as they were not tied by blood to the community of Spanish descent.

Yet the issue of African ancestry and the corresponding debates over the abolition of slavery elicited a range of opinion. Agustín Argüelles summed up liberal sentiment toward the slave trade in 1811: "The traffic in slaves is not only opposed to the purity and liberality of the sentiments of the Spanish Nation, but to the spirit of their religion. To trade in the blood of our brothers is horrible, it is an atrocity, it is inhuman."[57] Others noted the incongruence between slavery and natural law, and many liberal deputies believed Africans to be worthy of universal human rights. Abolishing slavery, however, proved divisive. In the spirit of enlightened science and with an eye toward increased productivity, Argüelles proposed that the abolition of the slave trade would encourage experimentation and lead to better methods of cultivation. Citing England's 1807 ban and the charismatic leadership of William Wilberforce, he predicted that economic progress would result from the elimination of such a barbaric form of commerce. Similarly pragmatic concerns as well as the salient example of Saint Domingue drove other liberal deputies to advocate caution, voicing grave concerns over manumission en masse. Proposals to abolish the trade in human beings ultimately failed, and the institution of slavery persisted.

In other ways, Spanish representatives opened a path for exemplary people who remained outside of strict definitions of national citizens to become Spanish. The Cortes explicitly allowed those of African origin to hold important rights as "Spanish subjects," including attending university and entering into the priesthood. In January 1812, the Cortes decreed: "The general and extraordinary Cortes wishes to facilitate the study of the sciences and access to ecclesiastical careers by its Spanish subjects that through whatever line trace their origin to Africa, so that each one is ultimately more useful to the State, resulting in the present decree which enables the aforementioned subjects, being endowed with commendable talents, to be admitted to the rolls and grades of universities, to be students of the seminaries, [and] to enter the priesthood."[58] In a catechism written in 1813, a liberal cleric captured the contradictions of the requirements of Spanish citizenship. The priest described the savage condition in which Africans lived, yet simultaneously noted that only skin color differentiated them from Europeans: "These disgraceful people [blacks], that are men like us, without much difference aside from their color, and the coarseness of the savage state in which they live, are driven like beasts to the markets, and sold with the opprobrium of humanity in America and in Europe, at times with less respect than a horse . . . our constitution concedes the rights of Spaniards to the unfortunate men of this class, that obtain their liberty in Spanish territory."[59] Such discourse posited difference while at the same time insisting that all peoples deserved rights as human beings. Radical American voices espoused the full spectrum of political rights for those of African descent, if only to bolster their population relative to that of the peninsula. One newspaper excoriated the deputies at Cádiz for excluding "those that through some line were natives of Africa from citizenship and active and passive representation."[60]

During the period prior to the emergence of a hardened and immutable scientific rendering of "race," a more fluid conception of difference predominated. Exceptional men of African descent, according to this view, possessed the abilities necessary to enter the priesthood and undertake higher education. Prior to their expulsion from Spain, Jews had been able to convert and symbolically transform themselves just as those of African origin could display their capacity to be Spanish via education or religious instruction. Spanishness thus remained open to a limited number of those outside of the community of descent who could demonstrate a willingness to re-create themselves as model Spaniards.

Within this construction of citizenship, Indians similarly could exhibit the traits of a Spaniard. Spanish visions of the indigenous of the New World were fundamentally tied to religious discourse. Herzog notes that "as [Indians] had converted to Catholicism, theoretically there was nothing to bar them—even during the colonial period—from membership in the community of Spanish natives."[61] The ideal of conversion certainly played a crucial role in defining the national community. Patricia Seed shows that the first centuries of Spanish colonial policy focused on "the need to create the natives as humans in order to render them dutiful subjects and tolerable Christians."[62] Debates centered on Indians' capacity to accept Christianity and thereby distinguish themselves from the base world of animals. Clearly, as Seed points out, these ideas were not generated in a dialogue with Indians, but were produced by colonists speaking for a non-European Other. A royalist Indian priest, writing in 1810, proclaimed the Indians in Spanish America to be righteous defenders of the faith and of the Spanish Monarchy in the face of the rebellion begun in "the corrupt town of *Dolores*." Speaking for his parishioners, he defended "our caste" as "the most humble children of religion . . . the most submissive and peaceful vassals of the Spanish Monarchy." He emphasized "our enlightenment and moderate, Christian prosperity," highlighting the fervent religious convictions of the Indian community.[63] Similar justifications came from Xalapa, as an important municipal official proclaimed that the *repúblicas de indios,* the local communities of Indians, would fight to the death in defense of God, King, and Country. He also emphasized that the Indians ardently desired the publication of a patriotic proclamation in the official gazette of the viceroyalty to "give unequivocal proof of the noble sentiments that animate them."[64]

Colonial ideas of difference between the Indians and European Spaniards influenced the writing of the Constitution of 1812 and the ways in which citizenship was constructed for the transatlantic Spanish Monarchy. The most extreme denigration of Indians portrayed them as closer to nature and to the primitive emotions associated with the natural world than the "civilized" Europeans. Spaniards seldom distinguished between the different cultures and languages of *indios*.[65] A similar depiction erased all differences between Africans with the catch-all referent of "hotentots." Juxtaposing their own social norms against a picture of primitive African customs, Spaniards could assert the grand principles of republican civilization: law and constitutional government.[66] Likewise, against a construction of Indians as barbarous natives, European Spaniards appeared as the bearers of civility. According to one account, written by merchants and *peninsulares* from New Spain and read aloud to all deputies in attendance on September 16, 1811, Indians had far more in common with monkeys than with sophisticated European Spaniards: "The parallel between the Spaniard and the Indian, isn't it a comparison between a pack of monkeys and an association, or republic, of urbane men?" The merchant guild consistently painted both the indigenous and *castas* as "drunkards . . . barbarous . . . [and] easily aroused by their passions." In the conclusion to the diatribe, they emphatically declared that "the mass of people composed of Indians and castes does not have the aptitude to be represented by people of their own species."[67] Such characterizations did not resonate with all of the factions at Cádiz, and enlightened proponents of Indian citizenship denounced the report.

According to the liberal narrative, Indians' inherent intellectual ability—in comparison with that of their European Spaniard counterparts—was tempered only by circumstantial factors. Many deputies claimed that the fact that most Indians lived in rural communities bereft of Spanish influence and inaccessible to schools demonstrated that the actual conditions in which Indians found themselves limited their potential to act as citizens. During discussions of a financial dispute between an Indian *cacique* (chief) and a female owner of a saltpeter mine in New Spain, the rights and obligations of Indians became the focal point of debate. The American deputy Florencio Castillo concluded that the Indians, due to their ignorance, should retain their historic economic privileges:

> I find nothing new in this decree, because the laws for Indians consider them equal in all regards to Spaniards, and open the door to them to employment and honors. That is to say, they can be admitted to the sacred orders, to schools, they can follow a career of the robe, etc.; however, I agree with Señor Morales that the privilege of minority should be preserved for them still, due to the crudeness which in general characterizes those natives, not because they are incapable—they are as rational as we are. In proof of this, I could cite various Indians who

> have made great progress in Letters, and have deserved to be decorated with the highest degrees of a university. Ignorance arises, in my opinion, when we cease to look after them, and due to the lack of schools provided by law, they have not been established in towns that have the funds to endow them.[68]

Similar to those who argued on behalf of allowing exceptional men of African origin into religious orders and the university system, the liberal deputy Castillo believed that environmental factors posed a barrier to the progress of Indians in achieving individual rights and duties as citizens of the Spanish Monarchy. While some Indians proved that they could indeed succeed in the Spanish colonial world of educated elites, most were dragged down by the weight of circumstance and limited opportunity. According to this logic, Indians had to remain under the tutelage of the benevolent Spaniards. Castillo proposed that the indigenous maintain their minority (*menoridad*) status and by doing so hold on to their Old Regime economic privileges.

The issue of class presented an additional problem, as those considered by law as minors did not have the right of representation. Traditionally, women, slaves, domestic servants, and males under the age of twenty-five did not qualify as *vecinos* (residents).[69] The definition of "minor," however, could also indicate dependent economic status. Only heads of household typically enjoyed the privileges of *vecindad*. Likewise, according to the Constitution of 1812, financial insolvency, debt, domestic service, or lack of employment could lead to the suspension of one's rights as a citizen.[70] According to a political catechism from the period: "It is necessary to have residency, that is, to be the head of the household, or to have a way of subsisting through industry, commerce or personal work, to be in possession of and to exercise the right of citizenship."[71] Status as a financially independent head of household clearly designated active from passive citizens.

Many peninsular deputies viewed economic and ethnic considerations as barriers to full citizenship, demonstrating the importance of class in the debates of the Cortes. Thus for Indians residing in Spanish America, being privileged members of a separate jurisdictional community conflicted with the legal definition of active citizenship. José Espiga, a clerical deputy from Catalonia, praised a hierarchical model of citizenship based upon property qualifications as appropriate to the structure of Spanish America. He conceded equal rights to Creoles but hesitated to apply the same standards to all the inhabitants of the New World: "I have presented these political dispositions only to show the great difference that there is between the right of naturalization and of the simple citizen and that of representation, and that Governments can augment or diminish this gap in accordance with varied circumstances. The most enlightened authors of public law wanted to establish land ownership as a qualification. And wouldn't this be a just qualification in an agricultural country? I believe that it would be as just as that of matrimony in a nation in which luxury, pleasure and vice have diminished the population. Representation is not open to all citizens essentially: it is the result of the qualifications and circumstances demanded by law."[72] To justify his position, Espiga claimed it represented continuity with earlier attempts at enlightened reform and the rational economic development of an agricultural country. He emphasized that property qualifications were just and reasonable in light of the rural nature of the American economy. Efforts to assert peninsular superiority and fears of an American voting bloc also played into the politics of American representation.[73] Many deputies put forward disparate solutions to the "American question" and attempted to quell peninsular concerns over the population of Spanish America. One proposal advocated separate representation for each "class" of inhabitants in the Americas—divided into Indians, Creoles, mestizos, and Europeans. A provision within this system also called for slaves to be able to cast votes for European representatives.[74]

While some deputies debated Indians' capacity to lift themselves out of the state of depravity and ignorance in which the majority found themselves, others insisted that Indians were, in fact, just as rational as European Spaniards. Speaking to this issue during discussions over the rights of Americans within the Spanish Monarchy, the Catalan deputy Felipe Aner firmly maintained: "There is no reason Indians should not be heard and judged in court like all other Spaniards, because we are all equal, all the more so because they will be given representation in the future Cortes, and this could not be if they were considered minors, because only those of age can be electors or Deputies."[75] The commission investigating issues relating to the overseas territories of the monarchy decreed unequivocally that, in terms of the law, "the Indians were equal to Spaniards in all capacities and in everything that did not oppose their privileges granted with just cause."[76] The Peruvian deputy Vicente Morales Duárez decried the denigration of Indians, contrasting contemporary enlightened currents of thought with the dominant ideas of the sixteenth century and the reaction provoked by the Black Legend across Europe: "I cannot tolerate the declarations I have just heard about the incapacity of the Indians. This vulgar belief from the sixteenth century, from the first days after the discovery of America, should not now be spread in the nineteenth century, where it deserves universal contempt. It had a shameful effect that we should not forget, namely: the immense multitude of censures and invectives spread by foreigners against the Spanish."[77] With considerable support in the Cortes, Indians did receive the rights of citizens, and participated as active citizens in the political process begun during this period of revolutionary activity.

The literature on caste and race in the Americas generally presents a shift from environmental and climatic factors as determinative of difference to the essentialism posited by architects of mid-nineteenth-century scientific racism.[78] The image of Indians put forward in the early nineteenth century across the Hispanic Atlantic world did not portend a transition to an ideology of immutable racial traits. Indicative of unstable and transitory differences, the figure of the Other—whether African, Indian, or Jew—generally constituted a being with the capacity to attain enlightenment and the right to act in the political sphere. According to Morales Duárez, "It is important to observe that there is a notable difference between lack of enlightenment and lack of capacity; between a lack of ideas and of words that proves the first and a lack of ability to acquire those ideas and those words which is understood by the second."[79] Clearly, this discourse did not essentialize difference but rather placed blame upon Spanish colonial authorities for not having established more effective political, social, and educational structures for its Indian subjects.

THE SINS OF WOMEN AND THE RUIN OF THE NATION

In contrast to the example of male Indians in the Americas, Spanish women remained outside the realm of liberal politics. Although female citizenship had been debated in revolutionary France, similar discussions did not take place during the sessions of the Cortes.[80] Women were barred from political participation entirely, although many dressed as men in order to witness the proceedings in Cádiz.[81] Similarly, although famous heroines such as Agustina de Aragón courageously took up arms in the heat of battle, females were rarely combatants in the war.[82] Women across the Spanish Monarchy were relegated to the private spaces of the home, as men argued that the grave danger posed by women appearing in public would sap the strength and fortitude of the nation. Concomitantly, the private sphere of domesticity shielded women from the polemics of the political world. Recent scholarship has established the discursive boundaries between the public political sphere, enlarged to include new classes of men during the nineteenth century, and the private domestic sphere of bourgeois women.[83] With language featuring prominently as a powerful tool of exclusion, practitioners of cultural history and postcolonial studies have begun to focus on discourse analysis and narrativity in understanding the emergence of "masculinist" liberal politics.[84] For example, Gayatri Spivak demonstrates that "imperialism's image as the establisher of the good society is marked by the espousal of the woman as *object* of protection from her own kind." Spivak calls for historians to analyze the "dissimulation of patriarchal strategy" in order to examine this process.[85]

As a political sphere was carved out of the Old Regime Spanish Monarchy, men and women from within the church and among the laity expressed concern over the place of women in society using the traditional language of sin. Benito Feijóo, one of the most influential enlightened clerics in eighteenth-century Spain, wrote a tract titled *In Defense of Women* in 1726. He summarized popular attitudes toward women: "Very often the duller parts of the common people see in women a horrible collection of vices . . . [but] very strong opinions of this sort can also be found in an infinite number of books."[86] Although enlightened female writers acknowledged Eve's original sin, Josefa Amar insisted that women, like the biblical Eve, displayed great curiosity and a passionate desire for knowledge. Amar, the first woman elected to the Sociedad Económica de Aragón, ardently advocated for the education of women in Enlightenment Spain. If equality of opportunity existed, she opined, women "would do just as well or better than men."[87]

The rise of nationalist sentiment signaled a shift in perceptions, and the rhetoric deployed after 1808 departed in significant ways from earlier discourses. Many clerics condemned women as symbols of national decline in the face of war with Napoleonic France, whereas earlier sermons largely drew upon religious themes to inculcate moral codes of conduct. During the first months of the French invasion in 1808, punctuated by fierce battles and growing resistance, Spanish priests nonetheless gave sermons castigating youths for their suggestive dress and profligate behavior in the streets.

While many made literal calls to arms across peninsular Spain, others exhorted parishioners to a spiritual war against the temptations of sin. In a description of libertine youths in Seville, one priest, in a sermon from

1808, painted a picture of unrestrained licentiousness: "A crowd of youths of both sexes ran through the streets and avenues [of Seville], engaging themselves in acts of lewdness. The color, slenderness and form of the pants, that shape the body obscenely, the unashamed and vile position of the hands, the tightness of the dresses on the women . . . the shining, unlaced shoes, the bareness of their arms, chests and shoulders, the shameful tricks to augment them, even the openings of the dress dishonestly placed . . . Such iniquity!"[88] Women were specifically targeted as exemplifying lewd, imprudent behavior, although the display of both the female and male body in public was described as shameful and immodest. While the cleric noted that "Napoleon and his troops are the only enemies that make war upon us," he focused his ire on the sins of the people: "It is then indispensable to take the weapons of spirituality in our hands, and try to defeat our principal enemies valiantly, which are our sins." Significantly, he not only demanded repentance for the sins of women but linked such ills to the state of the nation. The priest posed the question of responsibility for the French invasion: "Sevillanos, do you believe that our nakedness and lack of modesty could cause the ruin of the nation?"[89] Many clerics tied moral laxity to the degeneration of the polity. While men were called upon to fight a war of national liberation and to serve as political representatives in the construction of a new national state, women were increasingly viewed as a temptation to sin, as objects of male desire rather than as subjects of a new national narrative. The rise of liberalism paralleled the exclusion of women from the newly inaugurated political process in Spain.

The figure of the patriotic female appeared in sermons from the time, yet such rhetoric tended to be religious in nature. For example, in an unsigned document from 1815, "a Marian patriot" exhorted her companions in Mexico City to avoid sin and manifest the utmost piety to please God and preserve order in the kingdom. Similar to many documents from the time, the text blamed philosophes for denigrating sacred belief as mere superstition and scorning faith as fanaticism. The religious and patriotic duties of women converged in obligations to obey their divine mother and serve God in the fight against "the dreadful rebellion that has afflicted us for five years."[90] Unlike so many of her male counterparts, the author remained anonymous. Few women published materials that circulated within the Catholic public sphere, and religious instruction provided a kind of public platform largely closed to females.

Ideals of female beauty and modesty had not fundamentally changed since the Old Regime. Priests presented women as immodest and as harbingers of decline and decadence rather than as incarnations of a regenerative spirit. The archbishop of Mexico City, Francisco Xavier de Lizana y Beaumont, delineated the fundamental difference between natural beauty and the sins of sexual suggestion in a pastoral from 1808.[91] The uncovered body signified a dangerous, specifically feminine sexual danger, far more sinful than one's physical appearance.[92] According to church doctrine, women walking the streets in public wearing revealing clothes, in addition to those seeing them, had committed a mortal sin and thereby endangered the health and well-being of the community. For residents of cities across the Spanish Monarchy, the image of public women could portend both national decline and mortal sin, as "women dressed revealingly, with tight clothing, and with a style of walking both free and immodest, live in mortal sin."[93] Only a revival of religious devotion and moral rectitude could return the nation to its proper focus on the war against the French.

Similarly, ecclesiastics dichotomized the public role of men and the world of work with the private domestic sphere reserved for women. In a eulogy to María Isabel Francisca de Braganza y Borbón, the wife of Fernando VII, the archbishop of Guatemala, Ramón Francisco Casaus y Torres, consistently emphasized the feminine qualities of innocence and compassion. He highlighted the fact that she had conducted her affairs "without becoming involved in affairs of state (and not ever having an ambition to dominate)," as if to suggest that only men were qualified to hold public office and exercise the powers of state.[94] Thus, the highest rank to which the aristocratic women of the Spanish Monarchy could aspire—that of queen—reinforced female submission to an ambitious, powerful male counterpart.

Others disputed the notion that women could not govern or gain the public's trust. José Ruíz de Padrón, a clerical deputy from the Canary Islands, forcefully argued that a woman should serve as regent for Spain's constitutional monarchy during the debates of the Cortes in 1813. He premised his case upon historical precedent, citing Elizabeth of England and Catherine the Great, among others. As the king and royal family had been held in France since 1808, Ruíz de Padrón advocated in favor of Doña Carlota Joaquina de Borbón, the "virtuous Princess," who would observe the sacred Constitution. Two factors mitigated against her candidacy, however: her status as a foreigner and her sex. Ruíz de Padrón disputed that these factors represented obstacles, noting that she had been born and raised in Madrid and had demonstrated that she was a "verdadera española," a true Spanish woman, in spite of having married into the Portuguese royal family. Furthermore, her staff would have been comprised entirely of Spanish nationals. He described the assertion that a woman would be inept in government as "ridiculous" and so "absurd" that it did not merit a response.[95]

More commonly, priests presented the "effeminization" of the national people as a sign of weakness and moral inconstancy. The nation, according to this discourse, was in essence a masculine body that became exposed to penetration by its enemies vis-à-vis female corruption and degradation. The Archbishop Lizana y Beaumont warned against "the effeminization of the people" that had eroded the power of the church throughout history from Rome to Constantinople.[96] Citing the history of Muslim rule in Spain, Lizana y Beaumont argued that "Andalusia . . . became so effeminate that the men insulted their own sex in wanting to imitate the other," causing divine punishment to befall one of its foremost prelates in the form of a terrible disease. Bridging past and present, he decried the sinful and lascivious women of Mexico City: "Disgraceful women! You all conspire to your ruin, to the dishonor of your husbands, to the desolation of your houses: you and all those who promote extravagance and caprice conspire to exile our holy Religion to other parts so that this Kingdom is no longer home to the Church." Lizana y Beaumont appealed to his female parishioners to avert such a catastrophe and the fatal ruin of their fellow (male) citizens. He prescribed moderation in dress and style, cautioning women to avoid ostentatious displays of luxury: "I have no doubt that if women will moderate their excessive ways, and would not deceive the hearts of men, then so many souls would not be damned along with them."[97] Women, therefore, were admonished for courting sin in their flirtations with men. Symbolizing the nation's virtue, they were accordingly charged with its safety. Otherwise, the monarchy risked the ignominious fate of other effeminized peoples—decline and domination by those more powerful and, by definition, more masculine.

Conservative priests viewed the rise of improper behavior, especially among women, as an auxiliary to the epidemic of liberalism. In a letter expressing support for the Inquisition penned in December 1812, six bishops exhorted the clergy and the people to lead virtuous lives and avoid the political strife engulfing the nation: "Sermons and the most instructive lectures, the examples of the virtuous, and even of the Saints themselves, that have always served for the instruction and edification of the youth, are today ridiculed by the press: and everything displays to us that the young run a great risk of perversion, and the biggest threat to future generations, if at present measures are not taken to preserve them from the contagion that is carried to all parts, is the epidemic of such pestilent writing."[98] In their view, the press and the rise of the public sphere represented the greatest challenge to the traditional order of Spanish society. Conservatives feared the spread of liberal doctrine by way of the print media and its effects upon the Old Regime ideology of submission and deference to authority. Women, the lower classes, the lower castes, and those of African descent could all seek the same rights as citizens under a radical liberal regime such as that established during the height of the French Revolution in 1792. Absolutists equated Spanish liberals with French Jacobins: "The ferocious Jacobins of the French Revolution have many imitators in Spain. They want to impoverish the clergy, abolish the religious orders, do away with the Inquisition, leave the authority of the monarch in ruins, and annihilate the nobility."[99] Using the language of disease to describe the spread of liberal ideas, defenders of the Inquisition and of traditional notions of order and hierarchy launched a public campaign to demonize liberals and enlightened currents of thought, branding them as French and foreign, somehow divorced from innate Spanishness.

Other clerics went further in arguing that the French had sparked the perversion of customs and morals in the first place. Archbishop Lizana y Beaumont was convinced that the French were "the authors, the original inventors that, in order to destroy our faith and possess what is ours, have introduced and propagated the style, the perverse custom and the abominable and poisonous way that women leave their chest and arms uncovered in Mexico City."[100] In this sense, women, as the embodiment of national innocence and virtue to be protected at all costs, were urged to resist the foreign, deviant morality exported by the French. Likewise, their duty as "the devout sex," members of the gendered national community, was served by their modesty and piety.[101]

CONCLUSION

During the Trienio liberal of 1820–23, liberals again took power on the heels of a military uprising begun in Cádiz. Public disturbances accompanied the revolution in peninsular Spain, foreshadowing a transition from verbal sparring in printed broadsides and newspapers to confrontation and violence. One of the first popular expressions of support for the liberal regime, coming the day after the Constitution was reinstated, was an assault on the jails of the Inquisition. Attacks took place in Zaragoza,

Barcelona, Mallorca, and Seville and often focused on exposing the secret instruments of torture utilized by the Inquisitors.[102] In Valencia, immediately following the arrival and circulation of the news from Madrid's *Gazeta extraordinaria,* residents liberated people who had been held by the Inquisition since an aborted uprising on February 6, 1818. On March 9, the government decreed the abolition of the Inquisition, which this time elicited little public outcry or political debate. When the Constitution was reestablished publicly in Valencia on April 2, 1820, freed prisoners paraded through the street carrying olive and laurel branches as well as images hearkening back to ancient Rome's freed slaves.[103]

In the popular imagination, the Inquisition had been a central mechanism for enforcing the power of the absolutist monarchy since the sixteenth century. It not only marked the limits of religious tolerance but reflected larger discourses of inclusion and exclusion that came to define the transatlantic Spanish nation. Popular violence in 1820 was channeled solely toward the tribunal of the Old Regime church, and the symbolic public destruction of the weapons of the Inquisition has been interpreted as one of the first examples of modern anticlericalism in Spain. This was certainly not an accidental choice of targets, and it represented the weakness and atrophy of the crumbling institutions of absolutism in the face of popular uprisings. No longer did an absolutist regime hold unquestioned authority over obedient Spanish subjects, and those displaced from power were now beginning to be held accountable by popular representative government ruling legitimately in the name of the people.

During the wars of independence, the print culture of the Catholic public sphere reproduced political debates over the conflicting legacy of the Inquisition and over the meaning of nationality in the constitutional Spanish Monarchy. Regardless of whether Spaniards embodied a historic and pure religious or ethnic lineage, exclusive constructions of citizenship were tempered by exceptions and a fluid conception of identity. Stemming in part from colonial policies that allowed for passing and in-between categories, citizenship in 1812 did not essentialize a national, racial body. Contrasted with citizenship regimes in other liberal polities of the time, Spanish nationality tended toward inclusion, being based more upon religious requirements than upon ethnic identification. Despite the promise of liberalism, however, women during the Trienio continued to face barriers to active citizenship. In response to the question, "What is a Nation?" put forward in an 1822 issue of *Periódico de las Damas* (Ladies' Journal), the editor wrote: "A mass of men, brought together of their own volition, [living] under the general rules that they themselves have established."[104] Citing Locke's formulation of the social contract, the article explained, for a female audience, the development of different types of government, from despotism to parliamentarianism. No mention was made of women's role in politics at all.

Religious requirements for inclusion into the national body incited a long-lasting battle over the meaning and nature of a religious nation tied to the legacy of Inquisition. In addition, these requirements had the paradoxical effect of making citizenship more exclusive than if the basis for citizenship were purely consensual. Thus religion and a fluid notion of ethnicity provided for the broad inclusion of Indians while simultaneously barring all those outside of the Catholic community from Spanish citizenship. In sum, the embodiment of the Spanish citizen as a male Catholic resident of the dominions of the monarchy displayed the tensions inherent within Old Regime notions of *vecindad* and religious identity on one hand and Enlightenment principles of the autonomous individual on the other and represented a compromise between tradition and emerging liberal doctrine.

5

THE CHILDREN OF THE MADRE PATRIA

Revolution in New Spain

At the height of the Spanish uprising against Napoleon in 1811, one prominent Spanish American cleric lamented: "How painful it is to see these machinations and these fraudulent tricks that have been able to separate Spaniards from Spaniards, the American Spaniards from the European Spaniards, with whom they share the strongest bonds of nature and of Religion, how all have always formed the same Nation, the same family and the same body, under the command and under the shadow of the same Father King and Lord, who is at present FERNANDO VII, whose sacred name was resonating unanimously and uniformly until now."[1] In New Spain, similar affirmations rang out from the pulpits testifying to the bonds of fidelity between the New World and the Old: "Long live Jesus, long live our Catholic King FERNANDO VII; and his most dignified Viceroy in this America . . . and long live the indivisible Spanish Monarchy."[2] By 1812, many ecclesiastics adhered to the idea that "now there is no difference between a native of America, he that was born in Europe and he that has yet to discover his lineage; now there is no Atlantic, now there are not two continents, the Constitution united them."[3] Accordingly, there were not two separate poles of the Spanish Monarchy but one unified Hispanic Atlantic world under the banner of a liberal constitution.

The Constitution of 1812 became a rallying cry for Hispanic liberals in peninsular Spain as well as Spanish America. It had fundamentally realigned the basis of sovereignty and the definition of the nation. Swearing an oath of loyalty to the Constitution in the cathedral of Valladolid in Michoacán in 1813, the peninsular cleric Manuel de la Bárcena extolled the virtues of a unified Spanish nation under the rubric of constitutional monarchy and the Catholic religion: "All free men, born in and resident of the dominions of Spain, and all those that through both lineages trace their origins to Spanish territory, are citizens. . . . Ultimately, let us not forget what is first, because we are Christians before we are citizens: let us always agree on the divine article 12."[4] Seven years later, with the revolutionary Constitution once again installed, Bárcena renewed his pledge of fidelity in the same cathedral: "I have seen Spanish patriotism spread rapidly through the entire peninsula like an electric fire; and like lightning that comes from the east to the west passed over the ocean and lit up the Americas."[5] The liberal principles endorsed by the authors of the new Constitution established the radical idea of a transatlantic nation-state and ushered in the era of nationalism across the Hispanic Atlantic world.

By 1824, however, independence from Spain severed the ties of the monarchy and an inclusive Spanish identity encompassing the Americas as well as peninsular Spain. The Virgin of Guadalupe, which had been appropriated by royalists as well as insurgents in the period 1810–21, soon emerged as the symbol of the new Mexican nation.[6] "Long live the Virgin of Guadalupe" and "death to the gachupines" are the slogans that have in large part defined the legacy of the War of Independence in Mexico. Religious imagery that had served to unite Spaniards on both sides of the Atlantic fragmented into regional identifications in the Americas. Articulations of a broadly framed Spanish nationalism faded as Americans came to inscribe their nations with a new postcolonial identity.[7]

SHIFTING LOYALTIES, CHANGING BOUNDARIES

In the first two decades of the nineteenth century, however, the political boundaries of colonial viceroyalties had yet to be demarcated into national borders, and no nations can be said to have existed in Spanish America. François-Xavier Guerra, among others, maintains that Spain and Spanish America exhibited a great degree of political unity at the time of Napoleon's invasion of Spain. Guerra insists that "in none of the writings from this epoch does one find a mention of an American nation. When they speak of the nation, they always speak of the whole of the Monarchy."[8] In peninsular Spain between 1808 and the early 1820s, a consistent rhetoric of inclusion put forward notions that *americanos* and *peninsulares* shared the same rights and privileges under the Spanish Crown.[9] America formed part of the provincial makeup of the Spanish Monarchy, just as regions such as Catalonia and Galicia comprised the diverse landscape of peninsular Spain and were legally tied to the central government in Madrid.

According to a prominent Creole cleric, preaching in 1809 to parishioners in Mexico City: "You are all Mexicans: but you have not stopped being Spaniards. Was the Andalusian not born in Andalusia, the Biscayan in Biscay, the Castilian in Castile, and the Aragonese in Aragon?" He vehemently insisted that "all of the Provinces of Spain are more or less distant and separated from one another."[10] During this crucial defining epoch, competing nationalist discourses emerged throughout the various realms of the Spanish Monarchy within shared political and cultural traditions, grounded in a common Catholic faith and proclaimed in Article 12 of the Constitution. Yet only in the Americas did peripheral nationalisms develop that advocated separation from Spain, as other regional identities in peninsular Spain became subsumed within a broader Spanish nationalism throughout the first decades of the nineteenth century.

The language of nationalism in New Spain underwent a profound transformation during the period from 1810—with the first cry of Hidalgo's revolt—through 1821, when Agustín Iturbide proclaimed the Mexican empire.[11] Although Spain had been utilized as an inclusive symbol of the motherland at the outbreak of violence, many clerics began to emphasize an American identity during the war and subsequently came to articulate a Mexican nationalism that displayed tensions between a Spanish cultural heritage and the imperial Aztec past.[12] Yet others, such as Bárcena, maintained an emphasis on a civic Spanish nationalism within the American provinces and did not see contradictions between Spanish and American identities. Hybrid formations of national identity were expounded in sermons, catechisms, pamphlets, and periodicals that eulogized the people and the nation. Ideologues enjoyed the freedom to publish with impunity after 1810, an unintended consequence of the war. The opening of the Catholic public sphere provided a forum for the polemics of the time. In New Spain, royalists defending the viceregal state against insurrection as well as clerics influenced by Enlightenment thought advocated an inclusive Spanish polity as prescribed in the Constitution of 1812. From local parishes to archbishoprics, political debates over the meaning and nature of the nation resonated from pulpits and street corners, engaging the clergy and their diverse audience of parishioners.

The struggle that culminated in independence for Mexico, as a civil war with shades of social revolution, provided fertile ground for the development of competing discourses of national identity. The exigencies of war, new channels of communication, and the appeal of insurgent and autonomist ideology allowed for the transformation of regionalism into a distinctive Mexican national identity by the 1820s. As members of the clergy and as insurgent leaders, Miguel Hidalgo y Costilla and José María Morelos, along with many other insurrectionaries, successfully mobilized a militant base around class grievances rather than national allegiance at the beginning of the uprising. They played upon issues of oppression and injustice that mixed traditional notions of Spanish regional identity with New World signifiers. Autonomists at times actively conspired with the rebellion from within urban centers such as Mexico City, although many also worked within the constitutional system to advance a liberal, representative government. Groups such as the Guadalupes in New Spain pursued a middle ground between the armed struggle led by rural insurgents and loyalty to peninsular royalists.[13] Accordingly, both autonomists and insurgents built upon earlier conceptions of Enlightenment patriotism and contributed to notions of a separate political and cultural American identity that came to mark declarations and calls for independence by the end of the war.[14]

Regionalist discourses, which did not represent a rupture with earlier patterns of identification, ultimately became framed as nationalist referents, as *americanos* emphasized their differences with the metropole. This distancing was manifest in the language utilized by political elites as well as clerics in New Spain by the 1820s, as the usage of terms such as *españoles americanos* and *americanos* trailed off, replaced with particularist notions inherent within conceptions of Mexico as a nation. With an external enemy to fight in peninsular Spain, national identity coalesced in part around an oppositional form of identification, whereas civil war prevented a similar path from taking shape in the New World. Nationalist ideologies upholding difference between *peninsulares* and *americanos* gained adherents in the Americas and increasingly attracted political conservatives and traditionalists to a particularist agenda when the liberal Constitution was again proclaimed in 1820. This shift gave traction to ideals associated with the insurgents, many of whom had been accused of fomenting social revolution. The construction of nationality in Mexico was spurred by this unlikely coalition and allowed for the continued circulation of a nationalist discourse that began to displace the civic values of an inclusive transatlantic Spanish identity by the time independence had been achieved across most of Spanish America. Autonomists and insurgents propelled transitional conceptions of identity into the Catholic public sphere that had emerged in New Spain and across the Spanish Monarchy.

Latin American national histories, reified as the nations achieved independence, have often been studied apart from one another. Mexican nationalism has been analyzed as a natural outcome of the independence struggle that culminated in 1821, just as the other nationalist traditions born out of colonial Spanish America have laid claims to a unique past that justified political sovereignty. Such teleological narratives, however, have served to obscure central features of the struggles against Spain. Thus, that the priest Hidalgo rebelled in the name of Fernando VII and under the banner of the Catholic church did not seem contradictory to his followers at the time. That many elites wanted to place a Bourbon monarch on the Mexican throne in 1821 similarly appeared in line with nineteenth-century ideals of constitutional monarchy.[15] John Lynch, whose work is cited in such foundational works on nationalism as Benedict Anderson's *Imagined Communities,* argues that "Americans had begun to question the basis of their allegiance" to the Spanish Crown by the late eighteenth century. Accordingly, the "divided loyalties" of Creoles became cemented into the dictum emblematic of the time: "I am not a Spaniard, I am an American."[16] Lynch's thesis that a Creole elite fought against the recolonization of America by enlightened Bourbon ministers has since been challenged.[17] For example, Jaime Rodríguez argues forcefully that many political leaders throughout the Americas espoused autonomy within a composite Spanish Monarchy rather than outright independence.[18] Autonomists saw no inherent contradictions between an American and a Spanish identity. Eric Van Young downplays Creole activism and insists that few bonds linked the popular rural struggle with elite movements. Van Young posits continuities between Old Regime forms of protest and rebellion and the independence struggle.[19] The contingencies of Spanish American and Spanish notions of identity, what Lynch referred to as a *conciencia de sí,* must be explored in order to understand the multivalent aspects of what has been characterized as the "period of independence" in Latin America.

VISIONS OF THE VIRGIN MARY IN NATIONALIST DISCOURSES

Prior to the tumult of the wars of independence and the Napoleonic invasion of peninsular Spain, few clerics on either side of the Atlantic glorified the people as the nation. The structures of the Old Regime state and the hierarchical social order remained firmly entrenched. Yet in the aftermath of the French Revolution, a small number of patriotic ecclesiastics began to use such language in New Spain. Preaching in 1802, one priest dedicated his sermon to "[the] nation beloved and chosen by God."[20] In celebrating the day of Our Lady of the Pillar of Zaragoza, the cleric insisted that salvation lay in the merciful guidance of the Virgin Mary: "Princes, Priests, the Spanish people! There is our security, there our liberty, there our protection."[21] His appeal, addressed to "Spain, fortunate Spain," pointedly conjured the image of a unified transatlantic audience of parishioners who shared a single cultural landscape. The sermon did not differentiate between American and peninsular Spaniards. Assuming reverence and devotion to a peninsular image of the Virgin, the priest drew upon Spanish identity as a shared idiom. The sermon concluded: "This Virgin of the Pillar strengthens me: this Image consoles me. . . . Blessed, blessed you will be forever, oh Mother of the Spaniards, the sweetness of our life, the gateway of divine grace and of the sovereign country!"[22] This suggests that constructions of identity drew upon a wide range of symbols, including peninsular iconography, and were not limited to images or figures of local historical significance.

Although the Virgin of Guadalupe provided a distinctly American symbol for Hidalgo's uprising in 1810, sermons did not single out Guadalupe as a sacrosanct national icon prior to the outbreak of war. Guadalupe, first witnessed on the hill at Tepeyac, near Mexico City, had been named patroness of New Spain in 1746, a decision recognized by the pope eight years later. Throughout the eighteenth century, Guadalupe certainly retained the traits of a local devotional cult, specific to Mexico City and its environs. William Taylor argues that the cult spread slowly northward from the capital in the late eighteenth century only with the endorsement of influential members of the church hierarchy. The cult appears less as a spontaneous movement of the faithful than as an instrument sponsored and promoted by the viceregal authorities.[23] In Mexico City on December 12, 1778, during the festival day of the Virgin of Guadalupe, one peninsular cleric presented the patroness as the "Mother of the Mexicans." The sermon concluded: "What glory for the Mexicans that MARÍA elected their City, and that she built a Temple in it in which to show her mercy and compassion!"[24] Guadalupe served as an icon of local identity, a symbol of civic pride to the residents of the municipality. On the annual day of Guadalupe's commemoration in 1793, a peninsular cleric in San Luis Potosí celebrated the Virgin by extolling New Spain's transatlantic kinship: "We have been born from the Spanish tree that extends its roots from there to here." Accordingly, the spirit of religion had allowed their relationship to grow and to flourish, and the cult of Guadalupe functioned in a like manner to those of Our Lady of the Pillar in Aragon, Saint James in Galicia, and Saint Ignatius of Loyola in the Basque region.[25] Preaching in Valladolid, Michoacán, in 1808, José Díaz de Hortega echoed such sentiments, promising that Guadalupe had placed "both Spains under [her] protection . . . because, ultimately, it was the universal vote of all their inhabitants." He placed his faith in the hands of the patroness: "Yes, my Mother: Spain will triumph; tyranny will be humiliated."[26] Framed as a regional image with transatlantic roots, Guadalupano devotion did not translate into separatist aspirations before the wars of independence.

Prior to 1821, priests in New Spain continued to honor a myriad of Marian representations, including decidedly peninsular devotional cults such as those of Our Lady of the Pillar as well as Our Lady of Covadonga. One ecclesiastic linked the two together as divinely inspired protection for all "Spaniards, [sons of] the Marian Nation." Glorifying the Virgin of Covadonga in 1806 in Mexico City, he emphasized the spiritual debt Spaniards owed to Mary: "To you, in Zaragoza, they owed the reception of the divine faith, the true liberty of the sons of God, and to you they owe in Covadonga liberty from the yoke of the Saracen, the preservation of that religion you brought to them, so that you were . . . the tender Mother, you were the Defender, and you were also the Renowned Restorer." He equated the heroic defense of religion and the Spanish Monarchy with the Marian image from Covadonga, in Asturias, which had animated don Pelayo's battle against the Muslim yoke of oppression and led to a national rebirth in the eighth century.[27] Mary, the holy mother, inspired soldiers to fight against the enemies of religion in defense of their homeland as the "Liberator of the Spaniards."[28] She also represented a devotional figure of maternal strength, allowing her followers to imagine that they had been delivered and reborn into a holy land. Nationalists were able to utilize these signifiers to espouse a Spanish national identity during the wars of independence across Spanish America.

Other clerics emphasized various representations and attributes of Mary, from Our Lady of Carmen to the Virgin of Remedies, who offered divine protection and sanctity, especially in times of crisis and war.[29] In a sermon given in Mexico City in August 1810, Bernardo Antonio González Díaz venerated the Virgin of Remedies as "a Patron Saint that is superior in power to men and to the Angels, to the Authorities and to Thrones, and that God made Queen of Heaven and of the earth." Our Lady of Remedies had been a celebrated image from the Conquest and had been revered especially in seventeenth-century Puebla as la Conquistadora.[30] González Díaz, a peninsular cleric, praised Spain's conquest of America as a benign act legitimated by Christ and justified through religious conversion. His sermon not only extolled the virtues of Columbus and Pizarro but stated that the conquest was "in favor of the Mexicans." The Spanish victory, "throwing dust into the eyes of the Indians," allowed them to see the light of the faith, as they had been blind to their idolatries. Ultimately, the triumphs of the conquistadors contributed to "extending the religion of Jesus Christ over the ruins of the most barbarous and cruel superstition; and adding new Kingdoms to the Church and to Spain."[31] The ecclesiastic further opined that the battles then raging in peninsular Spain would be over soon: "We, the Spaniards . . . will be victorious and exalted, because we have not placed trust in our own forces, but in the protection of the Lord and of the Holy Mother."[32] Thus the French, along with Napoleon's cowardly allies, would be defeated under the guidance of Our Lady of Remedies. The importance of this sacred image during the Battle of Monte de las Cruces, outside Mexico City, and its subsequent deployment by royalist forces should not obscure the plurality of Marian representations celebrated in New Spain in the eighteenth and early nineteenth centuries.[33]

FAMILIAL METAPHORS OF AMERICAN AND MEXICAN IDENTITY

The language of kinship utilized by the clergy embraced the idea of peninsular Spain as the central maternal figure within a familial structure—the mother defined by her fertility as well as her wisdom. The bishop of Puebla, Manuel Ignacio González del Campillo, exhorted: "Break the wall that divides the daughter from the mother: then you would never hear the hateful names of Creoles and gachupines; we would all be Spaniards, some European and other Americans; but all true Spaniards."[34] As the legitimate children of the motherland, Americans were bound to Spain and could not justifiably break the bonds that tied them together as a family. As a teacher, the mother had instilled religion in her offspring as their defining trait from birth. Bárcena explicitly maintained that membership in the church preceded and in some ways overshadowed citizenship. Furthermore, he contended that "Catholicism is inseparable from the Spanish nation . . . he who is not Catholic is not a Spaniard."[35] For both the descendants of Spaniards as well as the Indians, the *peninsulares* had fostered the love of God, King, and Country throughout the diverse reaches of Spanish America. This became a common theme of sermons and religious instruction during the first years after the Napoleonic invasion of Spain.

The arrest of Viceroy Iturrigaray by *peninsulares* in September 1808 fundamentally altered the course of events in New Spain and undermined the rhetoric of Spanish benevolence. As Iturrigaray had been charged with convening a representative *junta,* he had unwittingly aroused the hostility of peninsular Spanish leaders, who feared a loss of status and authority under an American-dominated governing committee. The *ayuntamiento* had insisted that "in the absence or during the impediment [of the king], sovereignty lies represented in all the kingdom and the classes that form it."[36] Interpreting the detention as an attempt to silence the legitimate government, discontented elites began to establish secret networks of political allies through social networks and *tertulias.* The Junta Central in Spain did not uphold the ascendancy of the next viceroy, Pedro Garibay, and instead named Archbishop Lizana to the post in July 1809. The historian Virginia Guedea interprets the attempts to undermine the government of Viceroy Garibay, dominated by peninsular officials, and subsequent regimes as "that which gave rise to and initiated the armed struggle," with violence erupting after the "Grito de Dolores" (Cry of Dolores) and Hidalgo's insurrection of September 1810.[37]

Numerous conspiracies abounded in New Spain prior to Hidalgo's revolt, calling for increased autonomy within the Spanish Monarchy. The 1810 plot to overthrow peninsular authorities, hatched in Querétaro, was to have begun in December during the commemoration of a seventeenth-century miracle carried out by the Virgin of Candelaria in the town of San Juan de los Lagos. With their plans exposed in September, however, leaders took action in Dolores and did not adopt the banner of Our Lady of San Juan de los Lagos. Guadalupe, the enduring religious symbol of the period, might not have been the figurehead of the uprising had the revolt proceeded as planned.[38]

The immediate goals of the conspirators, including Hidalgo and Allende, were not unlike those of liberal agitators in peninsular Spain: Seize their enemies and form a representative *junta* in the name of Fernando VII.[39] Hidalgo framed a discourse of national identity, what Lynch referred to as "incipient nationalism," in terms strikingly similar to those articulated by royalist clerics and by the clergy in Spain.[40] A common language of Spanish nationalism, imbued with religious metaphors and references, began to be heard in sermons and calls to arms across the Spanish

Monarchy. Formal armies as well as guerrilla bands offered their services to the *patria* in the name of religion. On both sides of the Atlantic, soldiers' garb included caps with religious slogans emblazoned with images of the Virgin Mary and local saints.[41] Reports circulated of troops in Spain refusing to fight on Sundays and of their palpable discontent in the absence of a priest to give mass.[42] The trinity of God, King, and Country, with God often listed first among the three, provided ideological ammunition for those fighting the French in Spain as well as for insurgents battling the Spanish forces in New Spain. For example, Hidalgo insisted that "the object of our constant vigilance is to maintain our Religion, the King, the Country, and the purity of our customs."[43] Hidalgo had amassed as many as eight hundred men in Dolores and marched toward San Miguel el Grande and Guanajuato, convening tens of thousands of troops within the first month of the initial military campaigns. The dramatic withdrawal of insurgent forces from the hills outside Mexico City on November 3 was only the beginning of a prolonged ideological as well as military campaign.

Opponents of the uprising led by Hidalgo and Morelos condemned as sacrilege the bloody civil war that had broken out, and Hidalgo was excommunicated prior to his trial and execution. Yet they, too, justified their stance in the language of Catholic piety, upholding the pillars of church and state. The bishop of Michoacán, remaining loyal to the Crown, exhorted his parishioners to "understand the obligations that one has, as a true Christian, to God, King, and to the Country, and to each one of your fellow citizens. All of you can understand your true interests, and embrace the sure ways of achieving them."[44] Preaching in 1810 against Hidalgo in Guanajuato, the site of some of the first battles of the war, the friar Diego Miguel Bringas impugned the "traitors to America, to Spain, and to the Church" because they "declare war against their fathers, their sons, their brothers, their monarch, their country and against their sacred religion."[45] Each side accused the other of crimes against religion, claiming the exclusive right to speak in the name of the universal Catholic faith. Hidalgo railed against his enemies, the men who "are Catholic only to benefit themselves: their God is money." He concluded that "under the veil of Religion and of friendship they want to make you victims of their insatiable greed."[46]

In peninsular Spain, the French served as the primary targets of religious ire. Clerics unleashed a barrage of anti-French sentiment, imploring Spaniards to defend the nation against the enemies of religion and the bearers of atheism and revolution. Conservative clerics argued that the French symbolized all of the evils then poisoning European societies. In the aptly titled *Preservativo contra la irreligión* (Protection against Irreligion), Rafael de Vélez inveighed against the French: "In all of Europe they are known by the names of *the enlightened, materialists, atheists, unbelievers, libertines, masons, the impious.* Their doctrines against kings, authorities and religion merit these titles: and their works expose them at least as fanatics, misanthropic enemies of all society."[47] He rallied the faithful to the national cause with cries of "'Long live the Virgin Mary: long live Jesus Christ: long live their faith, their religion: long live Fernando VII: death to the French."[48] Vélez boasted that "all Spaniards heard nothing but cries of *long live Spain, religion will triumph, death to France.*"[49] Just as insurgents called for "death to the gachupines" in New Spain—some demanded that all Europeans be killed—peninsular Spaniards attacked the French in nationalistic terms that had not been used in the previous war of 1793–95.[50] The entire French nation had become the enemy of Spain rather than a select few impious individuals representing seditious causes.

In order to demonize those who fought against the uprising in New Spain, insurgents accused royalists of secretly conspiring with the French.[51] As in Spain, anti-French epithets became synonymous with atheism and hostility toward the Catholic church. In December 1810, the insurgent periodical *El Despertador Americano* claimed the bonds of the Hispanic family had frayed, as "Mother Spain . . . will remain reduced—oh painful humiliation—to the precarious state of a mere Colony of France."[52] Other editorials compared the convening of the Cortes of Cádiz to the assembly brought together in Bayonne, France, in 1808.[53] The Creole Bringas likewise portrayed Hidalgo and his followers as counterparts to Napoleon and the French, "penetrated by the spirit of the failed politics of the impious Napoleon Bonaparte," corrupting the Americas with rapacious French ideas of liberty and equality.[54] Conflating the enemy with the French proved to be a powerful ideological weapon, which in turn established the idea that Spaniards in general were tied to the illegitimate regime of Bonaparte that had to be defeated. Yet deputies in the Cortes in Cádiz expressed gratitude for the "heroic defenders of the Patria" in New Spain and the "fidelity of Mexico City." They clearly expected the royalists to prevail. Manuel García Herreros, deputy from Soria, viewed Hidalgo's rising as an isolated disturbance, judging that it "was not a general insurrection."[55]

During the early stages of the conflict prior to 1814, America represented a regional variant within the context of Spanish identity. Rarely did nationalists eulogize *el pueblo mexicano* as the font of a new nation.

The term for the "Mexican people" generally referred to the residents of Mexico City. The nation, on the other hand, composed of the people, was a contested amalgam of regional and religious sentiments that had not coalesced around a central defining feature. America remained the *patria chica,* with Spain as the symbol of a broader inclusive cultural identification. For example, even Hidalgo, as the leader of the uprising, articulated a form of American identity rather than a specifically Mexican nationalism. In a manifesto from 1811 written shortly before his execution, he extolled "America beloved country of mine! Americans, my compatriots, Europeans my progenitors and above all the Insurgents, my sympathetic partisans."[56] Royalist clerics such as the bishop of Puebla also showed an emotional attachment to America: "In the present epoch in which America has declared itself an integral part of the Monarchy . . . and in which the Cortes has been convoked for the first time . . . the mother country has received the clearest testimonies of the fidelity of America."[57] America was the locus of regional identity for both sides in the civil war.

The Constitution of 1812 offered the possibility of reconciliation between warring factions. By bringing together both sides of the transatlantic Spanish Monarchy under the auspices of constitutional government, liberals argued that the nation could once again function as an integrated polity. Representation and electoral politics promised to give a voice to the American provinces. Supporters of the constitutional regime such as Bárcena heralded the recovery of their ancient freedoms, referencing the captivity of the Israelites as a metaphor for the Spanish nation: "Chosen nation, now you leave captivity, you have reclaimed your rights [and] you are free." Bárcena implored parishioners to bridge the Atlantic divide between peninsular and American Spain and come together as a nation united by constitutional law: "Compatriots, this small volume that you have read contains the foundation upon which to raise the edifice of our prosperity and our glory: it is the admirable product of the wisdom of two worlds, the celestial tie that reunited Europe with America, it is the Spanish Constitution." No stronger attachment existed than that of the Constitution, upon which liberals pinned their hopes and ideals: "Brothers, the storm is terrible, we have no more of an anchor than the Constitution, all Spaniards hold steady in her; if you are not to drown without recourse."[58] The language of family underlined the ties between American and European Spaniards as brothers in the greater struggle against the French. In the midst of civil war and internal strife, the Constitution as a unifying symbol was proclaimed from pulpits across the Americas.

Other royalist clerics came closer to espousing a pronounced regional identity apart from a pan-American discourse. As an ardent supporter of the royalist cause, the liberal Bishop Manuel Abad Queipo argued that New Spain, an integral part of the composite Spanish Monarchy, served as the principal marker of supraregional identity rather than America. Speaking out against the rebels, Abad Queipo delineated the conditional structure of the national body by excluding those who had taken part in the uprising: "Puebla, Veracruz, Oaxaca and the internal Provinces have given respectively the same proof of loyalty and patriotism that the capital Mexico City has. These are the provinces that constitute the Nation or the people of New Spain."[59] This echoed the rhetoric of "good" and "bad" Spaniards that had become increasingly prominent after the Cortes abolished the Inquisition. Clerics and conservatives upheld the idea that loyalty would separate the "true" Spanish people from their enemies—both internal and external. In the first years of the civil war in New Spain, various conceptions of identity emerged along competing axes. Yet each drew upon a common nationalist idiom grounded in the idea of a confessional state.

REVOLUTION IN PUEBLA

In Puebla, royalists held out against rebel armies of between two thousand and four thousand men between 1811 and 1812. Insurgents took key towns in the province, such as Cuautla and Tehuacán, but did not effectively mobilize forces for an all-out attack on the city. By 1813, royalists counted more than seven thousand men at arms in the province, and Morelos had retreated south. The city of Puebla was strategically and economically important, with commercial ties to regional trading networks, a strong manufacturing base, including the production of cotton textiles, and a vibrant agricultural sector. The province recorded approximately 800,000 inhabitants in census figures from the late eighteenth and early nineteenth centuries, and the city itself was the second-largest in New Spain.[60] In contrast to peninsular Spain's relative homogeneity, *repúblicas de indios* marked rural New Spain, and the indigenous comprised 75 percent of Puebla's populace.[61] Although not connected to Hidalgo's conspiratorial axis of 1810, the intendancy of Puebla became the epicenter of civil war between insurgents, under Morelos, and supporters of the Spanish Monarchy by 1811 and 1812. Whereas nationalist rhetoric resituated historic regional bonds in the case of Valencia during the struggle against the French, autonomist sentiment dominated the public sphere in Puebla.

As news spread of the French takeover in 1808, *novohispanos* pledged their fidelity to the monarch. Americans shared the outrage and frustration felt by peninsular Spaniards, who saw their country overrun by a foreign army in the spring and summer of 1808. Displaying his sentimental attachment to the motherland, the Creole cleric Josef Demetrio Moreno y Buenvecino referred to Puebla as "the noble daughter of Spain that, penetrated by the most profound humiliation in observing the bloody and horrible scenes of combat and ruin . . . runs to the temple and prostrates herself in the sanctuary, to express outrage and to importune . . . the heavens."[62] The war powerfully affected Americans and peninsular Spaniards alike, albeit in different ways. In addition, despite the great distance separating Spain from the Americas and the distinctive aspects of regional economic and political development, similar ideologies informed the manifest revolutionary changes on both sides of the Hispanic Atlantic.

In Puebla, the *ayuntamiento* requested permission from Viceroy Iturrigaray to hold a public ceremony in honor of the king, Fernando VII, on July 28, 1808. With unrest increasing in the city due to the events in the peninsula, leaders proclaimed Fernando the legitimate monarch on August 31, following festivities held in Mexico City earlier that month.[63] In a demonstration of unity, uniformed bands of volunteers paraded through the streets to honor the new king. The Creole Bishop González del Campillo, in a sermon given shortly thereafter, proclaimed that divine protection would allow Spain to vanquish its most brutal enemies: "Spain lives, and was not submerged in the immense sea of perfidy, treason, violence and irreligion. . . . Spain is the City [Pueblo] of God."[64] He unequivocally stated allegiance to Fernando VII: "We are his faithful vassals and his beloved children . . . while he lives, he reigns over and governs us . . . or in his Royal Name the Supreme and Sovereign Junta of immortal Seville, recognized as such by all of those Kingdoms, and even by foreigners, and in the pacts and the new alliances that have been concluded recently, proclaims his Sovereignty."[65] The bishop continued to draw upon the metaphor of mother and child in articulating the relationship between the metropole and its overseas provinces: "To us, your Settlers and your children, nothing remains but the sad consolation of crying for the misfortunes and disgrace of our common Mother."[66] News from peninsular Spain circulated widely in the Americas. For instance, the *Diario de Valencia* (Valencia Daily), complete with coverage of the events of the "revolution" of 1808, was republished in Puebla in 1808.[67] Catechisms from across the Atlantic spread the idea that Napoleon and Murat threatened not only peninsular Spain but the Americas as well. Religious schools trained children to recite catechisms originally published in the peninsula, such as the *Catecismo político para la instrucción del Pueblo Español* (Political Catechism for the Instruction of the Spanish People), which had been reprinted in New Spain between 1808 and 1811. Reports highlighted instances of students marching through Mexico City singing, "Free us from Napoleon and from the French nation."[68] The response to the fundamental question of allegiance—What do you call yourselves?—reinforced fidelity to the *patria*. The definitive answer was: "Spaniard."[69]

While on the surface the situation in New Spain appeared stable, clerics such as the bishop of Puebla saw the dangers inherent within the new political ideologies that circulated freely across the Hispanic public sphere. In a sermon given in October 1808, he decried republicanism and the notion of popular sovereignty, warning parishioners not to be seduced by novel "revolutionary" ideals.[70] Although a majority of *novohispanos* upheld the legitimacy of the monarch and declared their loyalty to Spain, the liberal political revolutions that began in municipalities such as Valencia presented models for revolutionaries in New Spain. Two years later, royalists would condemn the treachery of Miguel Hidalgo and Ignacio Allende, the initial leaders of the rebellion against Spanish authorities in New Spain, and denounce them as partisans of "revolution."[71] The insurrection of Hidalgo and the uprising of Bolívar in Venezuela are generally equated with nineteenth-century Latin American "revolutions." Yet, in many ways, the insurgents did not monopolize the revolutionary paths of the disparate regions of Spanish America. Rebels and royalists alike extolled the sovereignty of the people.

By 1809, with the conflict in Spain painted as an epic struggle against a common enemy, clerics in New Spain emphasized the values of religiosity and fortitude as the measure of national character. Preaching in Puebla, Francisco Xavier Conde y Pineda described "a Catholic nation that happily stands out above the rest [and] a city so devoted and religious like this one, distinguished by its honorable loyalty . . . to the King and to the country." He pointed to the Junta Central as a bulwark of defense against the perfidious French: "And above all, the Junta Suprema Central gubernativa, that is for the enemy, and will be, a fatal reef where the furies of their insolent audacity will break, for us is an impregnable wall of defense, like the tree of life planted in the middle of paradise . . . restoring our forces and infusing them with the greatest vigor and support."[72] In March 1809, and again in May 1810, the Ayuntamiento of Puebla swore solemn oaths of allegiance to the Junta Central and the reconstituted authorities governing in the name of Fernando in peninsular Spain.[73] Americans viewed the Junta of Seville, and its successor, the Junta Central, as legitimate governing bodies because they had assumed power legally and in the name of the king.[74]

The crisis precipitated by the French invasion and the subsequent realignment of political forces led to the opening of the public sphere and to increased calls for representative government between 1808 and 1810.[75] In addition, conspiracies and rumors circulated throughout the Americas as dissidents pushed for autonomy and questioned the legitimacy of peninsular authority.[76] Poblanos, in elections for the Cortes, ultimately chose the Creole Antonio Joaquín Pérez Martínez, a canon and resident of the city.[77] Yet just as elected representatives began to gather in Cádiz to open the inaugural sessions of the Cortes on September 24, 1810, civil war broke out in New Spain. Hidalgo's rising in Dolores, in the intendancy of Guanajuato to the northwest of Puebla, threatened the viability of a transatlantic nation premised upon the ideals of liberal government.

In cities throughout the viceroyalty, municipal leaders hastily improvised defense forces to combat the advances of the insurgency. In accordance with a military plan drafted by the government in October, volunteers were enlisted in the Distinguished Patriotic Battalions of Fernando VII. By the spring of 1811, clerics in Puebla steadfastly preached the virtues of fidelity to the monarchy and the "obligation to love the Country and to secure its liberty and independence."[78] As evidence of their loyalty to the Crown, ecclesiastics had enshrined May 2 as a day of remembrance for "the first, illustrious victims of National Liberty sacrificed in Madrid," and records indicate Poblanos continued to honor the fallen in subsequent years.[79] In correspondence in March, the *ayuntamiento* expressed grave concern over "the painful circumstances faced by the city, with insurgents intending a cruel invasion." Like Bringas, one Creole Poblano rebuked the *caudillos* Hidalgo and Allende as men without principles, humanity, or religion.[80] Leaders implemented "prudent measures" to provide for armed regiments in the city in the name of "Religion, Loyalty and Patriotism."[81] Funds also were solicited to aid in the defense of peninsular Spain in April and May 1811. In June, the cathedral of Puebla focused on local recruitment and on a monthly donation to the Volunteers of Fernando VII.[82]

On March 19, 1812, representatives from the Americas and the peninsula who had served in the Cortes unveiled the Hispanic Constitution, written in Cádiz as Spanish, English, and guerrilla forces launched offensives against occupying French armies and civil war spread across the Americas. The Constitution enshrined the principles of liberal nationalism, born in struggles such as those of Valencia in 1808, and definitively declared both hemispheres equal parts of the national body. In Puebla and Valencia, constitutional adherence took the form of elections, held as insurgents were defeated in Puebla and in the aftermath of the French defeat in Valencia in 1813. By September 1812, the Constitution had been published in Mexico City, and Puebla began to discuss its implementation by October 14.[83] The town council made elaborate preparations, as prescribed in documents issued by the Cortes on May 2.

Cities such as Puebla carefully followed the extensive guidelines for the establishment of the Constitution, all done under the auspices of the church. At the beginning of November 1812, the viceroy presided over the consecration of liberal government in Puebla. Swearing public oaths of loyalty proceeded in stages, with the *cabildo* (town council) pledging adherence to the Constitution first at seven thirty in the morning in the presence of an ecclesiastic. The intendant, judges, and *regidores* (councilmen) vowed to uphold the Constitution immediately afterward. Remaining local officials and Indians then pledged their adherence, which was followed by a mass at the city's main cathedral to inaugurate the new charter. Parishioners were to take the vow in their respective parochial churches. At two thirty, citizens honored the publication of the Constitution in the main plaza. Everyone stood in silence while the governor took the Constitution in his hands, kissed it, symbolically touched it to his head, and gave it to the royal official in charge of publication. He solemnly ordered: "Publish, in conformity with the Sovereign will of the King, this precious Code, with which the Spanish Nation recovers its rights, liberty and independence, and strengthens its happiness and glory."[84] The day ended with a festive banquet, fireworks, and the ringing of church bells across the city.

"FRATRICIDAL WAR"

Despite the promulgation of the Constitution of 1812, intermittent warfare continued to expose the vulnerability of the transatlantic monarchy. Insurgents forged alliances across the spectrum of social class and occupation under the banner of the church and the king. Fernando VII, the desired candidate to the Spanish throne, retained an aura of inviolability and legitimacy as a monarch held against his will by Napoleon in France. Royalists as well as rebels fought in the name of the king, just as the uprising in Spain had been proclaimed to restore the throne to the Spanish Bourbons. The common ties of church and state grounded nationalist rhetoric on all sides in a tone of deference to traditional authorities. Bringas, a virulent critic of Hidalgo, went as far as to question why the insurgency led by Hidalgo would fight against the Spaniards in the name of Fernando VII: "Then it appears more natural that they would think to establish a monarchy independent of Spain."[85] Contemporaries such as Bringas publicly noted the contradictions inherent in the civil wars that had erupted across Spanish America.

When the absolutist state was restored in peninsular Spain in 1814, and key leaders of the insurgency had been executed or jailed, autonomists continued to struggle over whether to declare national sovereignty and define a new state outside the orbit of the Spanish Monarchy. José María Cos, a general in the insurgency by 1814, derided the return of Fernando VII as the most disastrous thing that could have befallen Spain. The king's scorn for liberal government was made apparent by his unrepentant decision to dismantle the institutional structures created by the Cortes. Thus, for American liberals like Cos, independence was the only remaining path forward. He predicted destruction and ruin for the "foolish Gachupines."[86] In his memoirs from the era, Servando Teresa de Mier similarly pointed to the turmoil and political unrest in peninsular Spain as the raison d'être of American independence movements. With the Constitution declared null and void in May 1814, Mier drew attention to the fact that those who "swore to obey the Constitution are [now] rebels and guilty of the crime of lèse-majesté."[87] Advocates of constitutionalism in the New World had no choice but to break with the peninsular absolutist regime. The instability in Madrid, epitomized by the failure to consolidate a liberal government which would encompass the entirety of the Spanish Monarchy, allowed American insurgents to continue to press for independence and undermine the royal authorities.

American conservatives painted constitutionalists as puppets of radical France. The liberal architects of the Constitution of 1812, accordingly, had plagiarized from the French charter of 1791, drafted by Jansenists, Deists, and Materialists.[88] One Creole cleric typified restoration sentiment in insisting that a plurality of the deputies in Cádiz had caused tremendous harm to the sovereign rights of the king, just as the works of Bayle, Rousseau, Voltaire, and Diderot had chipped away at the foundations of divine right monarchy in France. His apocalyptic sermon, given in December

1814 in Mexico City, pronounced Fernando VII the "liberator" of Spaniards whose country had been lost to *doceañista* "republicans."[89] The idea that the country had been dishonored by a minority faction in Cádiz became a leitmotif in the rhetoric of the supporters of the restored king.

As the war dragged on, discursive formulations of identity retained tensions between regionalism and nationalism. The 1814 Constitution of Apatzingán christened the nation as América Mexicana, a middle ground between the broader frame of Spanish America and the specificity and uniqueness of the capital city.[90] Detractors alternately referred to the rebels as representatives of "la nación americana" or of "la república mexicana," and they quickly declared the rebels to be enemies of society.[91] The prodigious amount of invective leveled against the insurgents testifies to the degree of sympathy and support they undoubtedly enjoyed in spite of their losses in the first years of armed struggle. Although a great deal of blood had been shed over five long years, they had not triumphed on the battlefield. Timothy Anna writes that it would have been clear to those living in 1815 "that independence was not the inevitable destiny" of Spanish America.[92]

Notwithstanding a resurgence of royalist forces in the intervening years, the familial metaphor of mother and child that had reinforced Spanish bonds across the Atlantic, with all of the territories united under the Bourbon monarchy, did not remain in common currency by the 1820s. Whereas many New World clerics had articulated a Spanish nationalism that emphasized the inclusiveness of Spanish identity for *españoles europeos* and *españoles americanos,* the opening of the public sphere allowed competing discourses of identity to circulate widely. Insurgents continued to emphasize difference throughout the course of the war. Hidalgo undermined notions of fraternal bonds and inclusion by arguing that European Spaniards were motivated simply by greed and had no profound connections to America. He decried the *peninsulares* who had come to America in search of riches: "Don't all the gachupines trample over us only to enrich themselves in America?"[93] With Fernando VII back in power, Simón Bolívar referred to Spain as an "unnatural stepmother" in 1815.[94] Royalist clerics reflexively responded by reemphasizing the familial bonds of church and state that made Spain and Spanish America a single political and cultural entity.

Epitomizing the language of particularist Mexican identity, periodicals heralded the founding of the Mexican Empire in 1821: "Unite, then, Anahuacenses, unite with indissoluble ties to your first Chief, to your Emperor . . . to he who broke the chain that linked the two hemispheres, he has made you free and independent."[95] No longer did an extended Spanish family bind together a transatlantic community, but Mexicans traced their heritage to pre-Hispanic roots. Other writers glorified the urban populace of Mexican cities and their heroic contributions to independence: "What do we say, what praise can we give to the plebeians of great cities like Puebla, Querétaro and others, that decidedly resisted the enemies, swelling the ranks of the Army of the Three Guarantees with timely emigrations?" Praising the insurgents as "liberators," the editorial firmly declared: "It is necessary to fill ourselves with a purely national spirit, very distant from parties and ridiculous illusions to enlighten us with candor and good faith." The author asserted that, for the first time, his compatriots were "free to think, and to cast into the world our ideas in printed letters to circulate through the tertulias and the taverns."[96]

The narrative of Mexican independence as an uninterrupted path toward freedom and enlightenment, however, does not conform to the complicated political history of the early 1820s. Key municipalities, such as Puebla, went to great lengths to reestablish constitutionalism under the rubric of a transatlantic Hispanic monarchy. On June 2, 1820, Puebla received notice that the viceroy, the Conde del Venadito, had pledged loyalty to the newly reinstated Constitution of 1812 in Mexico City. Leaders of the city immediately swore allegiance in the cathedral, followed by the recitation of Te Deum.[97] On June 10, the city council announced that *electores* would be chosen the following day, the first step in the three-tiered electoral process. Elections for *regidores* to serve on the *ayuntamiento* were held on June 13. Just as in 1812, all elections were conducted under the direction of parish churches. On June 19, the newly elected officials took a vow of loyalty to the Spanish Monarchy, a mirror image of the oath taken on January 1, 1813. "To religiously guard the Political Constitution of the Spanish Monarchy" was of primary importance. The notable difference between the two vows was the addition of a call "to guard this, Our City, and its rights and Privileges."[98] Citizens would thus demonstrate their fidelity to the Crown, to the nation, and to the municipality simultaneously by upholding justice and the law.

On August 23, Bishop Pérez Martínez delivered a sermon to sanctify the new government. He preached the merits of constitutionalism and elaborated upon the central tenets of Fernando VII's 1820 royal decree on the reinstatement of the Constitution of 1812. Pérez Martínez discussed various articles in detail, imploring "the Diocesan Prelates to ensure that all parish priests in the Monarchy . . . explain the political Constitution of the Nation to all their parishioners on Sundays and on festival days as part of their obligations."[99] In September, Pérez Martínez addressed the *electores* selected to choose deputies to serve in the Cortes in Madrid. Rather than dwelling on local concerns, he emphasized the civic values of the Spanish nation: "Señores Electores . . . what an opportune time for me to warn you, for you not to forget to sustain your rights and promote your happiness, now that you are going to serve the Nation and the Country as dignified representatives in the Cortes and the Provincial Diputación." "The deputies that you are going to elect," he continued, "will be charged with reestablishing Spain, peninsular and overseas, to all its dignity and grandeur."[100]

Yet the city of Puebla faced serious obstacles in attempting to maintain the familial ties of a transatlantic monarchy. Agustín Iturbide, the former royalist officer, marched on the city after declaring the Plan of Iguala in February. On March 5, 1821, the constitutional *ayuntamiento* rebuffed the proclamation of independence. By May, city officials had denounced the "perfidious Yturbide" and "his anticonstitutional project of independence." The following month, leaders recognized that armed conflict was imminent and focused on the defense of the city, acknowledging that "the Yndependientes want to invade it." Citing articles 8 and 9 of the Constitution of 1812 concerning the duties and obligations of the Spanish citizen, the *ayuntamiento* demanded that all "honorable residents" join in the formation of a provisional militia.[101] Despite their efforts, the council began to perceive a change in public sentiment and an increased level of support for the insurgents. On July 12, leaders bemoaned "the state of public opinion [and] the disasters that the inhabitants of the City began to experience with the threat of a siege by the Yndependientes, and little or no hope to resist it with success."[102]

Facing the prospect of a prolonged struggle against superior forces, Puebla surrendered on July 29. On August 5, the city's residents gave an oath of loyalty to Agustín Iturbide. Iturbide presided over an elaborate ceremony, with a crucifix adorning an altar and four lights placed aside it, as local officials swore allegiance to "the plan which read: Observe the Roman Catholic, apostolic Religion, without tolerance for any other faith, and sustain in every case the intimate union between Mexicans and Europeans."[103] Afterward, the popular classes followed suit, and a mass concluded the ritualized ceremonies.

By the early 1820s, the parent and child had parted ways, and nationalists had constructed a particularist Mexican identity apart from its Spanish progenitor. According to Ludovico de Lato Monte's catechism from 1821, Mexican independence literally signified breaking the bonds of dependency. Just as orphaned children required the tutelage of a mentor, the catechism claimed, a mature people no longer required guidance: "A recent or modern people need a much older people to serve as their tutor, to encourage and educate them until they have passed through the stage of being a pupil and begin to govern themselves." The catechism attributed New Spain's "absolute incapacity to govern themselves" in the past to a chronic lack of population and the scarcity of enlightened thinkers. What triggered the change and signaled Mexico's readiness to self-govern? According to Lato Monte, "the regeneration of Spain and its new constitution" had been the first test of independence.[104] Participation in the political process begun in 1809 rather than success on the battlefield had demonstrated a new sense of maturity and confidence. Lato Monte's tract explained that troops under Hidalgo and Morelos had played critical roles but had not maintained their discipline and had caused disorder throughout the land. Thus the *doceañista* promise of an inclusive liberalism, realized by the Constitution of 1812, had inaugurated Mexican independence.

Clerics praised Hidalgo and Morelos, rather than the Spanish kings, as the forefathers of the nation. One priest lauded "Hidalgo and Allende, the first fathers of the nation [patria]."[105] Another spoke of the unbroken series of events initiated by Hidalgo that had led to independence: "At the same time that Hidalgo began to execute his plan, and to enjoy in his heart the sweet pleasure of manifesting his zeal for the liberty of the Country, the passing of eleven years of internecine, fratricidal war was marked, whose blood ran through the divisions of reciprocal rancor, and will only serve to stain the pages of history."[106] In addition to glorifying Iturbide, clerics connected the events of the 1820s to Hidalgo's 1810 revolt and glossed over the intervening period, weaving a linear history of Mexican independence.

Aztec roots began to take precedence over a Spanish cultural legacy, and the Virgin of Guadalupe provided a foundation for a separate religious and national identity distanced from imperial Spain. Eighteenth-century historians of Spanish America increasingly looked to the pre-Conquest past and disparaged the absolutism of the Habsburgs, beginning with the reign of Carlos V in the early sixteenth century. Sermons and political tomes written during the War of Independence built upon the texts of prominent Enlightenment figures, such as Francisco Clavijero, by linking conceptions of a sovereign American state to Anáhuac, the kingdom of the Aztecs.[107] Influenced by priests such as Mier, whose inflammatory sermon given in 1794 placed St. Thomas in the Americas with Guadalupe as patron saint, the insurgent leader Morelos affirmed continuities with the Aztec past in his 1813 decree *Sentimientos de la nación* (Sentiments of the Nation).[108] Carlos María de Bustamante likewise conjured the "spirits" of mythical Aztec leaders such as Moctehuzoma in his address to the Congress of Chilpancingo in 1813.[109] According to Brading, "Creole patriotism, which began as the articulation of the social identity of American Spaniards, was here transmuted into the insurgent ideology of Mexican nationalism."[110] Although still oscillating between the language of American and Mexican identity, Morelos and other insurgents increasingly advanced an indigenous lineage for an American nation-state. Other contemporary narratives of the independence struggle continued to draw parallels between the Aztec empire and an independent Mexico. By 1821, ecclesiastics portrayed Emperor Agustín de Iturbide as heir to the Aztec throne, with references to the lands of Anáhuac added for emphasis: "This hero of the patria [Iturbide] speaks, and his words are like so many rays of light that penetrate to the most hidden corners of the expanses of Anáhuac."[111] Others were more definitive, reiterating the claim that a Mexican dynasty had been established in 1327, the date first put forward by Carlos de Sigüenza y Góngora in the seventeenth century. Thus one cleric announced to his parishioners that he intended to help carry out the divinely sanctioned project of "reintegrating ourselves into the Imperium of Anáhuac." Begun in "the year 1327, when the Mexican court was founded," the revolt led by Hidalgo and completed by Iturbide had provided a bridge for the history of the Mexican nation.[112] From the point of view of such nationalists, the Spanish Conquest had simply been an interregnum between the two historical Mexican kingdoms.

No longer were the heterogeneous saints from Aragon and Asturias eulogized in American churches. Priests offered reverence to the Virgin of Guadalupe as the liberator of Mexico from Spain. Priests reiterated calls for national liberation from the pulpit and sanctioned independence as a sacred rite of passage for a religious nation. Solemnly giving thanks to the heroes of 1821, one friar praised Juan Diego and the Virgin of Guadalupe as central figures in the independence struggle: "Do not forget that María Sma. de Guadalupe, keeping the kind word that she gave to our compatriot Juan Diego of watching over us all as the pious Mother, moved the hearts of the leaders, and of all the towns, so that in such a short period of time, and with such happiness, we achieved our liberty. It is, then, our principal obligation to give to the Omnipotent Lord humble thanks, and to give them also to María Sma. de Guadalupe."[113] By elevating Guadalupe to prominence as a national image of the Virgin Mary, clerics departed from earlier oratorical patterns. Whereas a number of Marian cults had flourished in the churches of New Spain and across Spanish America, Guadalupe came to hold a unique place in postindependence Mexico. Together with calls for religious regeneration, Guadalupano Catholicism provided powerful ideological content for a particularist Mexican nationalism to develop apart from Spain.

CONCLUSION: THE REVOLUTION OF 1820 AND MEXICAN INDEPENDENCE

The liberal revolution of 1820 that began in Cádiz with a military uprising of soldiers bound for duty in the Americas played a pivotal role in the events occurring in New Spain. While many in Spanish America immediately swore allegiance to the Constitution of 1812, others began to reassess the situation in light of the legislative agenda of the Cortes. Still denying Americans equal representation while ostensibly granting them a large degree of self-rule, peninsular liberals during the Trienio liberal (1820–23) alienated their American counterparts, many of whom came to espouse independence. Conservative clerics argued that Mexico had pursued independence in order to secure the Catholic faith from its Jacobin enemies: "We will respect the resolutions of the vicar of Jesus Christ: we will obey the councils, as our distinctive piety and faith have given us the glorious name of the most Catholic Mexican Empire. . . . We want *Independence* that frees us from all of the evils that beset Spain. . . . Long live the *Independence* that assures us of our religious existence."[114] By the early 1820s, conservatives as well as liberals could unite under the inclusiveness of a Mexican nation that embodied the representative principles of the Constitution of 1812 as well as its confessional underpinnings. The nation served as a unifying symbol of liberal intentions and traditional faith.

Even the peninsular Bárcena aligned himself with the cause of Mexican nationalism by 1823 in the wake of liberal reforms in Spain, conflating religious and national identity: "The holy Catholic religion . . . is the soul of this empire; yes, the faith of Jesus Christ is inseparable from it and is identified with the nation of Anáhuac; and he who is not an apostolic Christian is not a citizen of ours; he is not a Mexican."[115] His use of language mirrored that of his earlier sermons, with Mexico replacing the Spanish nation as the locus of identity. Similarly, the metaphor of the family had been reframed by this point: Now the children of colonial Spain had to break from their mother and assert their own individuality and identity. As heir to Spain's former greatness, Mexico had to declare its independence in order to protect the Catholic faith and serve as a bulwark against the enemies of the church. Conservative clerics were able to rally around the cause of Mexican nationalism by the 1820s in defense of religion, whereas a decade earlier many had decried the excesses of Hidalgo's supporters.

The language that circumscribed the new nations of Spanish America centered on religious identity and notions of sovereignty inherited from the Hispanic Enlightenment. The Mexican nation was constructed around the image of the Virgin of Guadalupe and an American cultural heritage.[116] While Catholicism had linked Spanish America to the metropole, a parallel identity forged in Enlightenment texts, in the pulpits, and on the battlefield began to separate the New World from peninsular Spain. Although nationalist discourses continued to be contested in the wake of independence, and the terms *americano* and *mexicano* were often interchangeable, notions of a separate identity began to supplant Spanish nationalist discourses by the 1820s, distinguishing modern Mexico from its colonial past.

State institutions and the cultural apparatus of the church were two of the central elements linking the communities of Spain with Spanish America, but important local distinctions ultimately differentiated the processes of national identification formation in the peninsula and the New World. Whereas Spanish regional identifications were marginalized during the struggle against the French, the hierarchical structures of the monarchy, based upon ideas of class, ethnicity, and birthplace, were transformed into fixed markers of regional American identity by the early 1820s. Insurgent clerics such as Hidalgo and Morelos successfully mobilized a militant base by playing upon these issues. They emphasized the oppression and injustice of the imperial relationship that appealed to a cross-class alliance of the marginalized poor, indigenous peasants and mulattos, clerics, landowners, and urban elites.[117]

Insurgent ideologues mixed traditional notions of Spanish identity with New World symbols, initiating a shift in patterns of identification. While clearly building upon notions of patriotism rooted in the Enlightenment, Creoles and *peninsulares*, autonomists and insurgents alike formulated the tropes of Mexican national identity. In peninsular Spain, the insurgency against the Napoleonic occupation served as the foundational myth of burgeoning discourses of national identity. Class-based grievances that had been staples of Old Regime mobilizations against the royal authorities were displaced by anti-French sentiment and outrage at the destruction and privation caused by the war. Class conflicts and regional identification were largely elided in favor of nationalist rhetoric that called for defending the Spanish church and nation against the godless French. Fighting against the Spanish royalists, however, rebels in New Spain emphasized populist causes and conflated class antagonisms with an identity that differentiated *americanos* from peninsular Spaniards.

An inclusive nationalism embracing both Europeans and Americans had fallen into disrepute by the time of the proclamation of an independent Mexican Empire in 1821. In sum, the dynamics of two simultaneous wars of independence in New Spain and Spain began to diverge as the two insurgencies forged distinct identities in opposition to their enemies. Yet religion continued to serve as a unifying force of identity, and the dominant Mexican nationalism that appeared by the early 1820s overlapped with Spanish nationalist discourses. If, as cultural historians maintain, one crucial component of "national identification is clearly . . . something transmitted from the past and secured as a collective belonging, something reproduced in myriad imperceptible ways, grounded in everydayness and mundane experience," then the idioms of nineteenth-century Mexican and Spanish nationalisms shared a common historical and cultural legacy that was not simply broken by independence.[118]

6

THE CULTURE AND POLITICS OF HISPANIC LIBERALISM

José Bravo, an outspoken liberal Spanish priest, composed a popular anthem of national resistance that paid tribute to Spanish valor in the face of tyranny. He dedicated his song to the "patriotic company . . . of military officials of Seville, brought together under the constitutional system." While his clarion call to arms, published in Seville in 1821, may have been written originally during the War of Independence and revived during the Trienio liberal of 1820–23, the battle hymn nonetheless recalled the guerrilla leader Ascencio Nebot's call to arms: "*Long live Spain: long live the Constitution.*" While Diego José de Cádiz celebrated the "Catholic soldier" as the icon of religious war, Bravo wrote verses enshrining the "constitutional soldier" as the archetypal Spanish hero who fought for the honor of the nation: "With union, strength and constancy / What tyrant will be able to defeat us? / The heavens part and you will see how he fights / The constitutional soldier."[1] Sung to unknown musical accompaniment, Bravo's song encapsulates a moment in which liberal nationalism had reemerged triumphantly. Rather than interpret the Trienio teleologically, as an ineluctable slide toward the absolutism and civil strife of the "ominous decade," this chapter focuses on recovering the liberal culture of the transatlantic Spanish Monarchy and its antecedents during the first decades of the nineteenth century.

Liberal nationalist sentiment flourished during the wars of independence across the Hispanic Atlantic, and conservative discourses deployed by absolutists in many ways paralleled liberal visions that first put forward a civic national project. Liberals established the foundational narrative of nationalist ideology and culture of the time, creating a paradigm of popular nationalism that served as a template for all competing political forces. Eric Hobsbawm maintains that "the modern nation was part of liberal ideology."[2] In Spain from 1808 onward, narratives of popular resistance, giving agency to the general will of the people, rhetorically situated *el pueblo* at the center of political discourse. All subsequent ideologies had to contend with notions of popular sovereignty and had to justify their claims by speaking to individual rights and the vote of the nation. Liberalism had infused Spanish nationalist ideology from the outset. Fernando VII's swift decree abolishing the constitutional government of the Spanish Monarchy in 1814 and the subsequent exile of prominent dissidents did not expunge liberalism in peninsular Spain or within the warring American provinces. To the contrary, the restoration of the Constitution of Cádiz in 1820 emboldened those previously silenced to embrace the liberal nationalism of the *doceañistas.* Liberals articulated an emotional attachment to the law and to ideals of civil liberty, which they traced to the glorious and sometimes tragic history of the Spanish people. They also glorified the heroic exploits of soldiers fighting to defend the nation, expressing the martial values of a nation born out of war. Couched in religious imagery and biblical metaphor, liberal nationalism found an outlet in the culture, the church, and the politics of the transatlantic Spanish Monarchy throughout the early 1820s.

According to Alberto Gil Novales, "the second liberal experiment was a decisive phase" in the history of modern Spain.[3] Rafael de Riego's *pronunciamiento* (proclamation) on January 1, 1820, the first successful politically motivated military rebellion in the history of modern Spain, built on a number of failed conspiracies between 1814 and 1818. Most had been influenced or inspired by liberals, some of whom were Freemasons, and had been carried out by military officers attempting to restore the constitutional order.[4] During the Trienio, patriotic societies diffused the radical ideology of liberalism, and a renascent free press served as a forum for increasingly polemical political debates. Yet popular support had not been mobilized to catapult new leaders to power. The success of Riego's uprising, despite a lukewarm reception in southern Spain where his battalion had been based, sparked a movement in the north to reestablish the local governing *juntas* that had been so successful in 1808. Alongside these regional organizations, a popular nationalist culture of songs, poems, and catechisms reemerged in addition to sermons and political tracts that once again eulogized the heroic Spanish people and their representative national government.

The revolution of 1820, which began in Cádiz when troops about to be deployed to Montevideo and the Río de la Plata rebelled, profoundly affected events across the Atlantic. Leaders such as Iturbide reassessed their allegiance to the Crown, hesitating to support the reinstated Constitution and its unabashed liberal principles. The Cortes convened in Madrid provided a last-ditch venue for the contentious debates over the possibilities of transatlantic representation, and Americans were frustrated in their attempts at reconciliation.[5] Even attempts to install a Spanish monarch on a New World throne were thwarted as Latin Americans consolidated independent national governments.

The church also proved to be a divisive factor during the Trienio. Reforms aimed at ecclesiastical privileges pushed many clerics toward a reactionary stance. The Cortes of 1820 passed a law closing a large number of monasteries, most of which housed monks and friars devoted to contemplation and prayer. Within two years, more than eight hundred had been shut down, although this represented fewer than half of the monastic communities in Spain. By 1822, with four liberal governments formed in less than three years, absolutist reaction reached peak levels. Jerónimo Merino, a former guerrilla leader against the French, had taken up arms against the constitutional regime in 1821 in Burgos. A royalist insurrection spearheaded by incursions of French troops in 1822 was followed by the proclamation of a regency in Urgel that included the bishop of Osma. According to many accounts, a former Trappist monk, Antonio Marañon, began a counterrevolutionary campaign in Catalonia by shouting, "Death to the Constitution!"[6] One newspaper article indicated that liberals in the city of Pamplona had to walk the streets after dark with care, peeking around corners to ensure their own safety.[7] Reactionary mobilizations were not confined to the north, as absolutists even staged an abortive uprising in Madrid in July 1822.

Yet the constitutional government enjoyed a large degree of popular support, demonstrated by protests in favor of Riego in Madrid on September 18, 1821, followed by urban unrest in Cádiz, Córdoba, Granada, Seville, La Coruña, Valencia, and Badajoz.[8] One contingent of loyal troops, quartered in Alicante, volunteered to march to Catalonia to stem the uprising. Writing to the Cortes, the lieutenant in charge offered to underwrite the campaign until they reached Catalan soil.[9] A third French invasion of Spain within the span of thirty years ended the Trienio in April 1823, and peninsular liberals again faced exile, imprisonment, and reprisals for another decade prior to their ascendancy in the 1830s. Yet Hispanic liberal nationalism, which put forward a reformed Catholicism and a constitutional tradition as the basis for revitalized popular political movements, was firmly ensconced across Spain and the new nations of Spanish America.

THE CULTURE OF LIBERAL NATIONALISM

During the six years of Fernando VII's first restoration, liberal clerics cultivated a national mythology surrounding the events of 1808 and the uprising against the French. Symbolic episodes of the war became immortalized as part of a national narrative giving agency to the heroic martyrs of the nation. The people, accordingly, had defeated the French despite overwhelming adversity. For the liberal cleric Alberto Pujol, preaching in Barcelona in 1816, the siege of the Catalan city of Gerona provided the context for a nationalist sermon in honor of the Spanish resistance to French tyranny. The military general of Gerona, Mariano Álvarez de Castro, who had been cut off by a surrounding army in 1809, refused to negotiate with the French and held out for seven months. Pujol implored parishioners to venerate the sacrifices made by Álvarez and his men. Addressing the fallen soldiers, he cried: "Noble Spaniards, receive posterity's praise; the Country places you within its pantheon of heroes. . . . Hear the magnanimous votes of all the people, like Lazarus resuscitated from the grave in which he lay, Álvarez must know rest and a place of light and clarity."[10] Although remembering a defining moment that epitomized the particular hardships faced by Catalans during the war with neighboring France, Pujol emphasized the national character of the war and portrayed the soldiers and Álvarez as "noble Spaniards" rather than as defenders of the *patria chica.* As provinces declared their independence in Spanish America, peninsular regionalisms remained a part of an inclusive Spanish nationalism. Furthermore, by simply recounting episodes of the war against the French during Fernando's restored absolutist regime, Pujol invoked memories of the liberal government in Cádiz founded upon the principle of national sovereignty.

Various localized episodes of violence, including el Dos de Mayo, were consistently characterized as part of a larger national uprising tied to the constitutional revolution in Cádiz. Sermons, songs, and poems described victims of French atrocities as courageous soldiers fighting to free Spain from captivity.[11] In 1811, the Cortes had declared May 2 a national holiday, decreeing a "commemoration of the fallen, of the first martyrs of Spanish liberty in Madrid."[12] Even during the restoration, public pronouncements by the religious on May 2 evoked the revolutionary spirit of the first *juntas* that brought down the Old Regime. The reactionary friar Facundo Sidro Vilarroig, in a "reflection" published on May 2, 1814, refuted the liberal legislation enacted in Cádiz, especially that pertaining to the church, as he celebrated the people who had risen up against tyranny six years earlier on the streets of Madrid.[13] Such an event could not be separated categorically from the context of liberal revolution.

Songs represented another form of historical memory, pointing to popular attitudes and modes of cultural production. Antonio Alcalá Galiano, contrasting early-nineteenth-century culture with that of later decades, emphasized the importance of "patriotic songs" during the Trienio as well as during the War of Independence.[14] By 1822, the radical liberalism of the *doceañistas* had been endorsed officially by a decree from Fernando VII declaring the "Himno de Riego" (Riego's Hymn) the national anthem.[15] During the annual commemoration of el Dos de Mayo in Madrid, an anthem titled "Himno patriótico" (Patriotic Hymn), composed by the liberal priest Antonio Sabiñón, was sung in honor of those who had died. The chorus began by emphasizing the importance of national history: "Renewing the august memory / Of that day of mourning and of dread." Subsequent verses honored those killed by the French during the insurrection: "And laurels of eternal victory / Give honor to the brave men, / Dying illustrious deaths then, / Fought to make Spain free."[16] The concluding stanza upheld the rights of the nation against tyranny: "If an insolent tyrant again / Casts off the rights of Spain / They will rise from where they had lain / To avenge the nation once more."[17] Rather than adhering to Old Regime notions of the absolute power of kings, divinely sanctioned by God, this nationalistic hymn defended the liberal theory of the people's right to suspend and revoke their contract with unjust rulers. Yet absolutist invective, in the vein of Villanueva's *Catecismo del estado* from 1793, continued to appeal to the divine rights of kings. One catechism stated: "There is no exception so that one may disobey their legitimate superior. . . . One should suffer injustice with patience."[18] Songs such as the "Himno patriótico," however, composed in a tradition of civic nationalism, in effect reminded future kings who might lean toward despotism of the history of resistance and rebellion symbolized by the uprising of 1808. Although written by a cleric, the "Himno patriótico" contained no religious references. Sabiñón paid homage to fallen soldiers and to the strength of Spanish arms, and he contrasted the love of the king with the hatred felt toward the despot Napoleon. Toward the end, euphoric chants of "Liberty!" signaled victory for the Spanish and likely rose to a crescendo before the penultimate chorus. In sum, the song contained few traditional tropes or lyrical flourishes typical of the Old Regime. Such cultural works marked el Dos de Mayo as a signifier of resistance against a foreign power as well as of national sovereignty, and the war against the French began to be associated with a liberal vision of Spanish nationalism.

The "National March," written during the War of Independence, called for national resistance on both sides of the Atlantic. Using the term *las Españas,* as the framers of the Constitution had in 1812, the battle hymn exhorted all Spaniards as citizens and as Catholics to rise up against the figure of the "infernal Napoleon." The song directly addressed the people as a body unified during a time of war. The third stanza appealed to the nation to protect the faith from a people that did not know God: "You defend the just cause, / And God himself provides his protection." Using popular rhetorical devices from the time, the composer portrayed Spaniards subject to French rule as "slaves" under the yoke of Napoleon. Biblical metaphors alluding to the captivity of the Israelites in Egypt became common currency during Spain's occupation, and notions of Spanish "slavery" abounded. But the march did not reproduce a conservative, reactionary nationalism. While the lyrics hinted at French revolutionary terror, the language of liberty, equality, and fraternity—as a competing legacy of the Revolution—also appeared in the song. Accordingly, verses praised the "fraternal Spanish people, / Who for their beloved King Fernando, / Will know to die heroically / For Independence and Religion / Always on the field of honor."[19] The idea of fraternity, in addition to the language of national sovereignty embodied in the term *el pueblo español,* resonated with the symbolism of the French Revolution.

Notably, the Spanish nation was conceived of in the plural as a transatlantic community under the umbrella of monarchy. The song began with the awakening of the nation, symbolized by the figure of the lion: "Now awakened from its lethargy / The Lion of the Spains, / And with horrible roars / Covers the land with fear." Whereas the lion had been languid, hinting at the perceived decadence and misrule of Carlos IV and Godoy, it would not remain passive in the face of foreign occupation. The song alternately used the nationalist language of *el pueblo español* as well as *el pueblo hispano.* Capturing the broadly inclusive civic nationalism of the period, the song envisioned the expansive lands of the Spanish Monarchy fighting together against a common enemy.[20] Admired throughout Europe as the standard-bearers of national resistance against Napoleon, the Hispanic people were engaged in a heroic struggle to be immortalized by future generations: "All of Europe, the entire world / Will be filled with admiration, / In contemplating the enthusiasm and great valor / Of the Hispanic people. / And the coming ages / Between terror and confusion / Will always respect humbly / The august name of Spaniard."[21] Although the nation was spread out over two hemispheres and separated by the Atlantic, its people were united as Spaniards.

Bravo's hymn also exemplified a liberal nationalism that denigrated conservative reaction to reform. Bravo pilloried the *serviles,* the conservative faction at Cádiz, positioning their views in opposition to ideals of liberty and freedom: "Love of the Country unites us / Against the blind and obstinate servil; / We grasp the sword and fight / For the Country and for liberty." As a liberal rallying cry, the song reflected the increasingly martial tone of the struggle over Spanish identity: "To arms, soldiers / Of the just and beneficent union, / To save the insulted Country, / Or die for the Constitution."[22] This militarism likewise was reflected in the "Himno de Riego," which had mandated an oath of loyalty to the *patria:* "We swear our loyalty / to vanquish or die."[23] With no open hostilities in peninsular Spain in 1820, and Fernando VII offering allegiance to the Constitution he had denounced only six years before, a metaphorical battle between *liberales* and *serviles* continued to be fought within the Catholic public sphere. Bravo's song, unlike that of Sabiñón, upheld the sacred bonds between God and the state, although the importance of fealty to the monarch was conspicuously absent. His "Himno patriótico" glorified national "honor and the formal oath that we have made to the Country and to God" but did not mention the king at all.[24] Such popular expressions of nationalism often conveyed liberal sentiment in addition to reviving the military spirit of 1808.

Theatrical works composed to provoke resistance to French incursions similarly espoused the ideals of liberal nationalism and national sovereignty. Often simple one-act dramas, partisan plays were staged in all parts of the monarchy between 1808 and 1810. In Puebla, *comedias* with titles such as *Fin de Napoladrón* (The End of Napoleon the Thief) and *Napoleón rabiando* (Napoleon Enraged) were staples of the stage, each production displaying a sense of camaraderie with peninsular Spain.[25] Historians have catalogued over one hundred such plays, and many, including both *Fin de Napoladrón* and *Napoleón rabiando,* were performed on both sides of the Atlantic.[26] *La sombra de Pelayo* (The Shadow of Pelayo), which opened in peninsular Spain and in New Spain in 1808 and 1810, respectively, narrated the French invasion as a confrontation between good and evil. An allegorical drama, the work presented Pelayo, the eighth-century warrior-king from Asturias, lamenting the fall of an enervated nation. As Pelayo had defeated the Moors and initiated the Reconquest in 718 after the demise of Visigothic Spain, the people had to rise up under the banner of Fernando VII in order to triumph against despotism and greed, the antagonists of the drama.

Most of these works decried the French occupation and mocked "Josef Botellas," purported to be a drunkard-king, as well as the Constitution of Bayonne, promulgated in July 1808 by French officials and Spanish notables.[27] The play *La quema de la constitución en aldea leal* (The Burning of the Constitution in a Loyal Village), for example, argued that a constitution that reflected the will of the people must be enacted in lieu of the "Constitución *Napoleoniana.*" One of the main characters, a local curate, insisted: "That constitution [of Bayonne] is better for burning than for reading." Speaking for the villagers, the parish priest did not advocate a return to the Old Regime or a simple restoration of the Spanish Monarchy, nor did he promote a secular republic on the model of the French revolutionary regime. He urged moderation, praying "that God would deliver us in safety to our King Fernando, and would inspire the wise of the Kingdom of Spain to propose a sound Constitution more in line with the interests of the King and of the country." While various characters accused the French of being corrupted by Judaism and sacrilege, their principal concern was that the Constitution had been "formed without the consent of the Spanish, outside of our Spain, and by a usurper of our Fernando's throne."[28] That the Constitution had not been sanctioned by the vote of the people represented the fundamental flaw in the document drawn up at Bayonne. In a catechism published in 1809 in Seville, similar arguments justified rejection of the Constitution of Bayonne. Because the nation had not given consent through legitimately elected representatives, the Constitution was null and void. In a traditional question-and-answer form, the catechism derided the new charter: "Q. Is the new constitution given to Spain from Bayonne a wise one? A. Miserable constitution! It is the fruit of audacity and stupidity, regrettably introduced with neither the consent nor the consultation of the Nation."[29] In this view, King Fernando VII did not embody traditional authority and command deference as the figure of the monarch had in the past; by 1808, the Spanish people were sovereign and legitimacy was conferred by the nation.

PREACHING CONSTITUTIONALISM IN 1812 AND 1820

Many popular catechisms from the Trienio synthesized tradition and liberalism by espousing a moderate form of constitutional monarchy based upon the ideals first consecrated at Cádiz in 1812. Catechisms presented formulaic dialogues between a teacher and student to be memorized and internalized. While eighteenth-century versions may have reached a limited audience of the literate educated classes, a profusion of catechisms was published with the opening of the public sphere and the establishment of press freedom.[30] By the early 1820s, in contrast to the dogmatic renditions of the Old Regime, many catechisms espoused liberal sentiments and upheld the Constitution of Cádiz as the pillar of a representative system based upon national sovereignty and religious uniformity. The curate Apolinar Contoni composed a catechism, to be recited by children taught at the parish church of St. James in the city of Baza in Andalusia, intended to instill the values of constitutionalism and citizenship in the future citizens of the town. He dedicated his verses to the local commander of the town's national militia, the defenders of the liberal regime inaugurated in 1820. According to Contoni, the Constitution, as a manifestation of the "character of the nation, [preserved] natural rights, and [adhered] to the one and only true religion of Jesus Christ." In response to a question on "the type of government the Constitution proposes," the student was to recite: "The government of the Spanish nation is a moderate, hereditary constitutional monarchy." The idea of moderation not only indicated a mixed government headed by a monarch and run by elected representatives, but pointed to the limited powers of the king within the constitutional system. Laws were passed in the name of the king, but certainly not by the king himself, as he remained a figurehead "in whose name the monarchical Government is run." The catechism ended by reiterating the natural affinity and congruence between religion and the constitutional regime, and between ideals of the good Christian and those of the national citizen: "The articles of our Constitution are perfectly in line with the Holy Gospel, in that he who is a good Christian is necessarily a good Constitutionalist."[31] No contradictions existed in this incorporation of the sacred into the realm of the law and the state. To the contrary, this demonstrated continuity with the past, which would allow the architects of constitutionalism to argue that liberalism was consistent with the history of Spain and its legacy of religious purity and medieval representative government.

Contoni's catechism built upon those written during the War of Independence and the moderate ideals first articulated by liberals in Cádiz. Published in 1813, the catechism composed by Seville's cathedral dean Manuel López Cepero, *Lecciones políticas para el uso de la juventud española* (Political Lessons for Use by Spanish Youth), outlined for students all of the key concepts and tenets of the Constitution. Written for boys ten to twelve years old, the lessons instructed the respondent to address his priest with reverence and respect. As a paternal figure, the priest referred to a student as "my son" and was addressed as "my father." In the introduction to the catechism, López Cepero underscored the importance of reaching all levels of Spanish society, regardless of educational background: "I have proposed to explain the fundamental principles of the social contract in a way that accommodates the abilities and the language of the most rustic pastor. . . . [T]hen . . . public teaching can move forward."[32] López Cepero envisioned his catechism—grounded in the ideals of the Rousseauian social contract as based upon the general will of the people—as bridging the divide between illiterate and literate, rural and urban.

One of the first lessons clarified the meaning of sovereignty, which was defined as the active exercise of the legislative function. Making and implementing the law symbolized the abstraction of sovereign power. The catechism maintained an egalitarian interpretation of this inalienable right: "Everyone takes part in sovereignty, in that it resides essentially in society, being so essential and inherent that it cannot be divided or alienated."[33] In turn, the exercise of sovereignty expressed the general will and contributed to the common good of society.

López Cepero warned against the excesses of democracy in order to emphasize the wise and just values enumerated in the Constitution of 1812. He insisted that democracy was a gateway to the chaos of anarchy and disorder—the inevitable result of a body politic that had ceased to obey the legitimately established authorities: "Democracy can quickly convert into Anarchy, which is the worst ill to befall a society, as all of the citizens are neither virtuous nor moderate." He condemned the forces of anarchy as "an assembly of men without order and without a leader, and in consequence without laws or authorities that they are made to obey."[34] He also pointed to the tendency toward arbitrary and despotic rule inherent within an aristocratic monarchy. López Cepero admonished tyrants who concentrated the power of three branches of government into one and forced inhabitants to live like slaves obeying the vicissitudes of their masters. The concomitant loss of civil liberties under such a regime posed just as much danger to society as did the inevitable descent into anarchy of democratic government. Therefore, López Cepero argued for a restoration of the fundamental laws of the kingdom and the reunion of the Cortes.

The Constitution of 1812 had been presented as a revival of a Spanish tradition of representative institutions. Within this interpretation, many public supporters of liberal government linked constitutionalism to a long line of customs and laws implemented by the Spanish Monarchy. López Cepero's catechism described the slow erosion of Spain's age-old traditions due to abuses and royal despotism: "The most ancient of these laws were not observed because the Kings' powers had been advancing little by little, and surpassed the privileges confided in them by the nation, until they became true despots and tyrants." To counterbalance the tyranny of royal prerogative, the Cortes, representing the nation, had to be recalled. In justifying the use of the term "Cortes," López Cepero's catechism compared Spain's tradition of representation to that of England: "We have made that word sacred through venerating its antiquity and by calling it the supreme Congress of the nation, in the same way that England calls it Parliament."[35] Clerics nonetheless emphasized the religious element of constitutional government, which distinguished Spanish liberalism from England's political ideology.

Many liberal clerics argued that the text of the Constitution served as the political form of the religious catechism. Preaching in Valladolid in 1812, after the French had abandoned the city at the end of July following the Battle of Arapiles, Manuel Martínez exhorted parishioners to read and study the Constitution like a catechism: "After the religious catechism, study, meditate on and ruminate on your rights and your social obligations, and you will know dignity. As you do with the religious catechism, put the Constitution into the hands of your sons and grandsons."[36] Only by doing so, he maintained, would the true nature of Spanish identity be revealed. Only then would the heroism of innumerable soldiers be honored as the tragic sacrifice necessary to lift the nation out of disgrace and servitude and usher in a new age of freedom and independence. In a refractory tone, Martínez exalted "the Spanish people": "Wise nation, only in recent times has your liberty, your independence and your sovereignty been shouted out loud." He described the people as the architects of the liberal revolution at Cádiz because they had set in motion an electoral process by making use of their sovereignty: "The nation exercises the most difficult and important part of sovereignty through their representatives, chosen by the citizens."[37] The act of electing officials made the people the centerpiece of the new liberal system. Sermons from 1808 attributed the initial spark of the uprising to a profound and latent Spanish nationalism awakened from years of slumber, while those of 1812 claimed the people had initiated and participated in representative, constitutional government as their forebears had in the past.

On March 15, 1820, the archbishop of Toledo, Luis de Borbón, inaugurated the second era of liberal government in Spain with a pastoral premised upon the powers of the people to build a powerful and just nation on the foundations of constitutional law and religious observance. The sermon displayed marked similarities to those preached in March 1812 and in the months following the initial promulgation of the Constitution, stressing the fundamental centrality of law as the defining force of Spanish liberalism. Equating the law with true freedom, he maintained the Hegelian proposition that "we are free through subordination to the laws."[38] Borbón repeatedly implored Spanish citizens to fulfill their contractual obligations and the promise of constitutionalism, concluding, "Our future from now on will depend in large part upon you." Accordingly, elections depended on the goodwill of the nation in order to succeed: "In our hands is the most important function, that of electing subjects, entrusting them with National representation." Fernando VII, in swearing an oath of loyalty to the Constitution, also exhorted Spaniards to exemplify its ideals, thereby "demonstrating to Europe a model of wisdom, order and perfect moderation."[39] Through moderate conduct and adherence to the law, the Spanish citizen was to identify with the political ideology consecrated in Cádiz. In New Spain, liberals similarly invested the law with great significance. In his catechism from 1821, Ludovico de Lato Monte asked, "What is understood by independence?" The response repeated the maxims of Hispanic liberalism: "It is the right of every people or nation to govern itself through its own laws and customs, without being subject to those of another."[40] The canon Ignacio María del Castillo also placed law at the heart of liberal Spanish nationalism. From his pulpit in Seville, he urged parishioners to engage with the new government and legal system. Castillo emphasized that "the uniformity of education, of principles, and of language; the identity in the laws and the government; the community of equality in utility and in taxes . . . when the sublime sentiments of the same divine and consoling Religion inflame our hearts . . . here you see that which is the Country, the true significance of this sweet and comforting word."[41] Such centralizing rhetoric encouraged the nationalization of Spain's citizens on the basis of equality under the law and religious uniformity.

Within this emerging narrative, Fernando VII appeared as a benign patriarch, misled by the counsel of his advisors. According to the liberal cleric Antonio Bernabéu, writing in 1820 to celebrate the revival of the Constitution and the end of the Inquisition, Fernando had been led astray: "Long live religion, but only the pure faith, without obstacles, without superstition or fanaticism; long live the wise Constitution of the monarchy; and long live don Fernando VII, the most felicitous and dignified of kings, because he knows that he was the most deceived among men."[42] The title of Bernabéu's pamphlet, *España venturosa por la vida de la Constitución y la muerte de la Inquisición* (Fortunate Spain for the Life of the Constitution and the Death of the Inquisition), resonated with a sentiment similar to that of Luis de Borbón's sermon from March of the same year. Spain's fortune, *la ventura,* was linked to that of its people, according to Borbón. This could also be turned on its head to signify that Spain was fortunate to have its people once again charged with the exercise of national sovereignty, as Bernabéu explained. Either way, the people, rather than the monarch, had taken the reins of power. As Fernando, like his father before him, had been the victim of ministerial despotism, the framers of the Constitution firmly established the principle of balanced and separate branches of government. Priests emphasized the passivity of Fernando VII in the face of ministerial machinations, showing the potential for abuse of power: "Six years of continuous warnings, that we can truly call signs of the predilection of God watching over Spain, were not enough to awaken the King from the profound lethargy in which those who abused his trust had submerged him."[43] To remedy the situation, liberals argued, the Constitution had to be reinstated and power divested from factions at court. According to one sermon, the Constitution provided the solution by declaring, "The figure of the King inviolable, discharging all of the responsibility of the Ministers, whose arbitrariness has been for too many centuries the origin, in large part, of our misfortunes: the Nation, through its representatives, freely elected by the towns, form the laws through which to govern and that are the expression of the general will."[44] The people, ardently voicing their opinions in favor of the Constitution, were given agency as the driving force behind the reestablishment of liberal government.

Conflicts punctuated the path of order and moderation preached by the king and clerics across the monarchy. The Old Regime ideal of obedience was resuscitated by liberals in order to insist upon allegiance to the constitutional order. In the midst of political and ideological struggles taking place within the Catholic public sphere, one periodical maintained that "obedience to the precepts of the law is that which forms true public opinion; outside of the law there is nothing more than crime and opprobrium."[45] With the upsurge of popular liberalism across the Spanish Monarchy, conservatives also upheld the principles of obedience and submission in opposition to the values of liberty and individual freedom. Writing from the bishopric of Ceuta in 1822, Rafael de Vélez described the identity of Spaniards as a function of the social mores of deference and hierarchy:

> Spanish gravity, our public decency, our urbanity and politics: the respect given to magistrates, submission to the civil laws we have always lived under; the love of our Kings, obedience to their orders and the dependence upon and subordination to those who govern the towns . . . these are the civic virtues that are distinctively Spanish, and the immediate fruits of the religious values that our fathers have always had plenty of; these values, I say, are disappearing, and are replaced by disorders, by vices, by crimes. . . . Spanish character is being disfigured, and presently voices are losing their own significance and meaning.[46]

Vélez consistently warned of the excesses of freedom and the dangers of impetuous action driven by passion. Luis de Borbón had offered a distinct view of the characteristics of the Spanish citizen—endowed with the responsibility to actively participate in the formation of the state—in sermons given during the Trienio. He insisted that constitutional government and natural rights gave Spaniards the freedom and responsibility to act rather than to passively obey: "Liberty is conceded to propose plans and projects for the common good, and to direct public opinion toward this same objective by word of mouth and in writing."[47] While upholding a religious obligation to submit to divine will and to respect authority, the liberal ideal of the active citizen contrasted sharply with Vélez's notions of the submissive, obedient subject, conforming to the Old Regime stereotype of a devout Spanish character.

The constituent Cortes and supporters of the Constitution came to be viewed as increasingly radical by opponents of liberalism throughout the period 1820–23. In Lérida, for example, the liberal canon Antonio Forriol's cry of "Constitution or death!" was denounced by the defenders of absolutism as a liberal call to arms.[48] The king's name was dropped from *doceañista* battle cries in favor of "the constitutional king," causing consternation among the allies of the monarch.[49] In addition, liberal factions of *moderados* (moderates) and *exaltados* (radicals) divided over the same issue of national sovereignty that had united them at Cádiz. The politics of constitutional government played out in an atmosphere of civil war in Spanish America and increasingly tense conflicts in peninsular Spain by 1822.

A counterrevolutionary uprising took place in Madrid on July 7, 1822, that had repercussions throughout the peninsula.[50] One newspaper account predicted the events would come to occupy a central place in the annals of modern Spanish history, providing incontrovertible proof that Spaniards would fight to remain free and independent under the auspices of benevolent constitutionalism.[51] In Valencia, the cleric and self-proclaimed citizen Miguel Cortés y López devoted a lengthy discourse to the "martyrs of Madrid," members of the local militia who died putting down the rebellion and defending the Constitution and the reforms that Spain needed in order to prosper.[52] In it, he presented a detailed plan of a monument to the constitutional *ayuntamiento* in Valencia. The proposed memorial, to be erected in the Field of Liberty, exalted those who died "in Madrid on the memorable day of July 7 defending the liberty of the Nation" as well as the men involved in the failed conspiracy of January 20, 1819, such as Bertrán de Lis.[53] A plaque was placed in the Citadel with an inscription dedicating the site to the "valiant sons of Padilla."[54] The cenotaph, although never completed, was a celebration of the civic values of Spanish constitutionalism, protected by Spanish arms. Cortés, who had been elected to the Diputación Provincial, the Provincial Council, criticized the reestablishment of absolutist government in 1814, claiming that Fernando VII's regime had reinstated arbitrariness, ignorance, slavery, feudalism, the Inquisition, and "political and ecclesiastical *ultracismo*."[55] Conversely, Cortés advocated universalism: "To the supporters of humanity, to the liberators of the country, to the defenders of the Constitution, to the models of the most exalted and just citizenship . . . we celebrate these honors. . . . Christian morality . . . teaches us that the first and principal object of our cult and veneration, after God, is the country. . . . Upon hearing this doctrine, I am persuaded that there isn't one among you who does not fall back on the memory of article 6 of our Constitution, which states that one of the principal obligations of all Spaniards is the love of the country."[56] Cannons were to be placed on each side of the monument, symbolizing the liberal commitment to die in defense of the sacred charter of 1812.

Cenotaph [to be] erected in the Field of Liberty in Valencia in honor of the Militia of Madrid (Valencia, 1822). From the Biblioteca Valenciana.

The violent imagery of a constitutional regime forged in the midst of war against France and reinstated by force of a military *pronunciamiento* was a defining feature of liberal rhetoric. Hearkening back to classical Rome, the liberal cleric Castillo romanticized the figure of the soldier fighting to defend the *patria,* and by extension the Constitution, in declaring to an assembled audience of militia volunteers: "How sweet, how honorable it is to make sacrifices and to die for the Country! This is an eternal truth, consecrated in the grandeur of the human lineage." He identified the *patria* with its laws and government, which had been worthy of the ultimate sacrifice to past generations: "Our Country, these laws, this Constitution was the crowning achievement of our ancestors; in their defense they heroically sacrificed their lives."[57] The popular uprising against French occupation had united nationalist Spaniards in a common cause, and the martial images of Spanish nationalism continued to resonate in the 1820s.

Together with an increasingly militarist rhetoric, a defensive tone characterized many sermons from the Trienio, with liberal clerics launching attacks on those who would malign the pious Constitution as prejudicial toward religion. Rather than referencing scripture or paying homage to saints or kings, many clerics began by addressing the acrimonious conflicts of the time. In March 1820, the bishop of Barcelona used a sermon to respond to charges that the Constitution undermined the historic traditions of religion and the Inquisition in Spain. The governing official in charge of Catalonia, quoted in the introduction to the sermon, firmly avowed that "even though the tribunal of the Inquisition does not exist, no Spaniard can commit a crime against our holy Religion and virtuous customs with impunity; these will be punished just like similar crimes with the rigor and form prescribed by our laws." Secular law also served as a bulwark against absolutist demands to revive the Inquisition, as the constitutional system did not allow for blasphemies against the established church. The bishop followed up by denouncing the lies and rumors about the Constitution: "they are falsehoods, calumnies, and subvert order, do not doubt that they can only be part of the most refined malice." How could these pernicious beliefs be spread, he asked, when "the first precept imposed is the punctual observance of the Catholic Religion"?[58] In Cádiz, the priest Antonio Romero similarly invoked the religious dimensions of the Constitution in a sermon inaugurating the second era of liberal government in 1820: "I have said . . . that the observance of the CONSTITUTION . . . unites us with our God; the Spanish people do not believe that this proposition is arbitrary or capricious."[59] Priests reflexively pointed to Article 12 of the Constitution in order to marshal evidence against conservative detractors. They sanctioned the constitutional regime by repeating the dictum that the Roman Catholic faith was, and would always be, the only religion professed within the boundaries of the Spanish Monarchy.

In 1821 in Seville, preaching on the first anniversary of the reestablishment of constitutional government, Ignacio Castillo delivered a powerful defense of liberalism. He insisted that the values elaborated in the Constitution, from religious uniformity to natural law, had been the animating forces during the war against Napoleon, "those that electrified Spaniards and produced that sublime uprising of the nation against the usurpations of Napoleon." Castillo attacked the principles of absolutism, even suggesting that a tyrant wielding unlimited power could permit religious tolerance against the will of the people. He lambasted absolutist pretensions to establish laws that merely expressed the will of the monarch and his ministers. While the Constitution explicitly stated that the Spanish nation was not and could not be the patrimony of any family or single person, Castillo asserted that an absolutist monarch considered the nation a royal birthright. He summed up his argument by pointing to the decadence and decline of Imperial Rome as an example of the abuse of power: "Happiness under absolute governments depends upon the character and condition of the Princes, and of their ministers, which can vary at any moment; the Augustuses are often succeeded by the Neros and the Caligulas: at the same time, with a Constitution, happiness is cemented by the bonds of laws which are always just and always permanent."[60] His defense of liberalism rested upon the ability to establish the constitutional system as an artifact of Spanish history, categorically different and separate from the revolutionary French model of government. He rhetorically addressed an audience doubting his claims: "Do not believe, Sirs, that this Constitution is a novelty introduced to the Spanish people to separate them from their ancient ideas and customs, an invention of the Cortes of Cádiz, a copy of the systems of the revolutionary Governments of France."[61] Accordingly, the Constitution did not represent a threat to the unique value of national history but served as a seamless link to the essence of the Spanish past.

Liberal clerics such as Castillo contributed to the construction of nationalist mythology dating the origin of the Spanish nation to the conversion of the Visigothic King Reccared in 587. While some clerics had made passing reference to the Visigoths during the War of Independence, they situated them within the larger trajectory of Spanish history. Martínez observed in 1812 that the contributions made by the Visigoths had almost been forgotten: "In our ancient and almost forgotten past, our legislators look for and find the fundamental laws of the monarchy, even though they are dispersed, in the laws of the Goths (that foolishly are called barbarians by those who have never studied their legislation), [and] in the venerated privileges (*fueros*) of Aragon and of Navarre, of León and of Castile."[62] During the Trienio, clerics adamantly defended the Constitution as a link to a unique Spanish historical tradition. Therefore, they were able to position constitutionalism as inherently Spanish rather than as a political import from France. In pointing to the importance of law and religion as the basis of constitutional monarchy, Castillo recognized the Visigoths as the architects of the original laws of the nation. No longer disparaged as barbarians, these kings were placed in the pantheon of national heroes. Whereas Miguel de Santander paid scant attention to the Visigoths or to the centuries preceding the Reconquest in calling for a return to representative government, Castillo placed "the Goths" at the birth of the nation: "This native code of laws . . . was born with the Visigothic monarchy." Further, he claimed that "the centuries of the Reccareds and of the Wambas immortalized the nation." Therefore, the Visigothic kings were in essence the "fathers of the nation (patria)."[63] According to José Álvarez Junco, the ideology of National-Catholicism that emerged by the late nineteenth century played upon similar themes in mythologizing Spain's medieval past and collective identification with the Catholic religion.[64] During the Trienio, prominent liberal clerics began to build on the idea of an essential Spanish nation founded in the remote centuries of the national past.

Peninsular liberals also increasingly hearkened back to the defeat of the Comuneros in 1521, as their American counterparts had done in the wake of Godoy's treachery and the French invasion in 1808. Castillo memorialized the Battle of Villalar from 1521, in which the nobility had aided the Habsburg Monarchy in putting down the vestiges of the Castilian uprising of 1520. He lamented the tragic losses of the age: "The privileges (*fueros*) and liberties of Castile were buried on the fatal battlefields of Villalar with their immortal defenders, and the Country, along with the sacred rights of the Spaniards, disappeared." Following their defeat, Spaniards were met with "unimpeded ministerial despotism," which sapped the nation's strength and its material resources.[65] Songs published during the Trienio, such as "To the Illustrious Comuneros," fostered the legacy of the uprising as a fight for freedom and ancient liberties against the imposition of foreign tyranny. Using pejoratives coined by the *doceañistas*, popular anthems belittled Habsburg Spain as little more than a "servil toy."[66] By sanctifying the rebellion of the Comuneros as a defining moment of national history, liberal clerics justified the return to constitutional government and presented three hundred years of history as the story of the inevitable triumph of the people's will to rule the nation.

MEXICAN NATIONALISM DURING THE TRIENIO

The characteristics of liberal Spanish nationalism overlapped with an emerging sense of American identity. As discussed in chapter 5, Mexican nationalists emphasized continuity with the imperial Aztec past as well as the emotional attachment to Mexican Catholicism symbolized by the Virgin of Guadalupe. Three hundred years of despotism had hindered political and economic development, according to the logic of nationalists on both sides of the Atlantic. Liberals also pointed to the tenets of civil liberty and equality under the law as fundamental aspects of the newly consecrated nation. In addition to appealing to historic and local traditions, the rallying cry of "religion, independence, and union" provided a unifying language for the disparate classes and ethnicities of the country. A catechism published in Mexico City in 1821, dedicated to Agustín Iturbide, listed the four principal foundations of Mexican independence: "their liberty: the form of their government: the religion that they should profess: and the closest union of all individuals."[67]

Cultural artifacts from the period demonstrate the interplay between the language and symbolism of Spanish and Mexican identities. One song published in 1821 in Mexico City ended with a similar refrain of "religion, liberty, union or death." The lyrics upheld the sacred bond of church and state, promising that all would swear allegiance to the new Empire before God. Heralding Iturbide as a "new Columbus," Mexicans savored their victory over the descendants of the original conquistadors. Having vanquished the oppressive Spanish lion, troops embraced America, their beloved *patria*.[68] A play from the same year, *México libre* (Free Mexico), written by Francisco Luis Ortega, similarly rendered the bellicose Spaniard, the offspring of Columbus, Cortés, and Pizarro, as the enemy of freedom and liberty. Drawing on neoclassical themes, with Mars and Mercury playing major roles in the one-act melodrama, Ortega opposed the characters America and Liberty against Despotism, Discord, Fanaticism, and Ignorance. Akin to the 1808 drama *La sombra de Pelayo*, Ortega's work presented simplistic dichotomies between good and evil, innocence and victimization. And just as *La sombra de Pelayo* looked back to the founding of the Asturian dynasty as a historical precedent to be emulated within the context of a contemporary struggle, *México libre* traced the origins of the Mexican Empire to Anáhuac, reborn after three hundred years of slumber. The play ended with the chorus crying out: "Long live our union and liberty, eternally."[69]

These elements strikingly resembled discourses deployed in peninsular Spain, as nationalists asserted continuities between a historical Spanish legal tradition and that of the Constitution of 1812 and upheld the centrality of the church and religious imagery as the basis of national identity. Liberals consistently identified the ideology of natural law and the contractual theory of national sovereignty as the inherent basis of Spanish government, grounded in age-old tradition going back to the sixth century. Just as Mexican nationalists began to foreground the legacy of Anáhuac and the neo-Aztec roots of Mexicanness, peninsular ideologues increasingly looked to the past as a justification of the present. In Seville in 1820, for example, Castillo repeatedly extolled the virtues of the *patria* in his sermon celebrating the reinstatement of the Constitution: "Isn't our Country that which has made us realize our dignity, our rights, and the inexpressible valor of our civil liberties and independence? And who if not the Country . . . presents us with eternal rewards vis-à-vis our holy Religion? . . . Great virtues, union and vigilance are that which have sheltered and secured our constitutional charter."[70] Significantly, the idea of "union," which figured prominently in Mexican nationalist discourse from the time, also served as a mobilizing rhetoric in Spain as absolutist uprisings in the north threatened to tear the nation apart. Facing provinces demanding a share of national sovereignty in Mexico and provincial unrest in peninsular Spain, nationalists across the Hispanic Atlantic invoked the causes of "union," independence, and religion. These unifying elements, in addition to the tenets of civil liberty and natural law, infused peninsular and American rhetoric from the early 1820s.

NEGOTIATING EMPIRE, INDEPENDENCE, AND IDENTITY

On the first day of preparatory sessions for the reunited Cortes of 1820, debate began over the issue of representation and the meaning of the transatlantic nation. Simply naming a commission of eight members stirred controversy over whether or not to consider equal representation between deputies from overseas and peninsular representatives: "Sr. Ramos García proposed that all the elections take place on the basis of equality between the European Spaniards and the Overseas Spaniards, which is opposed by, among others, the Conde de Toreno, saying that because all are deputies of the same Nation, it was indispensable that any expression that could contribute to making a distinction between American and European Spaniards disappear."[71] Peninsular deputies such as the Conde de Toreno justified opposition to proportional representation by highlighting the very definition of the Spanish nation, firmly denying that geography should determine the composition of small committees or the Cortes as a whole. As early as April 1820, Americans published tracts critical of peninsular machinations: "It is a sad thing . . . that America sees their right of representation attacked, reduced to less than one-quarter of the total, by altering the number of deputies decreed by the Constitution for the Peninsula."[72] The problem of American representation, with proposals to address the issue put forward again in July and August, continued to divide the deputies. The Cuban representative, for example, implored his peers to allow all former American deputies then in Spain to be admitted into the Cortes and not to pass any binding resolutions concerning American affairs until a minimum of two-thirds of American deputies were present.[73] Ironically, American pressure for equal representation allowed peninsular deputies to question their loyalty as Spaniards and as members of the nation. With ongoing fighting in Spanish America and political battles in the Cortes, discursive representations of the transatlantic Spanish Monarchy in New Spain increasingly emphasized the natural division of kingdoms separated by vast expanses of ocean.

By 1821, debates over the status of the Americas took on an increased urgency. The Viceroy of New Spain, the Conde del Venadito, writing from overseas in March, declared that Iturbide had "raised the flags of a new revolution under specious pretexts, planning acts that are irreconcilable with the dignity, decorum and interests of the Nation and of the King." Iturbide himself, after having "worked with efficiency and great success in favor of the cause of the King and of the Nation," had become "perfidious and ungrateful, forgetting his duties and abusing in a most outrageous way the trust deposited in him."[74] Deputies discussed the crisis at length, and José Mariano Michelena, the representative from Michoacán, emphasized the need to "establish an indissoluble union" between the overseas territories and the peninsula. Furthermore, he understood that competing factions in New Spain had come together in their struggle against the royalist forces, which constituted the most significant change that had occurred since the initial uprising. Michelena implored: "It is necessary to understand the gravity of the current situation and the strength of this insurrection. In those propositions that Iturbide makes, the servil party is combined with a diminished liberal party, and even the liberals that have maintained strength are not attacked head-on: one concludes that this revolution has a great moral force."[75] Vicente Sancho, a representative from Valencia, put forward the most succinct question for the government to decide: "Is this about the independence of America? Yes, or no?" In response, Juan Estéban Milla, elected from Guatemala, argued that while these recent events could not be ignored, "the Americans at present do not think about independence from the Metropole: no, there is nothing to fear. America is convinced and agrees that it is an absolute necessity to be intimately united with the madre Patria: these are their desires. . . .They want the same rights as their peninsular brothers . . . and in sum, they want a just and rational dependence, and do not ever want to be a slave."[76] Many of the important American deputies at the Cortes as late as June 1821 ardently advocated maintaining ties to the peninsula and to the constitutional regime reinstated in 1820. Eusebio Sánchez Pareja, representing New Spain, insisted that the Cortes devote more time to devising a plan to deal with the governance of America, provided that it conform to the Constitution.[77] Yet their rhetoric displayed marked differences from the idealism espoused by deputies during the first phase of constitutional government in 1812. Rather than deploying symbols of a united monarchy, in which the Atlantic no longer figured as a representation of a fragmented empire, deputies consistently invoked the distance of "2,000 leagues of immense seas separating New Spain from the peninsula."[78]

Events quickly transpired that undermined the autonomist plans presented in Madrid. By the close of 1821, Iturbide had declared a Mexican Empire and Spanish representatives in Veracruz had recognized Mexican independence. During the first years of civil war in the Americas, Spanish nationalists lauded the Constitution of 1812, which had erased the boundaries of colony and metropole and had united Spaniards from both hemispheres as one nation under an enlightened monarchy. The notion that the Atlantic no longer existed in the imagination of Spanish nationalists contrasted greatly with the language of Mexican nationalists by the 1820s. The friar Juan de Dios María Piñera, preaching in Guadalajara in 1822 to honor Iturbide as the liberator of the Mexican nation, focused on the violence and upheaval of the initial Conquest. A kingdom separated by an immense ocean from the imperial throne, he believed, inevitably would reclaim its independence and break its shackles and chains. Piñera portrayed three hundred years of history as a biblical tale of enslavement, with the nation ultimately freed from captivity by the heroism and martyrdom of Hidalgo: "The centuries had never seen such a violent and repugnant union of Kingdoms: divided by an immense ocean, placed by nature at enormous distances, and at opposing margins, it is apparent that Nature herself had destined them, not only for mutual separation, but also to a perpetual neglect . . . [which] condemned their miserable inhabitants to an enduring slavery. . . . This produced precisely abjection and grievances . . . until the day of September 16, 1810, when the priest from the town of Dolores proclaimed the independence of both worlds."[79] Whereas previous clerics had spoken of the debts owed to the Spaniards, as they had introduced religion, rational government, and the legitimacy of the monarchy, discursive renderings of the Mexican nation condemned the vestiges of Spanish rule. Tellingly, Piñera also placed blame upon "the indigenous," who had been "victims of their docility and obedience in the space of three centuries." Only with the leadership of the Creole Hidalgo did a true national uprising begin. In the end, he argued, "the prudent, and religious plan, published in Iguala on February 24, 1821 . . . should be viewed as the safeguard of the political edifice of Anáhuac."[80] Yet the Plan of Iguala, proclaimed by Iturbide and Vicente Guerrero, accorded legal primacy to the Constitution of 1812 and legitimacy to the monarch Fernando VII, to whom Iturbide swore allegiance, and emphasized the common Spanish lineage of all Americans. Ironically, as Americans embraced pre-Conquest indigenous roots, they did not shirk a Hispanic heritage.[81] The Plan of Iguala outlined the establishment of an independent state, declared religious uniformity and called for the convocation of a Cortes. While nationalists upbraided peninsular Spaniards and the legacy of three centuries of colonialism, the political architecture of the Mexican nation relied heavily on the Hispanic precedent of the Constitution of 1812.

Even with independence declared in 1821, Americans presented a project to establish an autonomous branch of the Spanish Monarchy in Mexico. Deputies listed their grievances and spoke out against peninsular dominance, yet appealed to the Cortes as Spaniards, endowed with the same fundamental rights enjoyed by all national citizens. They noted the great distance between the continents and the costs incurred on the transatlantic passage for deputies leaving their homes and families.[82] Above all, they demonstrated their desire to make the Constitution function effectively, and in order for it to work, they pressed for autonomy within the monarchy. On June 25, Miguel Ramos de Arispe put forward a plan for three distinct parliaments in Spanish America, in Mexico, Santa Fé (New Granada), and Lima. A subsequent modified proposal for a single American Cortes represented the final American attempt to retain a unified transatlantic monarchy.[83] On August 23, the Treaty of Córdoba, signed by

Iturbide, recognized the Mexican Empire "as a sovereign and independent nation."[84] By the end of 1821, American deputies withdrew from the proceedings in Madrid, and only those from Cuba, Puerto Rico, and the Philippines remained from the overseas territories.[85]

Between the Plan of Iguala of 1821 and the signing of the Constitution of 1824, Mexican nationalism continued to display tensions between separatism and a Hispanic liberalism shaped by transatlantic currents in Cádiz. Ivana Frasquet argues that "the creation of the new Mexican nation-state followed upon the guidelines established by the liberal legislation of Cádiz."[86] In addition to the political elements of nation building, the culture of a shared Catholic tradition profoundly impacted emerging national identities. This study began by tracing the transition from a purely religious conception of the chosen people, the people of God, to the liberal nationalist discourse of *el pueblo español*, with its implicit validation of national sovereignty. Despite its radical connotations, the term took hold among all Spanish nationalists regardless of political affiliation. In Mexico, nationalists came to frame a particularist discourse of national identity that shifted from *el pueblo americano* to *el pueblo mexicano* during the course of the civil war. Just as in peninsular Spain, religion continued to inform identity. For example, Iturbide was glorified as "el caudillo del Pueblo de Dios" in 1822 in Guadalajara to celebrate Mexican independence from Spain.[87] Newly independent Mexico was sanctified as "the humble and religious Mexican nation," just as Spanish clerics continued to refer to the nation as *el pueblo religioso*.[88] The entangled identities of Mexico and Spain, built upon a shared history and culture, only diverged insomuch as nationalists argued that their primordial roots and essential traits drew upon distinct and separate cultural traditions.[89] Yet a common political and religious culture, as much a product of American syncretism as it was of peninsular Spanish institutions, served as the foundational blueprint upon which national identities were constructed in the Hispanic Atlantic world.

CONCLUSION

On the eve of a third French invasion in the span of thirty years, and with the majority of *americanos* having definitively separated from the monarchy, Spaniards celebrated the anniversary of the Constitution of 1812 on March 19, 1823. In cities such as Valencia, all of the churches commemorated the solemnity of the occasion with Te Deums and the ringing of bells. Chants and singing likely pierced the night, and the streets were illuminated in a festive atmosphere.[90] In the song "To the Re-establishment of the Constitution," published in Valencia in 1822, the chorus playfully announces: "We will sing festive songs, / As the happy day has come / With the servil yoke undone, / The Spaniard now enjoys freedom." Similar to many other songs from the period, the composition offered reverence to the people and to God: "Enjoy sovereign power, / O Nation protected by heaven."[91] This festival day, as a glimpse into the final moments of the Trienio, illustrates the vibrant culture of liberal nationalism that had endured despite political conflicts and upheaval across the peninsula.

Although religion and monarchism were still able to unify Spaniards during the 1820s, the diminished role of the monarch as set forth in the Constitution of 1812 had the effect of relegating the king's authority to that of the Cortes, while Article 12 retained the historic role of the Catholic faith in a confessional state. Thus religion and the role of clerics in the political process continued to play a vital role in nationalization while the monarchy was undermined by liberalism as a unifying signifier. Fernando VII's vacillation regarding constitutional government and the violent retribution against liberals in 1814 and again in 1823 hardened political divisions and tarnished the symbolic figure of the king. Yet liberals such as Argüelles wrote in 1835 that Article 12 was "a grave, fatal error, the source of great ills."[92] Catholicism and ideals of spiritual uniformity had a paradoxical effect on identity formation across the Hispanic Atlantic world, cutting across class and ethnic divisions while at the same time stoking ideological battles over jurisdiction and sovereignty.

As a process rife with contradiction and controversy, the construction of national identities across the Spanish Monarchy did not abruptly falter with the restoration of 1823. Peninsular liberals ascended to power in 1834 and consolidated a governing regime by the 1840s in Spain, and liberals played a central role in creating the federal state in Mexico in 1824. The Constitution of 1824 in Mexico resolved tensions between the states and the federal government by proclaiming joint sovereignty with limited executive power. By the time of the moderate ascendancy in Spain in the 1840s, popular sovereignty had been watered down with a constitution that endowed both the Cortes and the monarch with sovereignty over the nation.[93] But heirs to the *exaltado* tradition still looked to the Constitution of 1812 as the foundational document of Hispanic liberalism.

Civil wars, imperial conflicts, and church-state strife engulfed Spain and Mexico throughout the long nineteenth century. In the 1830s and

1840s, divisions between moderate and more radical factions threatened the liberals' grip on power in both nations. The push for democracy and reform of moderate liberalism reached a climax in the nineteenth century with the "glorious" revolution of 1868 in Spain. Reaction against Spain's first republic followed with sovereign power again granted to the king and to the Cortes under the 1876 Constitution. In Mexico, Porfirio Díaz similarly stabilized the state under a liberal authoritarianism after 1876. As liberals struggled to preserve constitutional regimes and the people's voice in government, nationalism developed in tandem with the martial values of romanticized militarism.

Spain's imperial ambitions did not fade, as politicians continued to grapple with an empire that held representation in the Cortes until 1837.[94] Between decolonizations (1825–98), writes Christopher Schmidt-Nowara, Spanish nationalists commemorated the history of their Atlantic empire in order to construct a cohesive vision of Spanish identity, one that incorporated its contemporary overseas territories into the nation. Nationalists imagined such a polity by drawing upon the precedent of the Constitution of 1812 and the ideal of a transatlantic nation of Spanish citizens.[95] Imperial Mexico under Iturbide, on the other hand, did not maintain its dominance over restive regions such as Guatemala, and the United Provinces of Central America broke off after a short-lived union in 1822. By 1862, the French Empire, under Napoleon III, had invaded Mexico, and, despite the famous May 5 battle in Puebla, occupied the nation for five years.

A culture of religious devotion certainly infused articulations of Hispanic identity, and the conflicts of the religiously inspired wars of the 1820s and 1830s in Spain were tempered by the papal concordat of 1851. Not until 1868 was Spain conceived of as a nonconfessional state. Carlists, as staunch Catholics and as Spanish subjects, contested the legitimacy of the Spanish monarch in the 1830s and again in the 1870s.[96] Similarly, while the Constitution of 1857 in Mexico significantly restricted ecclesiastical privileges, church-state conflict fueled the War of the Reform which began that year.[97]

In the course of the nineteenth century, the language of popular sovereignty was not monopolized by either the Right or the Left, as Old Regime language and liberal narratives overlapped within the Catholic public sphere. The majority of Spaniards were not simply partisans of absolutism, as earlier histories suggest, and liberals did not reflect the utopian sentiments of a minority faction.[98] A growing body of work demonstrates that popular local movements contested both liberal and conservative nationalist discourses in the context of agrarian radicalism and communal organizing throughout the nineteenth century.[99] Despite such a proliferation of nationalist visions amidst rising corruption and a turn toward authoritarianism, neither Spain nor Mexico can be conceived of as a "failed" state that was destined to follow a course of political and cultural polarization due to divisions first manifest during the Cortes of Cádiz. Gabriel Lovett, in *Napoleon and the Birth of Modern Spain,* concludes that, by 1813, revolutionaries had fractured the nation, and "irreconcilable views" had crystallized. For Lovett, this "signalled the beginning of a civil war which . . . culminated in the terrible conflict of 1936–1939."[100] The lack of nationalist consensus in the nineteenth century revealed ideological struggles, contestation, and conflict, but it did not inevitably lead to the civil wars and revolutions of the twentieth century. Above all, this study recasts the effects of Spanish liberal nationalism across the diverse landscape of a composite monarchy rather than obscuring the period by highlighting a caustic legacy of violence and opprobrium. Nationalists rhetorically situated "the people" at the heart of narratives of national resistance, but just as significantly, they diffused their political messages, through an orally based culture and the print media, to a cross-class, transatlantic audience. Through songs, poems, plays, periodicals, catechisms, sermons, and political pamphlets, nationalists truly reached "the people." And by recapturing the religious component of identification with the nation-state, this work sheds light on the significant convergences between competing ideologies and nationalist visions.

From a perspective encompassing the long nineteenth century in Europe and the Atlantic world, Spain and Mexico in many ways typify the persistence of an Old Regime subjectivity pitted against liberalism and reform.[101] In France and throughout Europe, restored monarchies reestablished pillars of aristocratic societies and defended traditional privileges. Debates over the meaning of national identity took place within the context of reaction and reinvigorated conservatism. In addition, contemporary scholars have demonstrated that religion did not fade away during the nineteenth century against the onslaught of a secular culture rooted in the Enlightenment.[102] But that does not tell the whole story. Reformist clerics reframed conceptions of national identity, and some even adopted the radical standard of revolutionary politics. Within the Spanish Monarchy, liberal nationalism served as the legacy of an inclusive Spanish identity and influenced the discourses and development of nationalist rhetoric throughout the course of the nineteenth century. Rather than revealing national experiences as unique and exceptional and nationalism as a product of modernity, this study of national identity within the transatlantic Spanish Monarchy demonstrates the importance of reconceptualizing "secular" national identities and insular investigations of nationalism and religious culture in the nineteenth-century world. National identities, unstable and fluid rather than an inevitable outcome predicated upon modernization, continue to be contested in the present day, and religion has not disappeared as a marker of purportedly unique national histories and heritage.

EPILOGUE

The bicentennial commemorations of the events of 1808–12 took on increased significance as contemporary governments continued to grapple with the legacy of this defining moment in Atlantic history. From historical reenactments to official ceremonies and speeches, public remembrance tended toward the grandiloquent. Eulogizing the martyrs of "independence" in both Spain and the Americas, these spectacles often provided more of a window into contemporary attitudes than a nuanced understanding of the past. For example, in Valencia on June 30, 2007, the 199th anniversary of the defense of the city against the French in 1808, a weekend-long reenactment included anachronistic Carlist flags and choreographed chants of "Viva España, viva Valencia, viva el Rey," patriotic slogans unlikely to have been the universal rallying cries of the first battles of the independence struggle.[1] Likewise, the president of the Community of Madrid, Esperanza Aguirre, speaking in 2008 at a bicentennial ceremony honoring the victims of el Dos de Mayo, alluded to a kind of timeless Spanish identity: "The men and women that fought and died [on May 2, 1808] knew very well that they were Spaniards and had no doubts as to what Spain was."[2] This notion is echoed in the 2008 film *Sangre de mayo* (The Blood of May). Produced at a cost of €15 million and funded by Aguirre's Community of Madrid as a cinematic monument to el Dos de Mayo, the film draws upon Benito Pérez Galdós's *Episodios nacionales* (The National Episodes), the first of which were written and published in the late 1860s and 1870s. Carolyn Boyd has argued that Galdós's "popularity can be explained by the values and assumptions he shared with his contemporaries [such as] his belief in a durable and unique 'national physiognomy' that persisted beneath the surface disturbances of national life." In one of the climactic scenes of the film, a Spanish rebel implores Gabriel Araceli, the young protagonist, to take up arms against the French. As Araceli hesitates to join the struggle, the man derisively recites the words penned by Galdós: "You aren't a Spaniard. . . . You don't have a weapon? Take a stone and break the head of the first Frenchman you find ahead of you."[3] Thus the producers of the film replicate the idea that Spanish values are simple, and Spanish courage, as a reflection of an eternal national character, is indefatigable.

In Mexico, official independence celebrations annually invoke the supposed cry of Miguel Hidalgo y Costilla on September 16, 1810, in the village of Dolores: "¡Viva la independencia!"[4] This, too, was unlikely to have been shouted by anyone involved in the initial uprisings against Spanish authorities.[5] Glossing over the fluid nature of transatlantic identities characteristic of an earlier age allows for a teleological reading of events, connecting an ahistorical vision of the past with the present. Royalists and autonomists, by default, do not merit discussion, despite their ideological affinities with Hidalgo and subsequent *independientes.* Such positions appear akin to treason within contemporary nationalist narratives. Even Bolívar's pan-Americanism might seem quaint and outdated. Moving beyond a state-sponsored nationalist agenda, writers such as the Mexican author Carlos Fuentes have recognized that, with the bicentennial of Mexican independence approaching, Americans and Europeans alike are left with "more questions than with answers" as they consider the lasting impact of the nineteenth-century revolutions across Latin America.[6]

In contrast to the self-assured rhetoric of today's elected officials, this work has uncovered the contingent spaces of sociopolitical mobilization that allowed nationalisms to develop at the onset of the modern age. Older loyalties, from regionalism and patriotism to a deep-seated sense of Catholic identity, overlapped with a burgeoning liberal nationalism across the diverse territories of the Spanish Monarchy. These were not mutually exclusive discourses and in many ways complemented historic allegiances. Spaniards propagated ideologies premised upon a harmonious blend of regional, national, and religious references and symbols.[7]

As the liberal language of national sovereignty became enshrined in nationalist demands and proclamations, arguments over whether this new political order was transitory and circumstantial or permanent and revolutionary began to take shape in the diverse spaces of the Catholic public sphere. What has been obscured is the central role played by clerics, as well as the impact of religious imagery, within such conversations. While it generally has been recognized that conservative priests rallied around a traditional narrative of Catholic dogmatism and monarchism, shouting, "Long live the Church" and "Long live Fernando VII," liberal religious presented the people and the nation as a collective, unitary body. By 1808, alongside Old Regime rhetoric, a radical new understanding of personal and political relationships had emerged. No longer a loosely bounded territory or place of birth, the nation had become synonymous with its inhabitants. And the people came to be eulogized as the embodiment of the sovereign nation and the higher power to which the government must answer. In 1820, ecclesiastics issued cries of "Long live Religion" accompanied by "Long live the King through the Constitution."[8] The original language of monarchism had been transposed into a mobilizing tool of liberalism. Yet religion proved to be the glue that held together this new discursive formulation, as many nationalists from both sides of the Hispanic Atlantic believed that they had reconciled tensions between Old Regime Catholic spirituality and the radical secularism of popular sovereignty that grew out of the Enlightenment. Nationalisms and regimes of citizenship grounded in religiosity appealed to those who sought to moderate revolutions that too often appeared to mimic Jacobinism. Although this first era of constitutionalism came to an end with another French invasion—the third in a span of thirty years—and Americans began to consolidate independent republics in the 1820s, a popular culture of liberal nationalism endured throughout the nineteenth century in both Spain and in Mexico, informing debates within the public sphere for decades to come.

As commemorations spark a renewed interest in the history of nineteenth-century Spain and Spanish America, it is important to recognize the self-consciousness of the participants in the process of politicization and nationalization. Many commented upon their place in history and situated themselves as protagonists within a new national narrative that they were beginning to construct. In an oath-taking ceremony for the Constitution of 1812, a prayer given by the editor of the *Gazeta de la Mancha* memorialized the elected deputies of the Cortes as the original architects of the nation: "Eternal thanks to the religious and wise representatives of the august congress [of Cádiz]: they will be the sweet memory that will become the emblem of our posterity: their honor, their names and their praises will be material for the eternal stories of the Spanish generation."[9] Although this first period of liberalism was fraught with instability, forged as it was in the midst of wars on both sides of the Atlantic, the ideological foundations and nationalist script embedded within it outlasted the vicissitudes of its various champions throughout the course of the nineteenth century. Conversely, the issue of state-sponsored religion became increasingly problematic in an age of democracy and pluralism. An inclusive liberalism mixed with an exclusive religious requirement for citizenship marked the competing legacies of those who preached nationalisms across the transatlantic Spanish Monarchy.

NOTES

INTRODUCTION

1. Rafael de Vélez, *Preservativo contra la irreligión, o los planes de la Filosofía contra la Religión y el Estado, realizados por la Francia para subyugar la Europa, seguidos por Napoleón en la conquista de España, y dados a luz por algunos de nuestos sabios en perjuicio de nuestra patria* (1813), in *Colección Documental del Fraile* (C.D.F.), Servicio Histórico Militar, vol. 172, signatura 701, 1–8.

2. See Jean-René Aymes, *La Guerra de la Independencia en España (1808–1814)*, trans. Pierre Conard (Madrid, 1975), 24; Juan Pablo Fusi, *España: La evolución de la identidad nacional* (Madrid, 2000), 154–55; Brian Connaughton, *Ideología y sociedad en Guadalajara (1788–1853)* (Mexico City, 1992); Anthony W. Marx, *Faith in Nation: Exclusionary Origins of Nationalism* (Oxford, 2003), 184–86; Michael Burleigh, *Earthly Powers: The Clash of Religion and Politics in Europe, from the French Revolution to the Great War* (New York, 2005), 112; Charles Esdaile, *The Peninsular War: A New History* (New York, 2003), 508. José Antonio Portero's *Púlpito e ideología* exemplifies the historical discourse that posits a deeply conservative Spanish church that sought to maintain its power as it battled the incipient liberalism of the nineteenth century. According to Portero, "sermons transmit an ideology that expresses a total homogeneity that does not allow for fissures or heterodoxy" (Portero, *Púlpito e ideología en la España del siglo XIX* [Zaragoza, 1978], 12).

3. Vélez, *Preservativo contra la irreligión*, 12.

4. Adrian Shubert has drawn attention to the weakness of "secular nationalism [that] stands in stark contrast to the energy and enthusiasm with which the symbolic representation of Spain's religious identity was promoted." He maintains that "a secular national identity did not displace a religious one before the Civil War" (Shubert, *A Social History of Modern Spain* [London, 1990], 204–5).

5. Domenique de Pradt, *Europe and America, in 1821*, trans. J. D. Williams (London, 1822).

6. Álvaro Flórez Estrada, *Introducción para la historia de la Revolución de España* (London, 1810), 7.

7. Vicente Bernaldo de Quirós, *Sermón que en la función solemne celebrada por el ilustrísimo cabildo eclesiástico y el M.I. ayuntamiento constitucional, de la M.N.Y.L. ciudad de Motril, el día 23 de julio de 1820* (Granada, 1820).

8. Roberto Breña, *El primer liberalismo español y los procesos de emancipación de América, 1808–1824: Una revisión historiográfica del liberalismo hispánico* (Mexico City, 2006), 66, 72.

9. Josep M. Fradera, *Colonias para después de un imperio* (Barcelona, 2005), 62–64.

10. Jeremy Adelman, *Sovereignty and Revolution in the Iberian Atlantic* (Princeton, 2006), 344–45.

11. Deputies saw parallels between the "project to abolish forced labor in the New World . . . [and] the wishes of some Europeans to end seigniorial obligations in the Peninsula" (Jaime E. Rodríguez O., *The Independence of Spanish America* [Cambridge, U.K., 1998], 91).

12. Miguel Laborda y Galindo, *Oración que en el día 12 de marzo y templo metropolitano de Ntra. Sra. Del Pilar con motivo de haberse decidido el Rey Nuestro Señor a jurar la Constitución Política de la monarquía española,* in C.D.F., vol. 758, sig. 2709, 13.

13. Anthony Giddens, *The Consequences of Modernity* (Stanford, 1990).

14. François-Xavier Guerra, *Modernidad e independencias: Ensayos sobre las revoluciones hispánicas* (Mexico City, 1992).

15. Eric Van Young, *The Other Rebellion: Popular Violence, Ideology, and the Mexican Struggle for Independence 1810–1821* (Stanford, 2001), 62, 199. For works emphasizing peasant politicization in the case of the Spanish Monarchy, see Peter F. Guardino, *Peasants, Politics, and the Formation of Mexico's National State: Guerrero, 1806–1857* (Stanford, 1996); Peter F. Guardino, *The Time of Liberty: Popular Political Culture in Oaxaca, 1750–1850* (Durham, N.C., 2005); and Terry Rugeley, *Yucatán's Maya Peasantry and the Origins of the Caste War* (Austin, 1996).

16. Guerra, *Modernidad e independencias.*

17. Irene Castells and Antonio Moliner, *Crisis del antiguo régimen y revolución liberal en España (1789–1845)* (Barcelona, 2000), 10–11.

18. Scholars working on questions of nationalism and national identity often argue that a division exists between religious and national identification. Grounded implicitly or explicitly in modernization theory, such arguments posit an evolution from traditional religious belief to the modern identification with the nation-state. For example, from a perspective privileging the secularizing Enlightenment, Benedict Anderson remarks that "in Western Europe the eighteenth century marks not only the dawn of the age of nationalism but the dusk of religious modes of thought." Ernest Gellner similarly focuses on a transition from a "culture-religion" to a "culture-state," and maintains that "in the industrial world high cultures prevail, but they need a state not a church, and they need a state *each.*" Eugen Weber concludes his chapter on religious practice in late-nineteenth-century France with the claim that "phosphates, chemical fertilizers, and schooling had spelled the beginning of the end. . . . It was the requiem of nineteenth-century religion." George Mosse contends that nationalism in Germany was a "secular religion." This line of argument has its roots not only in modernization theory, however, but also in the writings of the most prominent nineteenth-century historians. Jules Michelet implored in 1831: "My noble country, you must take the place of the God who escapes us, that you may fill within us the immeasurable abyss which extinct Christianity has left there" (see Benedict Anderson, *Imagined Communities: Reflections on the Origin and Spread of Nationalism* [London, 1991], 11; Ernest Gellner, *Nations and Nationalism* [Ithaca, N.Y., 1983], 72–73; Eugen Weber, *Peasants into Frenchmen: The Modernization of Rural France, 1870–1914* [Stanford,

1976], 355–56; George L. Mosse, *The Nationalization of the Masses: Political Symbolism and Mass Movements in Germany from the Napoleonic Wars through the Third Reich* [New York, 1975]; and Michelet, cited in David A. Bell, *The Cult of the Nation in France: Inventing Nationalism, 1680–1800* [Cambridge, Mass., 2001], 23).

19. Xosé M. Núñez Seixas criticizes "modernisation theory [that] seems . . . to be used as a 'catch-all' concept which serves to explain an unknown process that lacks empirical research behind it" (see Núñez Seixas, *Historiographical Approaches to Nationalism in Spain* [Saarbrücken, 1993], 145).

20. Liah Greenfeld, *Nationalism: Five Roads to Modernity* (Cambridge, Mass., 1992), 18.

21. For Marxist-influenced works that highlight the economic failures of the bourgeoisie in Spain, see John F. Coverdale, *The Basque Phase of Spain's First Carlist War* (Princeton, 1984), 45–46; Alberto Gil Novales, *El Trienio Liberal* (Madrid, 1980); Carlos Marichal, *Spain (1834–1844): A New Society* (London, 1977), 4–5; Jordi Nadal, "A Century of Industrialization in Spain, 1833–1930," in *The Economic Modernization of Spain, 1830–1930*, ed. Nicolás Sánchez-Albornoz; trans. Karen Powers and Manuel Sañudo (New York, 1987), 63; Josep Fontana, *La quiebra de la monarquía absoluta 1814–1820* (Barcelona, 1971); and Antonio Elorza, *La ideología liberal en la Ilustración española* (Madrid, 1970). On the Spanish American "bourgeoisie," see Miguel Artola, *La burguesía revolucionaria* (Madrid, 1973), 38.

22. Marx, *Faith in Nation*, 184.

23. Cited in Isabel Burdiel, "Myths of Failure, Myths of Success: New Perspectives on Nineteenth-Century Spanish Liberalism," *Journal of Modern History* 70 (December 1998): 893. According to the dominant narrative, during the long nineteenth century, the largely rural population of Spain stagnated, as 65 percent of the workforce was employed in agriculture at the end of the eighteenth century as well as at the beginning of the twentieth. Structural conditions prevented nascent industrialists in Catalonia as well as mining and shipping interests in Asturias and Biscay from establishing bourgeois hegemony over the state and initiating full-scale industrialization in Spain. Spain's rural economy and traditional social and political structures impeded economic development and allowed for only incremental growth. On the nineteenth-century Spanish economy, see Vicente Pérez Moreda, "Spain's Demographic Modernization, 1800–1930," in *The Economic Modernization of Spain, 1830–1930*, 34.

24. Gellner, *Nations and Nationalism*, 78.

25. E. J. Hobsbawm, *Nations and Nationalism since 1780: Programme, Myth, Reality, 2nd* ed. (Cambridge, U.K., 1992), 16.

26. Borja de Riquer i Permanyer, "Sobre el lugar de los nacionalismos-regionalismos en la historia contemporánea española," *Historia Social* 7 (Spring–Summer, 1990): 120. Juan Pablo Fusi views Spain in 1900 as a consolidated nation and downplays the plurality of identities within its borders (see Fusi, "Revisionismo crítico e historia nacionalista [A propósito de un artículo de Borja de Riquer]," *Historia Social* 7 [Spring–Summer 1990]: 127–34).

27. Borja de Riquer i Permanyer, "La débil nacionalización española del siglo XIX," *Historia Social* 20 (Fall 1994): 113.

28. Raymond Carr points to the centralizing efforts of the liberals of Cádiz as "the root of the regionalist and nationalist movements of Catalonia and the Basque Provinces" (see Carr, *Spain 1808–1939* [Oxford, 1966], 99; and Gabriel H. Lovett, *Napoleon and the Birth*

of Modern Spain [New York, 1965], 1:847–48). Lucas Alamán denied that Hidalgo's revolt constituted a "heroic effort of a people who struggle for their liberty." For the Mexican poet López Velarde, the Revolution of 1910 "summed up and crystalized our modern meaning and spirit of nationality" (cited in Enrique Florescano, *National Narratives in Mexico: A History* [Norman, Okla., 2006], 311, 318).

29. Cited in Florescano, *National Narratives in Mexico,* 310.

30. For works on Basque and Catalan nationalism that put primacy on the effects of modernization, see Stanley G. Payne, *Basque Nationalism* (Reno, 1975); Marianne Heiberg, "Basques, Anti-Basques, and the Moral Community," in *Becoming National,* ed. Geoff Eley and Ronald Grigor Suny (New York, 1996), 330; John Sullivan, *ETA and Basque Nationalism: The Fight for Euskadi 1890–1986* (London, 1988); Daniele Conversi, *The Basques, the Catalans and Spain: Alternative Routes to Nationalist Mobilization* (Reno, 1997), 48; and Charles Esdaile, *Spain in the Liberal Age: From Constitution to Civil War, 1808–1939* (Oxford, 2000), 170.

31. For works challenging the paradigm of bourgeois revolution in Spain, see Richard Herr, *Rural Change and Royal Finances in Spain at the End of the Old Regime* (Berkeley and Los Angeles, 1989); Guerra, *Modernidad e independencias,* 13; Jesus Cruz, "Notability and Revolution: Social Origins of the Political Elite in Liberal Spain, 1800 to 1853," *Comparative Studies in Society and History* 36 (January 1994): 99; Jesus Cruz, *Gentlemen, Bourgeois, and Revolutionaries: Political Change and Cultural Persistence among the Spanish Dominant Groups 1750–1850* (New York, 1996); and Burdiel, "Myths of Failure, Myths of Success," 895, 911.

32. For reinterpretations of Spanish "failure," see, for example, David Ringrose, *Spain, Europe and the "Spanish Miracle" 1700–1900* (New York, 1996), 14–23; and Ferran Archilés and Manuel Martí, "Ethnicity, Region and Nation: Valencian Identity and the Spanish Nation-State," *Ethnic and Racial Studies* 24, no. 5 (2002): 783–84.

33. Prasenjit Duara, "Historicizing National Identity, or Who Imagines What and When," in *Becoming National,* ed. Eley and Suny, 151–77. For an argument drawing upon Duara, see Sandie Holguín, *Creating Spaniards: Culture and National Identity in Republican Spain* (Madison, 2002).

34. Dipesh Chakrabarty, *Provincializing Europe: Postcolonial Thought and Historical Difference* (Princeton, 2000), 12–13.

35. Ibid., 16.

36. See, for example, Linda Colley, *Britons: Forging the Nation 1707–1837* (New Haven, 1992); and Kathleen Wilson, *The Island Race: Englishness, Empire and Gender in the Eighteenth Century* (London, 2003), 84.

37. Kavita Philip, *Civilizing Natures: Race, Resources and Modernity in Colonial South India* (New Brunswick, N.J., 2004), 106. For critiques of Chakrabarty's thesis in relation to the case of India, see C. A. Bayly, *Origins of Nationality in South Asia: Patriotism and Ethical Government in the Making of Modern India* (Delhi, 1998), 83; and Sugata Bose, "Nation as Mother," in *Nationalism, Democracy and Development,* ed. Bose and Ayesha Jalal (Delhi, 1998), 59, 70.

38. On religious practices as "shared tradition," see Sonya Lipsett-Rivera, "Language of Body and Body as Language: Religious Thought and Cultural Syncretism," in *Religion in New Spain,* ed. Susan Schroeder and Stafford Poole (Albuquerque, 2007), 67.

39. Guerra, *Modernidad e independencias,* 20. Gabriel B. Paquette sees "the study of Spanish America as an integral, not parallel, part of Iberian History" (Paquette, *Enlightenment, Governance, and Reform in Spain and its Empire, 1759–1808* [New York, 2008], 153).

40. J. H. Elliott writes that "in this age of globalization we are all uneasily aware that national history is no longer enough" (see Elliott, "Atlantic History: A Circumnavigation," in *The British Atlantic World, 1500–1800,* ed. David Armitage and Michael J. Braddick [New York, 2002], 235).

41. Tamar Herzog, "Early Modern Spanish Citizenship: Inclusion and Exclusion in the Old and the New World," in *New World Orders: Violence, Sanction, and Authority in the Colonial Americas,* ed. John Smolenski and Thomas J. Humphrey (Philadelphia, 2005), 206.

42. E. Inman Fox focuses on "una identidad nacional que nacen en España con el Estado liberal hacia mediados del siglo XIX" (see Fox, *La invención de España* [Madrid, 1998], 11). José Álvarez Junco, on the other hand, has explored the cultural and political roots of *españolismo* during the entire span of the nineteenth century, giving the first decades a significance overlooked by other authors (see Álvarez Junco, *Mater dolorosa: La idea de España en el siglo XIX* [Madrid, 2001]).

43. Juan Rico, *Memorias históricas sobre la revolución de Valencia, que comprehenden desde el 23 de mayo de 1808 hasta fines del mismo año, y sobre la causa criminal formada contra el P. F. Juan Rico, el Brigadier D. Vicente González Moreno, el Comisario de Guerra D. Narciso Rubio, y otros* (Cádiz, 1811), iii.

44. Guardino, *Peasants, Politics, and the Formation of Mexico's National State,* 56. Emilio La Parra López argues that "the sermon constituted the only channel of news and of information for the people [and] there is no doubt the popular masses depended entirely, in this sense, on the clergy." He adds that "the mentality of the Spaniards was determined by the teaching imparted by ecclesiastics, which was decisive at all levels of education." Another scholar writes: "The pulpit is, with any doubt, the means of diffusing ideas that reached the largest number of people at the beginning of the nineteenth century in Spain" (see La Parra López, *El primer liberalismo español y la iglesia: Las Cortes de Cádiz* [Alicante, 1985], 8; and Mariano Álvarez García, *El clero de la Diócesis de Valladolid durante la Guerra de la Independencia* [Valladolid, 1981], 187).

45. Van Young, *The Other Rebellion,* 240.

46. William J. Callahan, *Church, Politics, and Society in Spain, 1750–1874* (Cambridge, Mass., 1984), 89, 87.

47. John Lawrence Tone, *The Fatal Knot: The Guerrilla War in Navarre and the Defeat of Napoleon in Spain* (Chapel Hill, 1994), 149.

48. Álvarez Junco, *Mater dolorosa,* 134.

49. See, for example, W. F. P. Napier, *History of the War in the Peninsula and in the South of France, from the Year 1807 to the Year 1814* (London, 1832), x.

50. *Diario de las Sesiones de las Cortes Generales y Extraordinarias* (D.S.C.G.E.), December 21, 1810.

51. James Wilmot Ormsby, *An Account of the Operations of the British Army, and of the State and Sentiments of the People of Portugal and Spain, during the Campaigns of the Years 1808 & 1809* (London, 1809), 2:3.

52. Ibid., 46.

53. José Blanco White, *Cartas de España* (Madrid, 1972), 41.

54. Pablo Arribas, cited in Manuel Moreno Alonso, *Los españoles durante la ocupación napoleónica: La vida cotidiana en la vorágine* (Málaga, 1997), 200.

55. Modesto Medrano, cited in Moreno Alonso, *Los españoles durante la ocupación napoleónica,* 200.

56. Gabriel H. Lovett, in describing "the Spanish character," highlights the importance of religious faith (Lovett, *Napoleon and the Birth of Modern Spain,* 1:82–84).

57. Moreno Alonso, *Los españoles durante la ocupación napoleónica,* 190.

58. Javier Herrero, *Los orígenes del pensamiento reaccionario español* (Madrid, 1971), 375.

59. José Antonio Maravall, "Sobre orígenes y sentido del catolicismo liberal en España," in *Homenaje a Aranguren* (Madrid, 1972), 230.

60. José Álvarez Junco, "The Nation-Building Process in Nineteenth-Century Spain," in *Nationalism and the Nation in the Iberian Peninsula: Competing and Conflicting Identities,* ed. Clare Mar-Molinero and Angel Smith (Oxford, 1996), 90. Eric Hobsbawm notes that "religion is a paradoxical cement for proto-nationalism, and indeed for modern nationalism," although he finds links between religious and national consciousness (Hobsbawm, *Nations and Nationalism since 1780,* 68).

61. See José María Portillo Valdés, *Revolución de nación: Orígenes de la cultura constitucional en España, 1780–1812* (Madrid, 2000), 21; and Theresa Ann Smith, *The Emerging Female Citizen: Gender and Enlightenment in Spain* (Berkeley and Los Angeles, 2006), 5.

62. D. A. Brading, *The Origins of Mexican Nationalism* (Cambridge, U.K., 1985), 3.

63. On the clergy in Valencia, see, for example, Luis Barbastro Gil, *Revolución liberal y reacción (1808–1833): Protagonismo ideológico del clero en la sociedad valenciana* (Alicante, 1987). On the idea of a sovereign people, see Edmund S. Morgan, *Inventing the People: The Rise of Popular Sovereignty in England and America* (New York, 1988).

64. Lloyd Kramer, "Habermas, History, and Critical Theory," in *Habermas and the Public Sphere,* ed. Craig Calhoun (Cambridge, Mass., 1992), 243.

65. Brian R. Hamnett, "Puebla: City and Province during the Independence Period, 1800–1824," in *La ciudad y el campo en la historia de México,* ed. Ricardo Sánchez, Eric Van Young, and Gisela Von Wobeser (Mexico City, 1992), 166.

66. Gyan Prakash writes: "nationalism . . . attributed agency and history to the subjected nation" (Prakash, "Subaltern Studies as Postcolonial Criticism," *American Historical Review* 99, no. 5 [December 1994]: 1475).

67. Juan Antonio Posse, *Discurso sobre la Constitución,* in *Memorias del cura liberal don Juan Antonio Posse con su Discurso sobre la Constitución de 1812,* ed. Richard Herr (Madrid, 1984), 262.

68. Guerra, *Modernidad e independencias,* 18. Guerra points to 1810 as the key date of rupture.

69. Van Young, *The Other Rebellion,* 240.

CHAPTER ONE

1. Francisco de S. Cyrilo, *El más noble desempeño de la promesa más generosa: Sermón panegyrico de Nuestra Señora de Guadalupe* (1779), in Colección LaFragua, la Benemérita Universidad Autónoma de Puebla (B.U.A.P.), 17.

2. José Cadalso, *Cartas Marruecas*, ed. S. Solé Camps and J. Palomar Ros (Madrid, 1986), 111.

3. Richard Herr, *The Eighteenth-Century Revolution in Spain* (Princeton, 1958), 444.

4. *Exhortación que ha hecho el Señor Conde de Zanoni Intendente interino* (June 2, 1794), in Biblioteca Valenciana (B.V.). Given during the war, this was a call for "una contribución voluntaria para formar fondo, y ocurrir con él al armamento, y demás auxilios que necesite el Cuerpo que se está erigiendo de Voluntarios honrados para la defensa de nuestras Costas, y socorro de nuestros Vecinos, si se viesen atacados con ventaja por la bárbara Nación Francesa."

5. The language of nationalism has been treated in works such as María Cruz Seoane, *El primer lenguaje constitucional español (Las Cortes de Cádiz)* (Madrid, 1968); Pierre Vilar, *Hidalgos, amotinados y guerrilleros: Pueblo y poderes en la historia de España* (Barcelona, 1982), 211–52; and Juan Francisco Fuentes, "Concepto de *pueblo* en el primer liberalismo español," *Trienio, Ilustración y Liberalismo* 12 (November 1988): 176–209. Yet none of these works examines the interplay between religion and discourses of national identity.

6. Bernardo Clemente de Sala, *La mayor felicidad de España* (Cádiz, 1778), in B.U.A.P., 13.

7. *Un hermitaño de Monserrat al futuro regente o presidente de la Suprema y Soberana Junta Central de España e Indias* (Madrid, 1808), in C.D.F., vol. 24, sig. 96, 6.

8. William Callahan maintains that authority had its limits in the early nineteenth century, and that Spanish missionaries "exercised a freedom of expression not found elsewhere in the Church" (see Callahan, *Church, Politics, and Society in Spain*, 65).

9. Ibid., 8–21.

10. William B. Taylor, *Magistrates of the Sacred: Priests and Parishioners in Eighteenth-Century Mexico* (Stanford, 1996), 78, 561.

11. Cited in Antonio Elorza, "Cristianismo ilustrado y reforma política en Fray Miguel de Santander," in *Cuadernos hispanoamericanos* 214 (October 1967): 84.

12. Elorza, "Cristianismo ilustrado y reforma política en Fray Miguel de Santander."

13. Joseph Townsend, *A Journey through Spain in the Years 1786 and 1787* (London, 1792), 147–48.

14. Bell, *The Cult of the Nation in France*, 20.

15. Bayly, *Origins of Nationality in South Asia*, vii, 1–2.

16. Brading, *The Origins of Mexican Nationalism;* Jorge Cañizares-Esguerra, *How to Write the History of the New World: Histories, Epistemologies, and Identities in the Eighteenth-Century Atlantic World* (Stanford, 2001). According to William Taylor, "very few [parish priests] were sons of the peasants and wage laborers who made up the large majority of the population. . . . [P]arish priests tended to be creoles—few Indians were ordained . . . and few American-born priests identified themselves as mestizos or other castas" (see Taylor, *Magistrates of the Sacred*, 97).

17. Cañizares-Esguerra, *How to Write the History of the New World*, 209.

18. Cañizares-Esguerra and Brading do not emphasize the links between Spanish American patriotic discourse and peninsular Spanish patriotism. Enlightenment philosophes derisively referred to both the New World and Spain and did not distinguish between effete Creoles and "oriental" Spaniards (see D. A. Brading, *The First America: The Spanish Monarchy, Creole Patriots and the Liberal State* [Cambridge, U.K., 1991], 445). Spaniards such as Juan Pablo Forner, who defended Spain by extolling its cultural merits,

appear only in the footnotes of Cañizares-Esguerra (see Cañizares-Esguerra, *How to Write the History of the New World,* 371–72).

19. Anderson, *Imagined Communities,* 47–65.

20. The first printing presses in Chile, for example, were set up in 1811 (David Bushnell, "The Independence of Spanish South America," in *The Independence of Latin America,* ed. Leslie Bethell (Cambridge, U.K., 1987), 127. Hidalgo's early efforts to recruit were hampered by the lack of a printing press (see Hugh Hamill Jr., *The Hidalgo Revolt: Prelude to Mexican Independence* [Gainesville, Fla., 1966], 127).

21. François-Xavier Guerra argues that "sermons, in all their forms, constituted an essential vehicle for the construction and diffusion of values and identities" (Guerra, "Forms of Communication, Political Spaces, and Cultural Identities in the Creation of Spanish American Nations," in *Beyond Imagined Communities: Reading and Writing the Nation in Nineteenth-Century Latin America,* ed. Sara Castro-Klarén and John Charles Chasteen (Washington, D.C., 2003), 8.

22. Carlos Herrejón Peredo, *Del sermón al discurso cívico: México, 1760–1834* (Zamora, Michoacán, 2003), 253.

23. Cited in Françoise Etienvre, *Centinela contra franceses: Edición, con introducción, notas y apéndices documentales por Françoise Etienvre* (London, 1988), 45.

24. Greenfeld argues that nationalism, as distinct from patriotism, "derives from membership in a 'people,' the fundamental characteristic of which is that it is defined as a 'nation'" (see Greenfeld, *Nationalism,* 7).

25. Emmanuel Joseph Sieyès, "What Is the Third Estate?" in *The Old Regime and the French Revolution,* ed. Keith Michael Baker (Chicago, 1987), 167.

26. Juan Pablo Forner, *Amor de la Patria: Discurso que en la Junta General pública que celebró La Real Sociedad Económica de Sevilla el día 23 de Noviembre de 1794 leyó D. Juan Pablo Forner, Fiscal del Crimen de la Real Audiencia y Director de la Sociedad,* in C.D.F., vol. 641, sig. 2364, 27.

27. Fusi, *España,* 125. Similarly, Maravall argues that "en España, la ideología 'nacional' presenta caracteres muy claros en los hombres de la Ilustración, y entre ellos, corresponde a Juan Pablo Forner un papel destacado" (José Antonio Maravall, "El sentimiento de nación en el siglo XVIII: La obra de Forner," *La Torre* [Puerto Rico], 15, no. 57 [1967]: 27).

28. Cadalso, *Cartas Marruecas,* 72, 77, 183. Juan Pablo Forner similarly argued that "el hombre es naturalmente un animal religioso" (see Forner, *Preservativo contra el Atheísmo* [Seville, 1795], in C.D.F., vol. 641, sig. 2365, 29).

29. Forner, *Amor de la Patria,* 12, 25–26.

30. Miguel de Santander, *Sermon IV: De San Roque, predicado en el convento de capuchinos de la ciudad de Toro el año de 1775,* in *Sermones panegíricos de varios misterios, festividades y santos* (Madrid, 1814), 2:54, 63.

31. Antonio Tavira, *Sermón que en la solemnidad de acción de gracias, que celebró la Villa de Madrid el día 13 de junio de 1784 en la iglesia de Santa María de la Almudena por el feliz nacimiento de los dos reales infantes Carlos y Felipe, y por la paz, dixo el Dr. D. Antonio Tavira, del orden de Santiago, Capellán de Honor y Predicador de S.M.,* in Joël Saugnieux, ed., *La Ilustración católica en España: Escritos de Antonio Tavira (1737–1807)* (Salamanca, 1986), 63, 68.

32. Juan de Sarria y Alderete, *Oración fúnebre que en las solemnes honras que se celebran todos los años en la santa Iglesia metropolitana de México a la gloriosa memoria de los difuntos militares que han seguido las triunfantes banderas españolas* (1791), in C.D.F., vol. 604, sig. 2193, 16–17.

33. Herr argues that enlightened reformers chose a path of laissez-fare liberalism and market forces rather than state intervention to rationalize agricultural production. In addition, the Jesuits, expelled in the aftermath of the Esquilache Riots in 1767, found their properties confiscated and sold, a precursor to the disentailment begun in 1798 (see Herr, *Rural Change and Royal Finances*).

34. Herr, *The Eighteenth-Century Revolution in Spain*, 84–85.

35. The enlightened friar Benito Feijóo similarly conceptualized the organic functioning of the state (see Mariana Terán Fuentes, "De nación española a federación mexicana: La opinión pública en la formación de la nación," in *Las nuevas naciones: España y México, 1808–1850*, ed. Jaime E. Rodríguez O. [Madrid, 2008], 127).

36. Joaquín Lorenzo Villanueva, *Catecismo del estado según los principios de la religión* (Madrid, 1793), 15.

37. Fr. Francisco Nuñez, *Oración que en las solemnes exequias que celebró por su ínclito Monarca Luis XV el mui amado, la Nación Francesa de esta ciudad de Sevilla, dixo el M. R. P. Fr. Francisco Nuñez*, in C.D.F., vol. 210, sig. 786, 3.

38. Miguel de Santander, *Sermón IV: Divinidad de la religión católica*, in *Sermones dogmáticos* (Madrid, 1805), 1:102.

39. Pamela Voekel, *Alone before God: The Religious Origins of Modernity in Mexico* (Durham, N.C., 2002).

40. Herr, *The Eighteenth-Century Revolution in Spain*, 440–41.

41. Charles C. Noel, "Clerics and Crown in Bourbon Spain, 1700–1808," in *Religion and Politics in Enlightenment Europe*, ed. James E. Bradley and Dale K. Van Kley (Notre Dame, Ind., 2001), 127. On French Jansenism, see Dale Van Kley, *The Religious Origins of the French Revolution: From Calvin to the Civil Constitution, 1560–1791* (New Haven, 1996).

42. Herr, *The Eighteenth-Century Revolution in Spain*, 17.

43. Voekel, *Alone before God;* Herrejón Peredo, *Del sermón al discurso cívico*, 243–45.

44. Voekel, *Alone before God*, 51.

45. José Ruiz de Conejares, *Sermón que en la solemne función con que se dio principio a la Real Congregación del Alumbrado y Vela Continua del Santísimo Sacramento del Altar* (México, 1793), cited in Herrejón Peredo, *Del sermón al discurso cívico*, 244–45.

46. David Zaret, "Religion, Science, and Printing in the Public Spheres in Seventeenth-Century England," in *Habermas and the Public Sphere*, ed. Calhoun, 221.

47. Anderson, *Imagined Communities*, 40.

48. *Cartas eclesiásticas de D. Joaquín Lorenzo Villanueva al Doctor D. Guillermo Díaz Luzeredi en defensa de las leyes que autorizan ahora al pueblo para que lea en su lengua la sagrada escritura* (1794), in C.D.F., vol. 153, sig. 659, v. See also Callahan, *Church, Politics, and Society in Spain*, 71.

49. Zaret, "Religion, Science, and Printing in the Public Spheres," 222.

50. Jaime E. Rodríguez O., "The Origins of Constitutionalism and Liberalism in Mexico," in *The Divine Charter: Constitutionalism and Liberalism in Nineteenth-Century Mexico*, ed. Rodríguez O. (Lanham, Md., 2005), 3–7.

51. Herr, *The Eighteenth-Century Revolution in Spain,* 176–79.

52. *Real decreto* (January 19, 1770), cited in Herr, *The Eighteenth-Century Revolution in Spain,* 176.

53. Tavira, *Sermón que en la solemnidad de acción de gracias,* 68.

54. Manuel Gil, *Oración fúnebre del Señor D. Carlos III* (Madrid, 1789), in C.D.F., vol. 648, sig. 2423, 27–28.

55. Ibid., 51–52.

56. Ibid., 57.

57. John Lynch, *Bourbon Spain 1700–1808* (Oxford, 1989), 379.

58. Miguel de Santander, *Tres exordios de otras tantas pláticas hechas en los tres días de rogativas públicas, que en cumplimiento de real orden de S.M. (que Dios guarde) hizo la ciudad de Toro en 24, 25, y 26 de agosto de 1794,* in *Sermones panegíricos,* 2:368.

59. Diego José de Cádiz, *El soldado-católico, en guerra de religión* (Córdoba, 1815), vol. 1, in C.D.F., vol. 502, sig. 1593, 7.

60. Cited in Manuel Ardit Lucas, *Revolución liberal y revuelta campesina: Un ensayo sobre la desintegración del régimen feudal en el País Valenciano (1793–1840)* (Barcelona, 1977), 89; Simón López, *Despertador cristiano-político* (1809), in C.D.F., vol. 43, sig. 257, 23.

61. Teodomiro Ignacio Díaz de la Vega, *Relación de las suntuosas exequias celebradas en Sevilla el día 8 de Junio de 1793 a expensas de varios españoles en la Iglesia de la Universidad Literaria por el alma de Luis XVI Rey Christianísimo de Francia, con la oración fúnebre que dixo El P. D. Teodomiro Ignacio Díaz de la Vega* (Seville), in C.D.F., vol. 648, sig. 2426, 10.

62. Vilar, *Hidalgos, amotinados y guerrilleros,* 178–79.

63. Juan Carlos de Coucy, *Carta pastoral del Ilustrísimo Señor Don Juan Carlos de Coucy, Obispo de la Rochela dirigida a los fieles de su diócesis desde España, con el motivo de las inquietudes de la Francia* (1793), in C.D.F., vol. 210, sig. 789, 26; *Declaración lamentable contra los Franceses hecha por el Obispo de la Rochela, residente en Guadalajara, en el mes de Febrero de 1793,* in C.D.F., vol. 210, sig. 790, 4–9.

64. Raphael Thomás Menéndez de Luarca, *Opúsculo Primero. El Reyno de Dios, y su justicia, obradora de la paz de Christo, Príncipe de la paz, exortación, que el Obispo de Santander hacia a sus Diocesanos, y por ellos a todos los Españoles, sobre guerrear, Fuertes en la Fé, las Guerras del Señor, contra sus enemigos los Franceses libres, año de 1794,* in *Opúsculos Christiano-Patrios,* in C.D.F., vol. 173, sig. 702, 45, 47, 161. Herr characterizes Menéndez de Luarca's tome as "an exorbitant, redundant, and ungrammatical hodgepodge" (Herr, *The Eighteenth-Century Revolution in Spain,* 309).

65. Diego José de Cádiz, *El soldado-católico,* pt. 1, 6, 10; pt. 2, 13. He used the term *patria* few times in the whole text, generally in part 2: 29, 32, 45, 52, 53, 82. See José Álvarez Junco, "El nacionalismo español como mito movilizador: Cuatro guerras," in *Cultura y movilización en la España contemporánea,* ed. Rafael Cruz and Manuel Pérez Ledesma (Madrid, 1997), 43.

66. Manuel Gil, *Oración fúnebre del Excelentísimo Señor D. Alexandro de O-Reilly* (Cádiz, 1794), in C.D.F., vol. 191, sig. 730, 94.

67. Miguel de Santander, *Exhortación que el autor hizo a sus paisanos, para la defensa de la patria, en la presente guerra, el año de 1795,* in *Sermones panegíricos,* 2:351.

68. Diego José de Cádiz, *Jesús María y Josef: Memorial que al Rey Nuestro Señor (que*

Dios guarde) sobre los medios espirituales para el buen éxito de la presente guerra contra la sediciosa asamblea de la Francia, año de 1794, se dirigía Por el M.R.P. Fr. Diego José de Cádiz (1813), in C.D.F., vol. 230, sig. 844, 29.

69. Villanueva, *Catecismo del estado,* xiii, 2, 301. This work has been described as representative of "el pensamiento reaccionario español de este momento, inspirado por la Iglesia" (see Antonio Morales Moya, "Los conflictos ideológicos en el siglo XVIII español," *Revista de Estudios Políticos* 80 [1993], 28–29).

70. Villanueva, *Catecismo del estado,* xxiv, 13, 93. "He seldom used *patria* (190, 243, 252, 268, 275), *España* (103, 237, 247), or *españoles,* included only twice in the whole volume, emphasizing the terms *estado* and *reyno* instead."

71. Elorza, "Cristianismo ilustrado y reforma política en Fray Miguel de Santander," 75.

72. Santander, *Sermón IV: Divinidad de la religión católica,* in *Sermones dogmáticos,* 1:103.

73. Santander, *Sermón III: Necesidad de una religión revelada,* in *Sermones dogmáticos,* 1:68–69.

74. Miguel de Santander, *Carta de un religioso español, amante de su patria, escrita a otro religioso amigo suyo sobre la constitución del reino y abuso del poder* (1798), in Elorza, "Cristianismo ilustrado y reforma política en Fray Miguel de Santander," 104–6, 102. Other enlightened figures, such as Jovellanos, looked to the French constitutional monarchy of 1791 as a model for state-building (see Gaspar Melchor de Jovellanos, *Letter on the French Revolution* (1794), in *Early Modern Spain: A Documentary History,* ed. Jon Cowans [Philadelphia, 2003]).

75. Miguel de Santander, *Del carácter del christiano,* in *Doctrinas y sermones para misión,* 2nd ed. (Madrid, 1802), 47–54.

76. Antonio Tavira, *Carta pastoral del 4 de junio de 1801,* in Saugnieux, *La Ilustración cristiana española,* 173, 174–75.

77. Josef María de Miera Pacheco, *Discurso predicado en la Real Capilla de San Antonio de Aranjuez, el día 18 de Marzo de 1805, por el Dr. D. Josef María de Miera Pacheco,* in C.D.F., vol. 35, sig. 210, 3, 20. By 1812, he publicly praised the wisdom of the Constitution (see José María de Miera Pacheco, *Oración que en la iglesia de Ntra. Sra. del Carmen de la villa de Estepa pronunció el doctor Don José María de Miera Pacheco* [Osuna, 1812], in *Colección Gómez Ímaz* [C.G.I.], Biblioteca Nacional, Madrid, 20).

78. *Semanario Patriótico,* no. 74, September 5, 1811.

79. Pedro Luis Blanco, *Don Pedro Luis Blanco, por la gracia de Dios y de la Santa Sede Apostólica, Conde de Colle, Señor de las Arrimadas y Vegamian, Obispo de la ciudad de León y su obispado, del Consejo de S.M. &c.* (León, 1808), in C.G.I., 17–18.

80. *La Junta General de Gobierno* (June 1, 1808), in *Guerra de la Independencia: Proclamas bandos y combatientes,* ed. Sabino Delgado (Madrid, 1979), 31.

81. Blanco, *Don Pedro Luis Blanco, por la gracia de Dios,* 13.

82. 1 Macc. 3:3–9 (Rev. English Bible).

83. In Mexico City, one cleric exhorted the Spanish lion to rise up and bring the legitimate king back to power, just as the "people of God" had during the times of the Maccabees (see Joseph Beristáin de Sousa, *Oración panegírico-eucarística* [Mexico City, 1809], in *Colección Lafragua* [C.L.], Biblioteca Nacional, Mexico City, vol. 438, 32).

84. 1 Macc. 3:43.

85. Manuel de la Virgen del Rosario, *Oración fúnebre que en las solemnes de los militares difuntos en la jornada de Baylén y anteriores* (Málaga, 1808), in C.D.F., vol. 16, sig. 31, 33.

86. Rosario, *Oración fúnebre,* 32.

87. Ignacio Gutiérrez y Polop, *España Regenerada. Discurso, que para reanimar a los españoles en defensa de la justa causa, dixo en la Iglesia parroquial de la Villa de Axpe* (1809), in C.D.F., vol. 35, signatura 208, 9. The prime minister under Carlos IV, Manuel Godoy, symbolized Spain's misfortune and received much of the blame for the French occupation. During the Motín de Aranjuez, in which Carlos IV abdicated in favor of his son Fernando, crowds rioted to protest against Godoy, whom they almost killed. In signing the Treaty of Fontainebleau in October 1807, Godoy had allowed twenty-eight thousand French troops to march toward Portugal through Spain's northern provinces. Napoleon justified the move by claiming an urgent need to halt all Portuguese trade with the English, which would thus weaken the last remaining obstacle to France's European hegemony. To sweeten the deal, the French secretly promised Godoy the southern territories of Alemtejo and Algarve from a Portugal to be apportioned after conquest. However, French troops under Junot not only took Portugal, hours after the royal family abandoned Lisbon and set sail for Brazil, but began to capture military outposts in Spain. In February 1808, a contingent of French soldiers employed a ruse to seize a fortress in Pamplona and subsequently moved southward. On March 23, 1808, just days after the events at Aranjuez, Joachim Murat, Napoleon's brother-in-law and recently appointed "Lieutenant of the Emperor in Spain," entered Madrid.

88. Gutiérrez y Polop, *España Regenerada,* 21, 15, 14, 12, 26. Díaz del Castillo, preaching in Mexico City, memorialized May 2, 1808, as the "Día que en la posteridad hará inmortal su memoría por la crueldad y tiranía del indigno Murat" (Manuel Díaz del Castillo, *Sermón político-moral, que en las solemnes rogaciones hechas procesionalmente desde la Santa Iglesia Metropolitana de México a la del Imperial Convento de N.P. Santo Domingo* [1809], in C.D.F., vol. 604, sig. 2199, 8). Napoleon offered the Spanish Crown to his brother Joseph, José I, on June 6, 1808.

89. D. F. J. de Molle, *Efectos de la lealtad y del valor heroyco de los Españoles: Por D.F.J. de Molle, Presbítero* (Málaga, 1809), in C.D.F., vol. 36, sig. 214.

90. Luis de Borbón, *Carta Pastoral del Eminentísimo Señor Arzobispo de Toledo* (1808), in C.D.F., vol. 529, sig. 1799, 22–23.

91. Francisco Xavier de Lizana y Beaumont, *Exhortación del Illmo. Señor Don Francisco Xavier de Lizana y Beaumont, Arzobispo de México, en que manifiesta la obligación de socorrer a la Nación Española en la actual guerra con la Francia* (Mexico City, 1808), in C.L., vol. 714.

92. Ramón Casaus Torres y Lasplazas, *Sermón en acción de gracias a Dios Nuestro Señor por las gloriosas hazañas de la invicta Nación Española para la restauración de la Monarquía, y restitución de nuestro amado soberano el Sr. D. Fernando VII. a su trono; para la libertad sagrada de ambos mundos, y conservación de la divina Religión en ellos* (Mexico City, 1808), in C.D.F., vol. 604, sig. 2195, 7–19.

93. *El Conciso,* no. 61, December 14, 1810.

94. Manuel María Rodríguez y Romero, *Sermón moral en que se reconviene a Sevilla* (Seville, 1808), in C.D.F., vol. 16, sig. 32, 33.

95. Tomás de Salas, *Carta Primera: El Verdadero Patriotismo Demostrado por el evan-*

gelio escritas por el P. Fr. Tomás de Salas, in *Cartas Patrióticas* (Seville, 1809), in C.D.F., vol. 61, sig. 285, 7.

96. Francisco Alvarado, *Sermón del glorioso martir e inquisidor San Pedro de Arbues, predicado en la aniversaria solemnidad que le consagra el Santo Tribunal de la Inquisición de Sevilla, en el Real Convento de San Pablo* (1809), in C.D.F., vol. 43, sig. 252, 6.

97. *La bestia de siete cabezas y diez cuernos o Napoleón Emperador de los Franceses. Exposición literal del capítulo XII del Apocalipsis por un presbítero andaluz, vecino de la Ciudad de Málaga* (1808), in C.D.F., vol. 16, sign. 30.

98. Ramón Casaus Torres y Lasplazas, *Oración fúnebre, que en las exequias generales, celebradas el día 12 de septiembre de 1808,* in C.D.F., vol. 604, sig. 2197, 14.

99. P. Maestro Salmón, *Resumen histórico de la Revolución de España año de 1808* (Cádiz, 1812), in C.D.F., vol. 932, sig. 3368, 256.

100. Díaz del Castillo, *Sermón político-moral,* 19.

101. López, *Despertador cristiano-político,* 24, 32, 23.

102. Joaquín Lorenzo Villanueva, *Las Angélicas Fuentes, o El Tomista en las Cortes* (Cádiz 1811), in C.G.I., 33.

103. Joaquín Lorenzo Villanueva, *El Jansenismo, dedicado al Filósofo Rancio: Por Ireneo Nystactes* (Cádiz, 1811), in C.G.I., 1.

104. D.S.C.G.E., December 21, 1810.

105. Manuel de Santo Tomás Traggia, *El Amigo de la Verdad,* no. 11 (Mallorca, 1812), in C.D.F., vol. 123, sig. 492.

106. Raphael Thomás Menéndez de Luarca, *Opúsculo VI: La España Futura, felíz, o infelíz en extremo, según lo que fuere el que al presente (Año de 1812) se piensa celebrar en ella Concilio Nacional: Y España, la España miserable; que, dibuja a tan distantes aspectos sobre el fondo del estado, en que yace, se presenta, solicitando sus mayores felicidades a los padres de la Iglesia, que deben componer aquel gran Congreso, y a los de la Patria, que deben tratar de que se celebre,* in *Opúsculos Christiano-Patrios,* in C.D.F., vol. 175, sig. 704, 38.

107. Luis Carrasco y Enciso, *Oración Eucarística por la libertad gloriosa y feliz restitución del Rey Nuestro Señor al trono augusto de sus mayores, que en la solemne función celebrada por el batallón tercero de patriotas distinguidos de Fernando Séptimo* (Mexico City, 1815), in B.U.A.P., 47.

108. Domingo de la Heras Ibarra, *Catecismo natural* (1814), cited in Vicente León Navarro, *La pasión por la libertad: Miguel Cortés y López (1777–1854)* (Valencia, 2003), 120.

109. *Reflexiones sobre el sermón que Fray Miguel de Santander, auxiliar de Zaragoza, predicó en la Iglesia de Pilar de dicha ciudad el 17 de Mayo de 1810, con motivo de la rendicion de Lérida a los franceses* (Cádiz), in C.G.I., 16–17.

110. Manuel Revuelta González, "Actitudes opuestas de dos obispos santanderinos ante la Guerra de la Independencia," in *La Guerra de la Independencia (1808–1814) y su momento histórico* (Santander, 1982), 2:665–85.

111. Examples abound of ecclesiastics who, in spite of collaborating with the French, came to support the Constitution of 1812 after the occupation ended (see Gérard Dufour, *Un liberal exaltado en Segovia: El canónigo Santiago Sedeño y Pastor [1769–1823]* [Valladolid, 1989]). For example, on July 17, 1821, the few *afrancesados* left in Cádiz celebrated Napoleon's death, and the funeral oration included a eulogy in honor of the Constitution of 1812 (*Diario de la ciudad de Valencia,* no. 95, August 4, 1821).

CHAPTER TWO

1. Manuel María Rodríguez y Romero, *Sermón moral en que se reconviene a Sevilla* (Seville, 1808), in C.D.F., vol. 16, sig. 32, 8.

2. *Proclama a los Españoles Americanos: Los Españoles de Europa* (Valencia, 1808), in C.D.F., vol. 27, sig. 183, 7.

3. See Scott Eastman, "*La que sostiene la península es guerra nacional:* Identidades colectivas en Valencia y Andalucía durante la Guerra de Independencia," *Historia y Política: Ideas, procesos y movimientos sociales* 14 (November 2005): 245–70.

4. The War of Independence took on increasing significance for nationalists by the 1830s. Published in 1835, the Conde de Toreno's *Historia del levantamiento, guerra y revolución de España* was one of the first histories to explicitly use the phrase "War of Independence." According to Álvarez Junco, the work of Toreno best represents the way in which the protagonists of the events themselves compiled their memories into an autobiographical as well as historical account of the war. In analyzing the historiography of the war, Toreno argues: "Ahora, haciendo corta pausa, séanos lícito examinar la opinión de ciertos escritores que, al ver tantas derrotas y dispersiones, han querido privar a los españoles de la gloria adquirida en la guerra de la Independencia." He does not use the new name exclusively, as he also refers to "la revolución" on page 107 (see José María Queipo de Llano, Conde de Toreno, *Historia del levantamiento, guerra y revolución de España* [Madrid, 1953], 181; and José Álvarez Junco, "La invención de la Guerra de la Independencia," *Studia Histórica-Historia Contemporánea* 12 [1994]: 84–85).

5. Valencia, the third-largest city in Spain at the time, had a population close to 100,000, followed by Seville, Granada, Córdoba, and Cádiz, each with between 50,000 and 90,000 residents. Out of a total Spanish population of 10.5 million (based on the census of 1797)—fast approaching 12 million by 1808—the region of Valencia recorded 825,059 inhabitants while Andalusia claimed 1,897,980 people, almost one-fifth of the total populace. The demographic and social composition of southern Spain and the Levant, despite discrepancies between the censuses of 1787 and 1797, generally points to a rising population as well as to increasing social inequality along with a manifest rural-urban divide (Ardit Lucas, *Revolución liberal y revuelta campesina,* 25–27; J. Vicens Vives, *Historia de España y América social y económica,* vol. 4, *Los Borbones. El siglo XVIII en España y América* [Barcelona, 1977], 4–10). See also Juan Plaza Prieto, *Estructura económica de España en el siglo XVIII* (Madrid, 1975), 146–89.

6. P. Maestro Salmón, *Resumen histórico de la Revolución de España,* vol. 3 (Cádiz, 1812), in C.D.F., vol. 934, sig. 3370, 300. In exploring the 1808 uprisings, Antonio Alcalá Galiano drew upon a series of "notable examples," beginning with the cases of Seville and Valencia and proceeding to Manuel Quintana's influential *Semanario Patriótico* (Antonio Alcalá Galiano, *Memorias de D. Antonio Alcalá Galiano,* in *Obras escogidas* [Madrid, 1955], 1:349).

7. Juan Rico, *Memorias históricas sobre la revolución de Valencia,* 84.

8. Ibid., iii.

9. Van Young comes to the opposite conclusion in studying the War of Independence in New Spain (see Van Young, *The Other Rebellion,* 3).

10. Xosé Nuñez Seixas, "The Region as *Essence* of the Fatherland: Regionalist Variants of Spanish Nationalism (1840–1936)," *European History Quarterly* 31, no. 4 (2001): 483. On

French regionalism, see Caroline Ford, *Creating the Nation in Provincial France: Religion and Political Identity in Brittany* (Princeton, 1993).

11. Peter Sahlins, *Boundaries: The Making of France and Spain in the Pyrenees* (Berkeley and Los Angeles, 1989).

12. Peter Sahlins, "The Nation in the Village: State-Building and Communal Struggles in the Catalan Borderland during the Eighteenth and Nineteenth Centuries," *Journal of Modern History* 60 (June 1988): 261. Colley follows Sahlins in articulating a vision of British national identity as "emerg[ing] alongside of, and not necessarily in competition with older, more organic attachments to England, Wales or Scotland, or to county or village" (see Colley, *Britons,* 18).

13. Josep Fradera has coined the term "double patriotism" to describe the development of Catalan identity within the spaces of Spanish politics and the spectrum of liberal values in nineteenth-century Spain (see Fradera, "El proyecto liberal catalán y los imperativos del doble patriotismo," *Ayer* 35 [1999]: 96).

14. Archilés and Martí, "Ethnicity, Region and Nation," 785.

15. Marx, *Faith in Nation,* 185–86. Ringrose challenges the idea of Spanish backwardness. As growing centers of trade and agriculture, Valencia and Andalusia displayed important similarities as well as the salient differences that marked the varied socioeconomic patterns of nineteenth-century Spain. Regional networks epitomized early modern Spanish commerce and did not function as a coherent "national" economy. Ringrose, in contrast to scholars who situate modernization as a central causal agent, observes that the processes of "industrialization and modernization did surprisingly little to alter the matrix of central places [urban networks] that had emerged in Europe by the sixteenth century." Valencia and cities as far south as Málaga had pronounced links to Mediterranean commerce centered in Barcelona. The free trade decree of 1778 opened the port of Alicante to American commerce, although Valencia did not enjoy the same privilege. By 1791–92, the Crown was receiving 19 percent of its income from American colonial trade and did not have to raise domestic taxes. Andalusia, in spite of its ties to the Americas from the ports of Seville and Cádiz, likewise witnessed "its urban network become more regionally oriented in the course of the eighteenth and nineteenth centuries." In Valencia, the cultivation of rice, grapes, olives, grains, and carob was balanced by woolen and silk textile production. As a percentage of the workforce as a whole, agricultural laborers comprised 64.7 percent and 67.3 percent of the active population in Andalusia and Valencia respectively in 1797, indicating the prominence of the rural agricultural sector in Spain at the time. The rural poor, especially in Andalusia, composed a growing class as social inequities exacerbated by the privatization of land became more pronounced (Ringrose, *Spain, Europe and the "Spanish Miracle,"* 111–12, 302, 307).

16. Riquer i Permanyer, "La débil nacionalización española del siglo XIX."

17. See John Breuilly, *Nationalism and the State* (New York, 1982). Breuilly argues that nationalism must be understood as a form of politics that develops in conjunction with the state.

18. Javier Varela, "Nación, patria y patriotismo en los orígenes del nacionalismo español," *Studia Histórica-Historia Contemporánea* 12 (1994): 34.

19. Núñez Seixas, *Historiographical Approaches to Nationalism in Spain,* 146.

20. Cadalso, *Cartas Marruecas,* 41.

21. Felipe Scio, *Sermón que inspirado de Dios, y por su mandato, predicó el profeta Jeremías, en la puerta del templo de Jerusalén, exhortando al pueblo a una sincera conversión, si no quería ser entregado en manos de sus enemigos . . . por un sacerdote deseoso del bien de la religión y de la patria* (Valencia, 1809), in C.D.F., vol. 43, sig. 254, 7.

22. *Real Decreto* (Madrid, March 16, 1808; Valencia, March 21, 1808), in B.V.

23. *Con fecha de ayer se sirvió S.M. dirigir al Excelentísimo Señor Duque del Infantado, Presidente del Consejo, el Real Decreto siguiente* (Madrid, April 8, 1808), in Archivo Histórico Municipal (A.H.M.), Valencia, Libros Capitulares, signatura D-204 (1808).

24. Flórez Estrada, *Introducción para la historia de la Revolución de España,* 117. The Conde de Toreno similarly wrote that the deaths of "los ilustres y beneméritos oficiales Daoiz y Velarde; honra y gloria de España, dechado de patriotismo, servirán de ejemplo a los amantes de la independencia y libertad nacional" (Toreno, *Historia del levantamiento, guerra y revolución de España,* 44).

25. John Lawrence Tone, "Spanish Women in the Resistance to Napoleon, 1808–1814," in *Constructing Spanish Womanhood: Female Identity in Modern Spain,* ed. Victoria Lorée Enders and Pamela Beth Radcliff (Albany, 1999), 261. Francisco Goya's visceral realism captured the killings in his ex post facto painting *El 3 de mayo.*

26. Miguel Artola, *La España de Fernando VII* (Madrid, 1968), 44. On May 3, the lead story in the *Diario de Madrid* focused on fishing techniques in China, which were supposedly unknown to Europeans at the time. By May 5, the religious, among others, were implored to "impede the excesses of the people [pueblo]" (*Diario de Madrid,* nos. 124, 126, May 3 & 5, 1808).

27. See Richard Hocquellet, *Résistance et révolution durant l'occupation napoléonienne en Espagne 1808–1812* (Paris, 2001), 140–54.

28. *Proclama* (1808), in Delgado, ed., *Guerra de la Independencia,* 99.

29. *Semanario Patriótico,* no. 12, November 17, 1808.

30. On elections in New Spain, see Nettie Lee Benson, "The Elections of 1809: Transforming Political Culture in New Spain," ed. Kathryn Vincent, *Mexican Studies* 20, no. 1 (Winter 2004): 1–20; Jaime E. Rodríguez O., "The Transition from Colony to Nation: New Spain, 1820–1821," in *Mexico in the Age of Democratic Revolutions, 1750–1850,* ed. Rodríguez O. (Boulder, 1994); and Rodríguez O., *The Independence of Spanish America,* 92–103.

31. Cited in Seoane, *El primer lenguaje constitucional español,* 55.

32. Cited in Joaquín Varela Suanzes-Carpegna, *La teoría del estado en los orígenes del constitucionalismo hispánico (Las Cortes de Cádiz)* (Madrid, 1983), 102.

33. *Constitución Política de la Monarquía Española* (Cádiz, 1812), in *Los inicios del constitucionalismo español: De las Cortes de Cádiz a la crisis de la monarquía absoluta (1808–1833)* (Valencia, 1980).

34. Jordana Dym, *From Sovereign Villages to National States: City, State, and Federation in Central America, 1759–1839* (Albuquerque, 2006).

35. Valencia housed 2,610 ecclesiastics within an overall population of just under 100,000 (Callahan, *Church, Politics, and Society in Spain,* 2).

36. Vicente Martínez Colomer, *Sucesos de Valencia desde el día 23 de mayo hasta el 28 de junio del año 1808* (Valencia, 1810), in C.L., vol. 185, 5. A statue of Domenech, flag in hand, heroically inspiring the people to war, stands next to the Torres de Quart (Quart Towers) in Valencia today.

37. In Valencia, one edict, published in the name of King Fernando VII, exhorted: "Por

la gracia de Dios, Rey de España, y en su Real Nombre el Excmo. Sr. Capitan General y Real Acuerdo, mandan: Que todos los Vecinos se tranquilicen y retiren á sus casas, pues siempre han velado por su bien estar y harán quanto puedan para que tengan efecto sus deseos é intenciones: Que se haga el alistamiento forzoso desde edad de 16 á 40 año" (*Suplemento al Diario de Valencia del martes 24 de mayo de 1808,* in A.H.M., Libros Capitulares, sig. D-204 [1808]).

38. *El pueblo,* in this instance, did not signify the nation as a whole but referred to the lowest classes or plebeians, consisting of *jornaleros,* laborers not affiliated with the guild structure and the urban poor. This was akin to Capmany's 1778 definition of *el pueblo.* Yet conceptions of the people quickly came to connote the nation in discourses articulated during the course of the War of Independence, and the radical transformation and elevation of commoners into archetypal members of the national community posed a clear threat to privileged elites.

39. Martínez Colomer, *Sucesos de Valencia,* 19–20. There were four members of the "ecclesiastical branch," four "curates," four "prelates," two clerics "from the Law College," and two clerical "representatives of the people" out of thirty-nine *junta* members. At the beginning of the nineteenth century in Spain as a whole, approximately 71.5 percent of the working (male) population was employed as artisans or agricultural laborers, including both renters and landless *jornaleros,* constituting the popular class. Ten percent can be classified as middle class, engaged in administration, a profession such as the law, medicine, or the army, while commerce, industry, and peasant smallholders comprised a mere 2.5 percent. Fourteen percent of the population can be identified as nobility, and 1.5 percent served in the ranks of the clergy, although nobles remained less than 1 percent of the population in Valencia and Andalusia.

40. Rico, *Memorias históricas sobre la revolución de Valencia,* 65.

41. Ibid., 37–38.

42. Martínez Colomer, *Sucesos de Valencia,* 17.

43. Rico, *Memorias históricas sobre la revolución de Valencia,* 17–18. Other contemporary accounts corroborate Rico's testimony. One cleric wrote: "Hoy es quando todo español conoce lo que es el *entusiasmo*. . . . Mientras carga su fusil de nuevo, me parece que mira hácia sus compañeros de armas. . . . ¡*Viva España*! grita con una fuerza inesperada, que lleva su eco hasta las filas más distantes, desde donde le responden unos: *viva la religión, y otros viva, viva* FERNANDO SÉPTIMO. " See Antonio Marqués y Espejo, *Higiene política de la España, ó medicina preservativa de los males con que la contagia la francia* (Valencia, 1808), in Biblioteca Universidad de Valencia (B.U.V.), 38.

44. Juan Rico (October 16, 1808), in A.H.M., Libros Capitulares, sig. D-204 (1808). Rico, among others, was taken prisoner in December 1808 and was transported to Mallorca for having disrupted the public order (see Ardit Lucas, *Revolución liberal y revuelta campesina,* 147–48).

45. Rico, *Memorias históricas sobre la revolución de Valencia,* 25.

46. Ibid., 26.

47. Ibid., 73.

48. Ardit claims they enlisted up to 9,800 men (Ardit Lucas, *Revolución liberal y revuelta campesina,* 140).

49. *Carta de Pedro Zanón, vicario de Bugarra* (June 15, 1808), in Archivo Diocesano de Valencia (A.D.V.), sig. 500/006.

50. Rico, *Memorias históricas sobre la revolución de Valencia,* 19.

51. Ibid., 64.

52. Ibid., 57.

53. In Seville, the regular clergy comprised 59 percent of the ecclesiastical community, and their eighty-four monasteries and convents played a more prominent role in religious services than did the thirty parish churches. The majority of both secular and regular clerics resided in urban Spain, often leaving rural parishes vacant. Inequalities in land distribution were mirrored in the concentrations of clergy across Spain. Whereas in the north, ratios of clergy to parishioners ranged from one to between two hundred and four hundred people, ratios reached one to more than one thousand people in Córdoba and Seville. Such figures mask a significant clerical presence within the cities, however. In spite of these extreme disparities, William Callahan maintains that "the eighteenth-century Church was omnipresent; no one escaped its influence" (Callahan, *Church, Politics, and Society in Spain,* 2).

54. Ambrosio de Valencina, *Los capuchinos de Andalucía en la guerra de la independencia* (Seville, 1910), 41–50.

55. Manuel Moreno Alonso's *Sevilla napoleónica* (Seville, 1995) focuses on the period of the French occupation.

56. Lovett, *Napoleon and the Birth of Modern Spain,* 1:166.

57. *Grito General de la Nación: Proclama de Sevilla,* in *Guerra de la Independencia,* ed. Delgado, 71.

58. Ibid., 75.

59. Martínez Colomer, *Sucesos de Valencia,* 13.

60. Ibid., 11.

61. Ibid., 16.

62. Violent episodes occurred all over Spain in reaction to potential disloyalty. On February 21, 1809, a member of the Cádiz Junta was accused of treason and murdered. A priest quelled the continuing violence, giving a speech castigating those who thought the Marqués de Villel, another representative in the new government, was a traitor (Valencina, *Los capuchinos de Andalucía,* 67).

63. Rico, *Memorias históricas sobre la revolución de Valencia,* 94–97.

64. *Manifiesto de la causa formada por el Señor Don José María Manescau, Alcalde del crimen de la real audienca de Valencia, por comisión de la Junta Suprema de Gobierno, contra el canónigo de S. Isidro D. Baltasar Calbo* (Valencia, August 14, 1808), in B.V., 8.

65. *Manifiesto de la causa formada por el Señor Don José María Manescau,* 15.

66. Ardit Lucas, *Revolución liberal y revuelta campesina,* 129–32.

67. *Manifiesto de la causa formada por el Señor Don José María Manescau,* 22.

68. *Excelentísimo Señor* (June 6, 1808), in A.H.M., Libros Capitulares, signatura D-204 (1808).

69. *Reglamento para la formación de compañías de vecinos honrados en el reyno de Valencia, que defiendan sus pueblos, y mantengan la quietud, titulándose: cuerpo de vecinos honrados y urbanos del reyno de Valencia* (Valencia, August 20, 1808), in A.H.M., Libros Capitulares, signatura D-204 (1808).

70. Rico, *Memorias históricas sobre la revolución de Valencia,* 97.

71. *Gazeta de Valencia,* no. 15, July 15, 1808.

72. *Nos D. Fr. Joaquín Company, por la gracia de Dios y de la Santa Sede Apostólica,*

Arzobispo de Valencia . . . a todos nuestros Diocesanos, salud y paz en nuestro Señor Jesu-Christo (Valencia, 1808), in C.D.F., vol. 35, sig. 207, 14.

73. Francisco Antonio Cebrián y Valda, *Carta Pastoral. Nos D. Francisco Antonio Cebrián y Valda . . . Obispo de Orihuela . . . A todos los Curas, Vicarios y Regentes de las Parroquias, y a todos los Prelados Regulares de los conventos de Religiosos de esta nuestra Diócesi* (*sic*). (Valencia, 1808), in C.D.F., vol. 43, sig. 256.

74. Vicente Facundo Labaig y Lassala, *Sermón en acción de gracias al patriarca San Josef por la defensa de Valencia contra el exército francés día 28 de junio 1808* (Valencia, 1808), in C.G.I., 5.

75. Ibid., 6.

76. Rodríguez y Romero, *Sermón moral en que se reconviene a Sevilla,* 8.

77. Labaig y Lassala, *Sermón en acción de gracias al patriarca San Josef,* 30.

78. Tone, "Spanish Women in the Resistance to Napoleon, 1808–1814."

79. Manuel Gil, *Proclama dirigida a los estudiantes de Sevilla exhortándolos a la lucha contra Napoleón* (Seville, 1809), in C.G.I.

80. *Manifiesto de la Junta Suprema de Sevilla,* in *Guerra de la Independencia,* ed. Delgado, 91.

81. *Manifiesto de la Nación Española a la Europa,* in C.D.F., vol. 16, sig. 26, 21.

82. Rosario, *Oración fúnebre,* 30.

83. Molle, *Efectos de la lealtad y del valor heroyco de los Españoles.*

84. Juan Acisclo de Vera y Delgado, *Exhortación del Serenísimo Señor D. Juan Acisclo de Vera y Delgado, Arzobispo de Laodicea, Presidente de la Suprema Junta Central Gubernativa del Reyno, a sus amados españoles* (Cádiz, 1809), in C.D.F., vol. 43, sig. 260, 21.

85. Francisco Xavier de Lizana y Beaumont, *Exhortación del Illmo. Señor Don Francisco Xavier de Lizana y Beaumont, Arzobispo de México, en que manifiesta la obligación de socorrer a la Nación Española en la actual guerra con la Francia* (Mexico City, 1808), in C.L., vol. 714.

86. On the guerrillas in Spain, see Tone, *The Fatal Knot.*

87. Ardit Lucas, *Revolución liberal y revuelta campesina,* 211–12.

88. Charles J. Esdaile, *Fighting Napoleon: Guerrillas, Bandits and Adventurers in Spain 1808–1814* (New Haven, 2004), 176. Esdaile refers to him as Agustín Nebot.

89. *Gazeta del Reyno de Valencia,* no. 36, May 8, 1813, in C.G.I., 193–94.

90. Ascensio Nebot, *Artículo Remitido* (Valencia, March 30, 1820), in B.V.

91. *Valencianos* (Valencia, 1810), in B.V. The Bayonne Constitution of July 7, 1808, established a constitutional monarchy with Catholicism, enshrined in Article 1 as the religion of state, as its centerpiece. A Senate and a three-tiered Cortes, or Parliament, constituted the legislative branch. American viceroyalties and the Philippines received minority representation in the Cortes and enjoyed the same rights as the metropole, according to Articles 87 and 92.

92. Ibid.

93. Joaquín Company, *Exhortación que dirige el Arzobispo de Valencia á los Vocales congregados en esta Capital, para el nombramiento de Diputados de las Cortes que van á celebrarse* (1810), in B.V., 11–12.

94. The French occupation of Valencia had not taken place without incident, and residents were killed by firing squad in January 1812. Five of the victims were nationalist clerics, including Friar Faustino Igual. According to one account, "Si todos hubieran sido

Iguales, no se hubiera perdido Valencia." The author played upon the term *igual,* or same, in underscoring the ideals of liberty and equality that had animated the popular struggle against the French (see José Tomás Nebot, *Memorias históricas de la vida y muerte de los MM. RR. PP. Fr. Pedro Pasqual Rubert . . . Fr. Josef de Xérica . . . Fr. Faustino Igual . . . Fr. Gabriel Pichó . . . y Fr. Vicente Bonet . . . fusilados por los Franceses en Murviedro, el 18 de Enero de 1812; y del Presbítero Don Juan Bautista Casañs, fusilado junto al Convento del Remedio en 29 de Enero del mismo año* [Valencia, 1813], in C.D.F., vol. 353, sig. 1223, 11–12; and *Muerte de los cinco mártires de la Patria, víctimas de la rendición de Valencia* [1814], in C.D.F., vol. 353, sig. 1224).

95. Joaquín Centelles y Nuñez, *Efemerides ó bien sean sucesos memorables ocurridos en Valencia, desde 1. de Enero de 1801 hasta fin de Diciembre de 1825,* in B.U.V.

96. *Sigue la orden general de hoy 18 de marzo de 1813,* in C.D.F., vol. 862, sig. 3153. Conservatives also heralded the anniversary of March 19, equating it with the day of Fernando's return to Spanish territory in 1814: "The day has finally arrived in which the heroic people [pueblo] of Madrid, always constant in their most profound love toward their idolized Fernando, repeated the scene that they bestowed upon the Nation in March of 1808" (*Atalaya de la Mancha,* no. 76, April 1, 1814).

97. *Sigue la orden general de hoy 18 de marzo de 1813.*

98. Facundo Sidro Vilarroig, *Memoria de los regocijos públicos que en obsequio del rey nuestro señor D. Fernando VII. En su tránsito por esta capital* (Valencia, 1814), in B.V., 47–48.

99. Ibid., 46.

100. Joaquín Sanchis Albella, *La actividad precisa en el día, convertida en elogio de la tropa, para honor del gran Lord Wellington* (Valencia, 1814), in B.V.

101. While in Valencia, Fernando was given the influential *Manifiesto de los persas,* which advocated a return to monarchy and an unimpeded royal prerogative.

102. Sidro Vilarroig, *Memoria de los regocijos públicos,* 106–7. See also Centelles y Nuñez, *Efemerides ó bien sean sucesos memorables ocurridos en Valencia.*

103. Antonio Alcalá Galiano, *De nuestras costumbres políticas,* in *Obras escogidas,* 2:463.

104. Molle, *Efectos de la lealtad y del valor heroyco de los Españoles.*

105. Emile Durkheim, *The Elementary Forms of the Religious Life,* trans. Joseph Ward Swain (New York, 1965), 482.

106. *¿Qué se debe a Valencia?: O sean reflexiones sobre los esfuerzos que ha hecho esta providencia en la presente guerra* (Valencia, 1808), in C.D.F., vol. 27, sig. 167, 9–22.

CHAPTER THREE

1. Juan Pablo Constans, *Plan sobre el modo de formar un Exército de Cruzados en la Provincia de Cataluña* (June 22, 1809), in Archivo Histórico Nacional (A.H.N.), Madrid, Estado, legajo 41C.

2. Molle, *Efectos de la lealtad y del valor heroyco de los Españoles.*

3. *El Robespierre Español,* no. 14 (Cádiz, 1811).

4. Santander, *Del carácter del christiano.*

5. Keith Michael Baker, "Defining the Public Sphere in Eighteenth-Century France: Variations on a Theme by Habermas," in *Habermas and the Public Sphere,* ed. Calhoun, 192.

6. Jürgen Habermas argues that the public sphere, consisting of arenas of Enlightenment sociability such as the salon and the newspaper, first took root in Britain and France during the eighteenth century. Habermas conceives of the public sphere—a topic much debated since his work was first published in German in 1962—as a functional system in which rational-critical debate in public forums undermined the legitimacy of Old Regime monarchies and paved the way for the liberal republics of the nineteenth century. He constructs an argument based upon a philosophy of communication that brought about consensus and conflict resolution. The public sphere incorporated universal norms as a framework to solve political and social problems. Habermas's adherence to an ideal of universal normative solutions to complex social ills derives in large part from his grounding in Kantian epistemology and an idealized vision of the Enlightenment public sphere, the historical backdrop to the rise of bourgeois public space. Yet he decries the irrational and divisive nature of nineteenth-century party politics, and describes the broadening of the public sphere as the harbinger of "public opinion [as] a coercive force, whereas it had once been supposed to dissolve any kind of coercion into the compulsion of reason." Following Marxist cultural analysis, Habermas views art, culture, and public opinion as subject to the authority of the Old Regime order. He posits a "monopoly of interpretation" not limited to the pulpit and the laws of the state (Habermas, *The Structural Transformation of the Public Sphere: An Inquiry into a Category of Bourgeois Society,* trans. Thomas Burger [Cambridge, Mass., 1989], 36–37, 133).

7. Geoff Eley, "Nations, Publics, and Political Cultures: Placing Habermas in the Nineteenth Century," in *Habermas and the Public Sphere,* ed. Calhoun, 296–97.

8. Marx, *Faith in Nation,* 186. Furthermore, Max Weber suggested that Calvinist ethics contributed to a positive view of the accumulation of wealth (see Weber, *The Protestant Ethic and the Spirit of Capitalism,* trans. Talcott Parsons [New York, 1976], 42; and Anthony Giddens, introduction to Weber, *The Protestant Ethic,* 1–12).

9. Zaret, "Religion, Science, and Printing in the Public Spheres," 213. Habermas essentially disentangles the church from an emergent public sphere in civil society. Zaret argues that "Habermas's account glosses over the relevance of religion for the emergence of a public sphere in politics at a time when religious discourse was a, if not the, predominant means by which individuals defined and debated issues in this sphere." Yet even in expanding the theoretical reach of a Habermasian conception to include the religious foundations of a public sphere in seventeenth-century England, scholars such as Zaret have not considered the context of an emergent public sphere, including popular religious practices and the public space of the church, in the Hispanic Atlantic world. Zaret presents Protestantism as an exceptional case of early dissent, in which the questioning of scripture, lay initiative, and adherence to reason (within limits) held special appeal in sixteenth- and seventeenth-century Puritan England. He also concludes that the religious foundations of contract theory between earthbound individuals and a heavenly contractor paved the way for the subsequent development of classical liberalism.

10. On scientific aspects of the Hispanic Enlightenment, see Jorge Cañizares-Esguerra, "La Ilustración hispanoamericana: Una caracterización," in *Revolución, independencia y las nuevas naciones de América,* ed. Jaime E. Rodríguez O. (Madrid, 2005), 87–98.

11. Alcalá Galiano, *Memorias de D. Antonio Alcalá Galiano,* in *Obras escogidas,* 1:314, 385.

12. Ibid., 392, 315.

13. Habermas, *The Structural Transformation of the Public Sphere,* 27.

14. On the Catholic public sphere, see Scott Eastman, "Las identidades nacionales en el marco de una esfera pública católica: España y Nueva España durante las guerras de independencia," in *Las nuevas naciones: España y México, 1808–1850,* ed. Jaime E. Rodríguez O. (Madrid, 2008), 75–97.

15. Portillo Valdés, *Revolución de nación,* 27; Brian Connaughton, "Los curas y la feligresía ciudadana en México, siglo XIX," in *Las nuevas naciones,* ed. Rodríguez O., 241–72.

16. D.S.C.G.E., October 16, 1810.

17. Flórez Estrada, *Introducción para la historia de la Revolución de España,* 45.

18. Bartolomé Gallardo, *Diccionario crítico-burlesco: Diccionario razonado manual para inteligencia de ciertos escritores que por equivocación han nacido en España* (Madrid, 1820), 101–2. *Liberal,* signifying a political party, was a Spanish neologism at the time (see Richard Herr, "Flow and Ebb 1700–1833," in *Spain: A History,* ed. Raymond Carr [Oxford, 2000], 198).

19. *Semanario Patriótico,* no. 9, October 27, 1808.

20. Gallardo, *Diccionario crítico-burlesco,* 103.

21. Ibid., 106–7. Jailed in 1811, Gallardo stood accused of being "atrociously subversive . . . and insulting to different Ministers of the Ecclesiastical Hierarchy and Religious orders" (cited in Lovett, *Napoleon and the Birth of Modern Spain,* 2: 472–73).

22. *Prospecto para la Gazeta de Valencia.*

23. For the press in Spanish America at this time, see Rodríguez O., *The Independence of Spanish America,* 37–39; and Guerra, *Modernidad e independencias,* 286, 297.

24. María Cruz Seoane, *Historia del periodismo en España,* vol. 2, *El siglo XIX* (Madrid, 1983), 30.

25. *Semanario Patriótico,* no. 1, September 1, 1808.

26. *El Voto de la Nación Española,* no. 1, December 13, 1809, 5.

27. *Semanario Patriótico,* no. 3, September 15, 1808.

28. Ibid., no. 2, September 8, 1808.

29. Ibid., no. 3, September 15, 1808.

30. Ibid., no. 4, September 22, 1808.

31. Ibid., no. 9, October 27, 1808.

32. Ibid., no. 3, September 15, 1808.

33. Javier Fernández Sebastián, "España, monarquía y nación: Cuatro concepciones de la comunidad política española entre el Antiguo Régimen y la Revolución liberal," *Studia Histórica-Historia Contemporánea* 12 (1994): 45–74.

34. Juan de Escoiquiz, *Representación escrita por el Señor D. Juan de Escoiquiz, Maestro del Señor D. Fernando VII, siendo Príncipe de Asturias, principal fundamento de la causa del Escorial, por haberla hallado en poder de S.A. para entregarla al Señor Don Carlos IV* (Cádiz, 1809), in C.D.F., vol. 43, sig. 249. Escoiquiz, a priest, recommended inundating Spain with catechisms, booklets, and periodicals in order to extol the Spanish national spirit during the war against the French (see Dorothy Tanck de Estrada, "Los catecismos políticos: De la revolución francesa al México independiente," in *La revolución francesa en México,* ed. Solange Alberro, Alicia Hernández Chavez, and Elías Trabulse [Mexico City, 1992], 66).

35. Manuel Abad Queipo, *Carta pastoral del Ilustrísimo Señor Obispo electo y Gobernador del Obispado de Michoacán* (Valladolid, 1812), in C.D.F., vol. 607, sig. 2252, 22.

36. Manuel Díaz del Castillo, *Sermón político-moral, que en las solemnes rogaciones hechas procesionalmente desde la Santa Iglesia Metropolitana de México a la del Imperial Convento de N.P. Santo Domingo* (1809), in C.D.F., vol. 604, sig. 2199, 6. The Junta Central declared the Indies an integral component of the monarchy, definitively not colonies, on January 22, 1809.

37. Manuel Abad Queipo, *Don Manuel Abad Queipo, Canónigo Penitenciario de esta Santa Iglesia, Obispo electo y Gobernador del Obispado de Michoacán, a todos sus habitantes salud y paz en nuestro Señor Jesuchristo* (Valladolid, 1811), in C.D.F., vol. 604, sig. 2202, 15.

38. Álvarez Junco, *Mater dolorosa*, 219–21.

39. *Semanario Patriótico*, no. 1, September 1, 1808.

40. Santander, *Carta de un religioso español*, 102–6. José Marchena, in a pamphlet published in France in 1792, also advocated convoking the Cortes: "Let *Cortes, Cortes* be the universal cry" (see *A la nación española* [Bayonne, 1792], cited in Herr, *The Eighteenth-Century Revolution in Spain*, 276).

41. *El Voto de la Nación Española*, no. 5, January 10, 1810.

42. For the case of elections in Oaxaca, see Jaime E. Rodríguez O., "'Ningun pueblo es superior a otro': Oaxaca y el federalismo mexicano," in *Poder y legitimidad en México, siglo XIX: Instituciones y cultura política*, ed. Brian Connaughton (Mexico City, 2003).

43. José Francisco Arroyo, cited in Jaime E. Rodríguez O., *"Rey, religión, yndependencia y unión": El proceso de la independencia de Guadalajara* (Mexico City, 2003), 32.

44. Manuel Martínez, *Discurso que en la solemnidad de jurarse la Constitución política de la monarquía española por el clero, pueblo y todas las autoridades de la ciudad de Valladolid en la Santa Iglesia Catedral* (1812), in Álvarez García, *El clero de la Diócesis de Valladolid*, 231.

45. Ramón Solís, *El Cádiz de las Cortes: La vida de una ciudad en los años de 1810 a 1813* (Madrid, 2000), 301.

46. Rodríguez O., *The Independence of Spanish America*, 64–74; Virginia Guedea, *En busca de un gobierno alterno: Los Guadalupes de México* (Mexico City, 1992), 12.

47. Ramón Huarte, *Don Ramón Huarte, Alcalde primero por S.M. de ésta Ciudad y su jurisdicción, y encargado de la intendencia de ésta Provincia de Michoacán* (December 31, 1810), in *Colección de documentos para la historia de la guerra de independencia de México*, ed. J. E. Hernández y Dávalos (Liechtenstein, 1968), 2:314.

48. Francisco Xavier Venegas, *D. Francisco Xavier Venegas* (November 14, 1810), in *Colección de documentos para la historia de la guerra de independencia de México*, ed. Hernández y Dávalos, 2:222.

49. *Gachupín* was a derisive term for European-born Spaniards.

50. *Ilustrador Americano*, no. 22, August 8, 1812.

51. Manuel de la Bárcena, *Sermón que en la jura del señor Don Fernando VII* (Mexico City, 1808), in C.L., vol. 1432, 14.

52. Joseph Mariano Beristáin de Sousa, *Discurso político-moral y cristiano* (Mexico City, 1809), in C.L., vol. 11, 8.

53. *Ilustrador Americano*, no. 5, June 10, 1812.

54. Ibid.

55. *Semanario Patriótico Americano, plan de este periódico.*

56. *Semanario Patriótico Americano*, no. 1, 1812.

57. Solís, *El Cádiz de las Cortes,* 238.

58. Seoane, *Historia del periodismo en España,* 2: 41.

59. *El Redactor General,* no. 1, June 15, 1811.

60. Solís, *El Cádiz de las Cortes,* 463.

61. Henry F. Schulte, *The Spanish Press 1470–1966: Print, Power, and Politics* (Urbana, Ill., 1968), 129; Solís, *El Cádiz de las Cortes,* 451.

62. Alcalá Galiano, *Memorias de D. Antonio Alcalá Galiano,* in *Obras escogidas,* 1:387.

63. *El Conciso* no. 17, September 26, 1810.

64. Ibid., *El Conciso,* no. 18, September 28, 1810; ibid., no. 26, October 12, 1810.

65. Ibid., no. 18, September 28, 1810.

66. Ibid., no. 22, October 4, 1810.

67. Ibid., no. 30, October 20, 1810.

68. D.S.C.G.E., October 17, 1810.

69. *El Conciso,* no. 30, October 20, 1810.

70. *El Robespierre Español,* no. 15 (Cádiz, 1811).

71. D.S.C.G.E., October 21, 1810.

72. *El Conciso,* no. 30, October 20, 1810.

73. D.S.C.G.E., July 6, 1811.

74. Seoane, *Historia del periodismo en España,* 2:47–48.

75. *El Robespierre Español,* no. 14 (Cádiz, 1811).

76. Ibid.

77. Jean-Jacques Rousseau, *On the Social Contract,* trans. Donald A. Cress (Indianapolis, 1987), 30.

78. *El Robespierre Español,* no. 15 (Cádiz, 1811).

79. Ibid.

80. Ibid.

81. Ibid.

82. *El Vencedor Católico por el amante de la Religión, y de la Patria* (Seville, 1809), in C.D.F., vol. 42, sig. 240, I. Traggia began his journalistic career at the *Diario de Valencia* in 1792 (see Alberto Pacho Polvorinos, "Original proyecto de Cruzada presentado por el P. Manuel de Traggia a la Junta Central," in *La Guerra de la Independencia (1808–1814) y su momento histórico* (Santander, 1982), 2:707–23.

83. *El Despertador Americano,* no. 2, December 27, 1810.

84. Ibid., no. 4, January 3, 1811.

85. Miguel Santos Villa, *Sermón que en los solemnes cultos que se tributaron a San Francisco Xavier por haberse libertado esta ciudad de Valladolid de los estragos con que la amenazaban los insurgentes* (Mexico City, 1811), in C.L., vol. 1280, 25.

86. *Semanario Patriótico,* no. 3, September 15, 1808.

87. Ibid., no. 74, September 5, 1811.

88. *El Robespierre Español,* no. 13 (Cádiz, 1811).

89. Gallardo defined friars as "a species of vile and contemptible animals that live a life of leisure" (see Gallardo, *Diccionario crítico-burlesco,* 54).

90. Ibid., xxi.

91. Gallardo and other liberals used the term *servil* to represent conservatives, whom they viewed as abject and literally vile—a play on the separation of the word *servil* into *ser,*

to be, and *vil,* vile. He defined the ideology of liberals by highlighting "the panic and terror that the idea of liberal men gives to the serviles, that is to say, to those who honor the title of servants" (ibid., 97–98).

92. *El Conciso,* no. 19, March 19, 1812.

93. Manuel de la Bárcena, *Exhortación que hizo al tiempo de jurarse la Constitución Española, en la catedral de Valladolid de Michoacán* (Mexico City, 1813), in C.D.F., vol. 607, sig. 2253, 2.

94. *Constitución Política de la Monarquía Española.*

95. *Semanario Patriótico,* no. 74, September 5, 1811.

96. Joaquín Lorenzo Villanueva, *Discurso que restituida a la ciudad de Valencia la Audiencia Territorial, pronunció al tiempo de su apertura D. Lorenzo Villanueva, ministro más antiguo, el día 27 de julio del año 1813* (Valencia), in C.G.I., 9.

97. Ibid., 18.

98. See, for example, Rodríguez O., *"Rey, religión, yndependencia y unión,"* 32.

99. *La Regencia del Reyno se ha servido dirigirme el Decreto que sigue* (Cádiz, 1812), in Archivo Municipal de Puebla (A.M.P.), Libro de Cabildos, 81 (1812).

100. *D. Manuel Fernando Ruíz del Burgo* (September 10, 1812), in C.D.F., vol. 862, sig. 3153.

101. Abad Queipo, *Don Manuel Abad Queipo, Canónigo Penitenciario de esta Santa Iglesia,* 13. The term "extraordinary representation" was also used to describe the convocation of the Estates-General in 1789 (see Sieyès, "What Is the Third Estate?" 178–79).

102. Abad Queipo, *Don Manuel Abad Queipo, Canónigo Penitenciario de esta Santa Iglesia,* 7–8.

103. Rodríguez O., *"Rey, religión, yndependencia y unión,"* 35.

CHAPTER FOUR

1. *Informe sobre el Tribunal de la Inquisición* (Cádiz, 1812), in C.D.F., 61, 66.

2. *Apología de la Inquisición: Respuesta a las reflexiones que hacen contra ella el Semanario patriótico número 61, y el periódico titulado el Español número 13, y breve aviso a los Señores Arzobispos, Obispos y Diputados en Cortes* (Cádiz, 1811), in C.D.F., vol. 650, sig. 2436, 32.

3. William H. Prescott, *History of the Reign of Philip the Second of Spain* (Boston, 1855), cited in Richard L. Kagan, "Prescott's Paradigm: American Historical Scholarship and the Decline of Spain," *American Historical Review* 101, no. 2 (April 1996): 430.

4. Pierre Rosanvallon, cited in Charles Tilly, "The Emergence of Citizenship in France and Elsewhere," in *Citizenship, Identity and Social History,* ed. Tilly (Cambridge, U.K., 1996), 228.

5. Charles Tilly, "Citizenship, Identity and Social History," in *Citizenship, Identity and Social History,* ed. Tilly, 11.

6. Michael P. Fitzsimmons, "The National Assembly and the Invention of Citizenship," in *The French Revolution and the Meaning of Citizenship,* ed. Renée Waldinger, Philip Dawson, and Isser Woloch (Westport, Conn., 1993), 37.

7. Rogers Brubaker, *Citizenship and Nationhood in France and Germany* (Cambridge, Mass., 1992), 14.

8. Geoff Eley and Ronald Grigor Suny, "Introduction: From the Moment of Social History to the Work of Cultural Representation," in *Becoming National,* ed. Eley and Ronald Suny (New York, 1996), 4–5; Hans Kohn, *The Idea of Nationalism: A Study in Its Origins and Background* (New York, 1944). Accordingly, civic nationalism appeared as an outgrowth of the French revolutionary model of the sovereign people as national citizens. Ethnic nationalism, on the other hand, has often been tied to Germany and an exaltation of the uniqueness of a particular people. In order to avoid a false dichotomy, however, this chapter problematizes the notion that civic and ethnic nationalisms are tied to specific national histories.

9. Tamar Herzog, *Defining Nations: Immigrants and Citizens in Early Modern Spain and Spanish America* (New Haven, 2003). In a review essay, Stephen Jacobson argues that "the difference between these two regimes—between *vecino* and 'citizen' (*ciudadano*)—mirrors the distinction between 'kingdom' and 'nation.' Between this early modern regime and the Constitution of 1812, it is night and day" (see Jacobson, "'The Head and Heart of Spain': New perspectives on nationalism and nationhood," *Social History* 29, no. 3 [August 2004]: 405).

10. Antonio de Capmany, *Centinela contra franceses,* in *Centinela contra franceses: Edición, con introducción, notas y apéndices documentales por Françoise Etienvre,* ed. Françoise Etienvre (London, 1988), 81.

11. Facundo Sidro Vilarroig, *Reflexiones Cristiano-Políticas acerca de las nuevas Cortes, libertad de imprenta, eclesiásticos, militares, nobles, y Santa Inquisición* (Valencia, 1814), in C.D.F., vol. 924, sig. 3348, 7.

12. *Instrucción pastoral de los Ilustrísimos Señores Obispos de Lérida, Tortosa, Barcelona, Urgel, Teruel, y Pamplona: Al clero y pueblo de sus diócesis* (Mallorca, 1813), in C.D.F., vol. 345, sig. 1163, 187.

13. *Apología de la Inquisición* (emphasis mine), 5.

14. Ibid., 8.

15. *Informe sobre el Tribunal de la Inquisición,* 4.

16. Ibid., 38–39.

17. See Jordana Dym, "La soberanía de los pueblos: Ciudad e independencia en Centroamérica, 1808–1823," in *Revolución, independencia y las nuevas naciones de América,* ed. Rodríguez O., 312.

18. *Informe sobre el Tribunal de la Inquisición,* 46–47.

19. Ibid., 55.

20. Ibid., 53–54.

21. Henry Kamen, *The Spanish Inquisition: A Historical Revision* (New Haven, 1997), 79.

22. Juan Antonio Posse, *Discurso sobre la Constitución,* in *Memorias del cura liberal don Juan Antonio Posse con su Discurso sobre la Constitución de 1812,* ed. Richard Herr (Madrid, 1984), 268. Juan Antonio Llorente claimed that the Inquisition was responsible for the deaths of three hundred thousand people (see Llorente, *The History of the Inquisition of Spain* [Philadelphia, 1843], 5).

23. Kamen, *The Spanish Inquisition,* 60.

24. Ibid., 203.

25. *Informe sobre el Tribunal de la Inquisición,* 59–60.

26. Herrero, *Los orígenes del pensamiento reaccionario español,* 380–81.

27. *Semanario Patriótico Americano,* no.10, September 20, 1812.

28. *Dictamen del Doctor D. Antonio José Ruíz de Padrón, ministro calificado del Santo Oficio, Abad de Villamartin de Valdeorres, y diputado en Cortes por las islas Canarias, que se leyó en la sesión pública de 18 de enero sobre el tribunal de la Inquisición* (Cádiz, 1813), in C.G.I., 63–64.

29. La Parra López, *El primer liberalismo español y la iglesia,* 213–16. In the aftermath of the debates, Juan Antonio Llorente noted: "I have the satisfaction to be able to declare, that this triumph of reason and humanity was principally owing to the documents I furnished, and which became known to the public in 1812. . . . [B]ut they were not cited, because I was then a counsellor of state to King Joseph" (see Llorente, *The History of the Inquisition of Spain,* 204).

30. *Representación que el Ilustrísimo Señor Obsipo de Segovia ha hecho al augusto Congreso de las Cortes, pidiendo el restablecimiento del Santo Tribunal de la Inquisición: Dala a luz un español, amante de la religión* (Cádiz, 1812), in C.D.F., vol. 650, sig. 2440, 7–11.

31. *Carta sobre el establecimiento del Tribunal de la Inquisición: Por el Dr. D. Blas Ostolaza, Capellán dè Honor y Confesor de S. M. C. El Sr. D. Fernando 7 y Diputado en Cortes* (Cádiz, 1811), in C.D.F., vol. 650, sig. 2437, 8, 15.

32. *Apología de la Inquisición,* 9.

33. Callahan, *Church, Politics, and Society in Spain,* 102.

34. Raul Morodo and Elías Díaz, "Tendencias y grupos políticos en las Cortes de Cádiz y en las de 1820," *Cuadernos Hispanoamericanos* 201 (1966): 637–75.

35. La Parra López, *El primer liberalismo español y la Iglesia,* 214.

36. *El Procurador General de la Nación y del Rey,* no. 116, January 24, 1813; Morodo and Díaz, "Tendencias y grupos políticos en las Cortes de Cádiz; Federico Suárez, *Las Cortes de Cádiz* (Madrid, 1982), 28–48. Clerics voting in favor of abolishing the Inquisition: Andueza, Presbítero, Peru; Calello, Canónigo, Asturias; Castillo, Presbítero, Guatemala; Couto, Cura, New Spain; Espiga, Presbítero, Catalonia; Gallego, Presbítero, León; Gordillo, Presbítero, Canaries; Goyanes, Presbítero, León; Llarena, Canaries; Muñoz Torrero, Presbítero, Extremadura; O'Gavan, Presbítero, Cuba; Oliveros, Canónigo, Extremadura; Pascual, Canónigo, Aragon; Ramos Arispe, Presbítero, New Spain; Rivas, Cura Párroco, Balearics; Ruíz de Padrón, Presbítero, Canaries; Traver, Presbítero, Valencia; Villanueva, Presbítero, Valencia; Zufriátegui, Presbítero, Montevideo.

37. Kamen, *The Spanish Inquisition,* 17, 57.

38. For a discussion of the ideology of *limpieza de sangre,* see Gonzalo Álvarez Chillida, *El antisemitismo en España: La imagen del judío (1812–2002)* (Madrid, 2002), 43–44.

39. Ibid., 22.

40. María Elena Martínez, "Guardian of the Christian Society: The Holy Office of the Inquisition—Racism, Judaizing, and Gambling," in *Religion in New Spain,* ed. Schroeder and Poole (Albuquerque, 2007), 198.

41. Robert Miles and Malcolm Brown, *Racism,* 2nd ed. (London, 2003), 30.

42. On the first decades of the Inquisition in Spain, see Kamen, *The Spanish Inquisition,* 56–65.

43. D.S.C.G.E., September 4, 1811.

44. Ibid., December 17, 1810.

45. López, *Despertador cristiano-político,* 24.

46. *La quema de la constitución en aldea leal por el Doct. Don Patricio Español* (1808), in C.D.F., vol. 55, sig. 273.

47. On oppositional national identity, see Sahlins, *Boundaries.*

48. Álvarez Chillida, *El antisemitismo en España,* 44. Álvarez Chillida argues that "el resultado de esta contraposición entre españoles-cristianos y extranjeros-judíos/moros en el imaginario popular terminó por convertir al judío en un ser mítico que englobaba a todo no cristiano que no fuera musulmán."

49. *Diario de las Sesiones de las Cortes Generales y Extraordinarias: Sobre el Tribunal de la Inquisición,* January 20, 1813.

50. Joyce E. Chaplin, "Race," in *The British Atlantic World, 1500–1800,* ed. Armitage and Braddick, 154, 165.

51. Jorge Cañizares-Esguerra maintains that Europeans first articulated essentialist visions of racial difference in the seventeenth century during debates over the effects of the New World on biological development. Despite the articulation of such views reifying different racial bodies, he contends, the ideas of Creole scholars did not play a substantial role in the subsequent rise of scientific knowledge and racial classification (see Cañizares-Esguerra, "New World, New Stars: Patriotic Astrology and the Invention of Indian and Creole Bodies in Colonial Spanish America, 1600–1650," *American Historical Review* 104, no. 1 [February, 1999]: 33–68).

52. Magali M. Carrera, *Imagining Identity in New Spain: Race, Lineage, and the Colonial Body in Portraiture and Casta Paintings* (Austin, 2003), 5.

53. Ann Twinam, *Public Lives Private Secrets: Gender, Honor, Sexuality, and Illegitimacy in Colonial Spanish America* (Stanford, 1999), 25.

54. On performative aspects of *casta* categories in colonial society, see Rachel O'Toole, "Castas y representación en Trujillo colonial," in *Más allá de la dominación y la resistencia: Estudios de historia peruana, siglos XVI–XX,* ed. Paulo Drinot and Leo Garofalo (Lima, 2005), 48–76.

55. For a discussion of a case from the 1770s in Mallorca, see Herzog, *Defining Nations,* 125.

56. *Constitución Política de la Monarquía Española.*

57. D.S.C.G.E., April 2, 1811.

58. Ibid., January 26, 1812.

59. Manuel López Cepero, *Lecciones políticas para el uso de la juventud española* (Seville, 1813), in *Catecismos políticos españoles arreglados a las constituciones del siglo XIX* (Madrid, 1989), 159–60.

60. *Semanario Patriótico Americano,* no.10, September 20, 1812.

61. Herzog, *Defining Nations,* 156–57.

62. Patricia Seed, "'Are These Not Also Men?': The Indians' Humanity and Capacity for Spanish Civilization," *Journal of Latin American Studies* 25, no. 3 (October 1993): 651.

63. *Proclama de un cura indio del obispado de Valladolid, a todos los padres curas y vicarios indios, y a nuestros hijos los caziques gobernadores y demás indios de esta América* (1810), in C.L., vol. 181, 1–7.

64. Bernardo de los Cobos, *Exmo. Sr.* (November 1, 1810), in *Colección de documentos para la historia de la guerra de independencia de México,* ed. Hernández y Dávalos, 2:244.

65. Rather than using the blanket term *indio,* some Spaniards differentiated between

settled and nomadic Indians. Liberals such as the *novohispano* deputy Ramos de Arispe described the nomadic Indians in his province of Coahuila as "naciones bárbaras que se han extinguido" (see Miguel Ramos de Arispe, *Memoria, que el Doctor D. Miguel Ramos de Arispe, cura de Borbón, y Diputado en las presentes Cortes Generales y Extraordinarias de España por la Provinica de Coahuila, una de las cuatro internas del oriente en el Reyno de México, presenta a el Augusto Congreso,* in C.D.F., vol. 608, sig. 2286, 5).

66. D.S.C.G.E., April 3, 1811. The deputy Terrero urged punishment for all those who refused to sanctify the essential laws of the monarchy: "Se le debería mandar á vivir entre los hotentotes ó cafres. De ella misma procede el que el Rey no sea ni pueda decirse señor de vidas y haciendas, ni que esto tenga lugar en una nación civilizada."

67. *Informe del Real Tribunal del Consulado de México sobre la incapacidad de los habitantes de N.E. para nombrar representantes á las Córtes,* in *Colección de documentos para la historia de la guerra de independencia de México,* ed. Hernández y Davalos, 2:463–66; Rodríguez O., *The Independence of Spanish America,* 84–85.

68. D.S.C.G.E., August 21, 1811.

69. Herzog, *Defining Nations,* 26.

70. This was similar to distinctions made between active and passive citizens during the French Revolution (see P. Dawson, "Active Citizen," in *Historical Dictionary of the French Revolution,* ed. Samuel Scott and Barry Rothaus [Westport, Conn., 1985], 4–5).

71. López Ceprero, *Lecciones políticas para el uso de la juventud española,* 162.

72. D.S.C.G.E., January 9, 1811.

73. Manuel Chust, *La cuestión nacional americana en las Cortes de Cádiz* (Valencia, 1999).

74. Domingo García Quintana, D.S.C.G.E., January 9, 1811.

75. D.S.C.G.E., August 21, 1811.

76. Ibid.

77. Ibid.

78. Irene Silverblatt posits that "race and caste were not separate systems, but interpenetrating" (see Silverblatt, *Modern Inquisitions: Peru and the Colonial Origins of the Civilized World* [Durham, N.C., 2004], 17).

79. D.S.C.G.E., August 21, 1811.

80. See, for example, Dominique Godineau, *The Women of Paris and Their French Revolution,* trans. Katherine Streip (Berkeley and Los Angeles, 1998).

81. Seoane, *Historia del periodismo en España,* 2:104.

82. Tone, "Spanish Women in the Resistance to Napoleon, 1808–1814," 266–67.

83. For the case of Spain, see Anna Aguado, "Liberalismos y ciudadanía femenina en la formación de la sociedad burguesa," in *La trascendencia del liberalismo doceañista en España y en América,* ed. Manuel Chust and Ivana Frasquet (Valencia, 2004), 211–31. Joan Landes argues that "the exclusion of women from the bourgeois public was not incidental but central to its incarnation," and the public sphere was essentially a "masculinist" space (see Landes, *Women and the Public Sphere in the Age of the French Revolution* [Ithaca, 1988], 7; Mary P. Ryan, "Gender and Public Access: Women's Politics in Nineteenth-Century America," in *Habermas and the Public Sphere,* ed. Calhoun, 259–88; and Leonore Davidoff and Catherine Hall, *Family Fortunes: Men and Women of the English Middle Class, 1780–1850* [Chicago, 1987], 28–35).

84. Rebecca Earle notes that all Colombian constitutions written between 1810 and

1819 equated citizenship with the essential qualities of a father, son, brother, and husband (see Earle, *The Return of the Native: Indians and Myth-Making in Spanish America, 1810–1930* [Durham, N.C., 2007], 13).

85. Gayatri Chakravorty Spivak, "Can the Subaltern Speak?" in *Marxism and the Interpretation of Cultures,* ed. Cary Nelson and Lawrence Grossberg (Urbana, Ill., 1988), 296–99.

86. Benito Feijóo, *In Defense of Women* (1737), in *Early Modern Spain,* ed. Cowans, 210.

87. Josefa Amar, *In Defense of the Talent of Women* (1786), in *Early Modern Spain,* ed. Cowans, 240–41.

88. *Proclama espiritual: Discurso muy preciso de leer en las actuales circunstancias. Se da a luz por un sacerdote que desea con eficacia la salvación de la Patria* (Seville, 1808), in C.D.F., vol. 198, sig. 743, 12.

89. Ibid., 3, 14.

90. *Exhortación de una patriota mariana a las señoras sus compañeras* (1815), in C.L., vol. 442, 2.

91. See Herrejón Peredo, *Del sermón al discurso cívico,* 245–51.

92. Francisco Xavier de Lizana y Beaumont, *Instrucción pastoral del illmo. Señor Don Francisco Xavier de Lizana y Beaumont. Arzobispo de México* (Mexico City, 1808), in C.L., vol. 714, 21.

93. *Proclama espiritual: Discurso muy preciso de leer en las actuales circunstancias,* 12–15.

94. Ramón Francisco Casaus y Torres, *Oración fúnebre, que en las solemnes y reales honras de la Reyna nuestra Señora Doña María Isabel Francisca de Braganza y Borbón* (1819), in C.L., vol. 706, 22.

95. José Ruíz de Padrón, *Dictámen de Don Antonio José Ruíz de Padrón, diputado por Canarias, proponiendo para regenta del reyno a la Serenísima Señora Doña Carlota Joaquina de Borbón, Princesa del Brasil, e Infanta de las Españas, entregado a uno de los secretarios de las Cortes Generales y Extraordinarias para leerse en una de las sesiones de marzo de 1813* (Madrid, 1814), in C.D.F., vol. 297, sig. 1028.

96. Francisco Xavier de Lizana y Beaumont, *Carta pastoral que el illmo. Señor D. D. Francisco Xavier de Lizana y Beaumont, por la gracia de Dios, y de la santa sede apostólica, arzobispo de México, del consejo de S.M. &c. dirige a sus diocesanos sobre la santidad de nuestra sagrada Religión* (Mexico City, 1807), in C.L., vol. 714, 21–22.

97. Ibid., 21–23.

98. *Instrucción pastoral de los Ilustrísimos Señores Obispos de Lérida, Tortosa, Barcelona, Urgel, Teruel, y Pamplona,* 188.

99. *Apología de la Inquisición,* 43.

100. Lizana y Beaumont, *Instrucción pastoral,* 37.

101. Ibid., 3.

102. Juan Sisinio Pérez Garzón, "Curas y liberales en la revolución burguesa," in "El Anticlericalismo," ed. Rafael Cruz, *Ayer* 27 (Madrid, 1997), 72–73.

103. Centelles y Nuñez, *Efemerides ó bien sean sucesos memorables ocurridos en Valencia.*

104. *Periódico de las Damas,* no. 3 (1822). Women faced an increasingly limited role within the nineteenth-century public sphere in Spain (see Smith, *The Emerging Female Citizen*).

CHAPTER FIVE

1. Francisco Pantaleón de Uztáriz, *Pastoral del Illmo. Sr. D. Luis Gonzaga de la Encina. Dignísimo Obispo de Arequipa, del consejo de S.M. &c. con motivo de la Instrucción dada por Napoleón Emperador de los franceses a sus Emisarios para las Américas* (1811), in C.D.F., vol. 606, signatura 2235, 10.

2. Antonio Bergosa y Jordán, *Exhortación cristiana y patriótica, que hizo en la Santa Iglesia Metropolitana de México su Arzobispo electo el Ilustrísimo Señor Doctor Don Antonio Bergosa y Jordán, en la Misa solemne del Espíritu Santo, que se celebró con motivo de la elección de Diputados a Cortes, en 18 de Julio de 1813,* in C.D.F., vol. 604, sig. 2206, 12.

3. Bárcena, *Exhortación que hizo al tiempo de jurarse la Constitución Española, en la catedral de Valladolid de Michoacán,* 4.

4. Ibid. Alfredo Ávila qualifies Bárcena, a peninsular whose entire career was spent in America, as a pragmatic advocate of *gaditano* liberalism (see Ávila, "El cristiano constitucional: Libertad, derecho y naturaleza en la retórica de Manuel de la Bárcena," *Estudios de Historia Moderna y Contemporánea de México* 25 [January–June 2003]: 1–41).

5. Manuel de la Bárcena, *Exhortación que hizo al tiempo de jurarse la Constitución Política de la Monarquía Española* (Mexico City, 1820), in C.L., vol. 149, 13.

6. William B. Taylor, "The Virgin of Guadalupe in New Spain: An Inquiry into the Social History of Marian Devotion," *American Ethnologist* 14, no. 1 (February 1987): 23–24.

7. See Scott Eastman, "'America Has Escaped from Our Hands:' Rethinking Empire, Identity and Independence during the *Trienio Liberal* in Spain, 1820-1823," *European History Quarterly* 41, no. 3 (2011): 428–43.

8. Guerra, *Modernidad e independencias,* 20, 159.

9. See, for example, *Proclama a los Españoles Americanos. Los Españoles de Europa* (Valencia, 1808), in C.D.F., vol. 27, sig. 183. See also Chust, *La cuestión nacional americana en las Cortes de Cádiz,* 143.

10. Beristáin de Sousa, *Discurso político-moral y cristiano,* 17–18. Beristáin was originally from Puebla.

11. Hamill describes the ideology of cleric and insurgent leader Miguel Hidalgo in terms of "incipient nationalism" in *The Hidalgo Revolt,* 40.

12. Jorge E. Traslosheros, "Santa María de Guadalupe: Hispánica, novohispana y mexicana: Tres sermones y tres voces: 1770–1818," *Estudios de Historia Novohispana* 18 (1998): 83–103; Mariana Terán Fuentes, *El artificio de la fe* (Zacatecas, 2002), 221.

13. Guedea, *En busca de un gobierno alterno.*

14. On "Creole patriotism," see Cañizares-Esguerra, *How to Write the History of the New World.* Rebecca Earle writes that "the uniformity of creole culture across Spanish America—itself continually strengthened by transnational contact between individual writers and politicians—helped form a language of elite nationalism that became the lingua franca of the entire continent" (Earle, *The Return of the Native,* 18).

15. With the Constitution of 1812 proclaimed in Peru in September, 1820, San Martín similarly sought a Spanish monarch for the throne (see Natalia Sobrevilla Perea, "Batallas por la legitimidad: Constitucionalismo y conflicto político en el Perú del siglo XIX [1812–1860]," *Revista de Indias* 69, no. 246 [2009]: 106–7).

16. John Lynch, *The Spanish American Revolutions 1808–1826,* 2nd ed. (New York, 1986), 1–2.

17. For works that link the Bourbon reforms with the struggle for independence, see Nancy M. Farriss, *Crown and Clergy in Colonial Mexico: The Crisis of Ecclesiastical Privilege* (London, 1968); and Taylor, *Magistrates of the Sacred.*

18. Rodríguez O., *The Independence of Spanish America.* For other works on autonomists in Spanish America, see Chust, *La cuestión nacional americana en las Cortes de Cádiz;* and Jaime E. Rodríguez O., "From Royal Subject to Republican Citizen: The Role of the Autonomists in the Independence of Mexico," in *The Independence of Mexico and the Creation of the New Nation,* ed. Rodríguez O. (Los Angeles, 1989).

19. Van Young, *The Other Rebellion.*

20. Ramón Casaus Torres y las Plazas, *Sermón panegírico de nuestra Señora del Pilar de Zaragoza* (Mexico City, 1803), in C.L., vol. 558, 1.

21. Ibid., 5–6.

22. Ibid., 1, 36.

23. Taylor, "The Virgin of Guadalupe in New Spain," 15. Brian Hamnett, on the other hand, argues that the Virgin of the Remedies "reflected the devotional patterns of the institutional Church; Guadalupe those of the general body of faithful" (see Hamnett, *Roots of Insurgency: Mexican Regions, 1750–1824* [Cambridge, U.K., 1986], 16).

24. S. Cyrilo, *El más noble desempeño de la promesa más generosa,* 11–21.

25. Antonio López Murto, *El incomparable patronato mariano, sermón panegírico de María Santísima de Guadalupe* (Mexico City, 1793), in B.U.A.P., 2–4.

26. José Díaz de Hortega, *Sermón que el día 13 de setiembre* (sic), *último del solemne novenario, celebrado en el Convento de PP Dieguinos de Nuestra Señora de Guadalupe . . . de la Ciudad de Valladolid de Michoacán para implorar el auxilio divino en las necesidades presentes de la monarquía* (Mexico City, 1808), in B.U.A.P., 15–16.

27. On the nationalist mythology of Our Lady of Covadonga in Spain, see Carolyn P. Boyd, "The Second Battle of Covadonga: The Politics of Commemoration in Modern Spain," *History & Memory* 14, no. 1/2 (Fall 2002): 37–64.

28. Joseph Ignacio Heredia y Sarmiento, *Sermón panegírico de nuestra Señora de Covadonga* (Mexico City, 1807), in C.L., vol. 1342, 26, ii.

29. See, for example, Ramón Casaus Torres y Lasplazas, *Sermón de nuestra señora del Carmen* (Mexico City, 1809), in B.U.A.P.

30. Brading, *The First America,* 351.

31. Bernardo Antonio González Díaz, *Sermón que en las públicas, solemnes y devotas rogativas hechas a María Santísima de los Remedios, por la muy noble y fidelísima Ciudad de México* (Mexico City, 1810), in B.U.A.P., 16.

32. Ibid., 10–14.

33. Hamnett writes that "too much has been made of the supposed rivalry between a *mestizo* cult of Guadalupe and a Spanish *Virgen de los Remedios*" (Hamnett, *Roots of Insurgency,* 15). On the number of Marian cults in New Spain, see Taylor, *Magistrates of the Sacred,* 282. Guardino notes: "In Antequera, the feast of Guadalupe had previously been overshadowed by the annual feast of the Virgin of Soledad" (Guardino, *The Time of Liberty,* 135).

34. Manuel Ignacio González del Campillo, *Pastoral que el ilustrísimo señor Dor. D. Manuel Ignacio González del Campillo dignísimo obispo de la Puebla de los Angeles dirige a sus diocesanos* (1810), in C.L., vol. 995, 12.

35. Bárcena, *Exhortación que hizo al tiempo de jurarse la Constitución Política de la Monarquía Española,* 8–9.

36. Cited in Rodríguez O., *The Independence of Spanish America,* 53.

37. Guedea, *En busca de un gobierno alterno,* 9.

38. Hamill, *The Hidalgo* Revolt, 114.

39. Ibid., 120.

40. José Antonio Serrano Ortega, "El discurso de la unión: El patriotismo novohispano en la propaganda realista durante el movimiento insurgente de Hidalgo," *Estudios de Historia Novohispana* 14 (1994): 157–77.

41. Alcalá Galiano, *Memorias de D. Antonio Alcalá Galiano,* in *Obras escogidas,* 1:353.

42. Moreno Alonso, *Los españoles durante la ocupación napoleónica,* 195.

43. Miguel Hidalgo y Costilla, *Manifiesto del Sr. Hidalgo* (1811), in *Colección de documentos para la historia de la guerra de independencia de México,* ed. Hernández y Dávalos, 1:119.

44. Manuel Abad Queipo, *Edicto instructivo que el Ilustrísimo Señor Don Manuel Abad Queypo* (Mexico City, 1810), in C.L., vol. 995, 23.

45. Diego Miguel Bringas, *Sermón que en la Reconquista de Guanaxuato, predicó extemporáneamente en la Iglesia Parroquial de dicha ciudad, el Padre Fr. Diego Miguel Bringas* (1810), in C.D.F., vol. 604, sig. 2200, 36.

46. Miguel Hidalgo y Costilla, *Manifiesto del Sr. Hidalgo y Costilla,* in *Colección de documentos para la historia de la guerra de independencia de México,* ed. Hernández y Dávalos, 1:125.

47. Vélez, *Preservativo contra la irreligión,* 2.

48. Ibid., 116.

49. Ibid., 122.

50. Álvarez Junco, *Mater dolorosa,* 339.

51. Guardino, *Peasants, Politics, and the Formation of Mexico's National State,* 67.

52. *El Despertador Americano,* no. 2, December 27, 1810.

53. *Semanario Patriótico Americano,* no.10, September 20, 1812.

54. Bringas, *Sermón que en la Reconquista de Guanaxuato,* 4.

55. D.S.C.G.E., April 29, 1811.

56. Hidalgo y Costilla, *Manifiesto del Sr. Hidalgo* (1811), 59. Many saw no inherent contradictions between the cry of "VIVA LA AMÉRICA," which began an 1810 exhortation, and that of "VIVA LA ESPAÑA CONSTANTE," which concluded it (*Foncerrada Michoacanense, oidor de México habla a sus compatriotras por la felicidad pública* [1810], in C.D.F., vol. 605, sig. 2217, 3, 15).

57. González del Campillo, *Pastoral que el ilustrísimo señor Dor. D. Manuel Ignacio González del Campillo,* 11.

58. Bárcena, *Exhortación que hizo al tiempo de jurarse la Constitución Española, en la catedral de Valladolid de Michoacán,* 2, 6.

59. Abad Queipo, *Don Manuel Abad Queipo, Canónigo Penitenciario de esta Santa Iglesia,* 4.

60. Puebla was New Spain's second-most important economic region (see Hamnett, "Puebla: City and Province during the Independence Period," 166).

61. Hamnett, *Roots of Insurgency,* 11.

62. Josef Demetrio Moreno y Buenvecino, *Oración panegírico moral pronunciada en la Santa Iglesia Catedral de la Puebla de los Angeles, por su prebendado don Josef Demetrio Moreno y Buenvecino, el 7 de mayo de 1809 . . . implorando la divina clemencia a favor de los sucesos de ambas españas* (Mexico City, 1809), in B.U.A.P., 10.

63. Reinhard Liehr, *Ayuntamiento y oligarquía en Puebla, 1787–1810,* vol. 2 (Mexico City, 1976), 143–44.

64. Manuel Ignacio González del Campillo, *Exhortación del Ilustrísimo Señor Obispo de Puebla a sus diocesanos* (1808), in C.D.F., vol. 35, sig. 206, 12, 16.

65. Ibid., 35–36.

66. Ibid., 6.

67. See *Unos diarios de Valencia que fueron reimpresos en Puebla* (Puebla, 1808), in Biblioteca Palafoxiana (B.P.), Puebla.

68. Cited in Tanck de Estrada, "Los catecismos políticos," 69. On the *Catecismo político para la instrucción del Pueblo Español,* see Alfonso Capitán Díaz, *Los catecismos políticos en España (1808–1822)* (Granada, 1978).

69. *Catecismo civil y breve compendio de las obligaciones del español* (Puebla, reprint, 1808), cited in Tanck de Estrada, "Los catecismos políticos," 68.

70. González del Campillo, *Exhortación del Ilustrísimo Señor Obispo de Puebla,* 38–39. Inquisitors in New Spain decreed in August 1808 that popular sovereignty constituted a heresy.

71. See, for example, *Pública Vindicación del Ilustre Ayuntamiento de Santa Fe de Guanaxuato justificando su conducta moral y política en la entrada y crímenes que cometieron en aquella ciudad las huestes insurgentes agabilladas por sus corifeos Miguel Hidalgo, Ignacio Allende* (1811), in C.D.F., vol. 638, sig. 2356, 4.

72. Francisco Xavier Conde y Pineda, *Oración moral deprecativa a la milagrosa imagen de Jesus Nazareno, que se venera en la parroquia de Señor San Josef de la Ciudad de Puebla* (México, 1809), 12, in B.U.A.P.

73. Liehr, *Ayuntamiento y oligarquía en Puebla,* 2: 148.

74. In the majority of cases, American *juntas* recognized the legitimacy of the Junta Central, and earlier on, the Junta of Seville. Manuel Chust, "Un bienio trascendental: 1808–1810," in *1808: La eclosión juntera en el mundo hispano,* coord. Manuel Chust (Mexico City, 2007), 23.

75. Portillo Valdés, *Revolución de nación.*

76. Guedea, *En busca de un gobierno alterno;* Guardino, *The Time of Liberty,* 126.

77. Liehr, *Ayuntamiento y oligarquía en Puebla,* 2: 149. Two of the final three candidates were clerics.

78. Archivo del Cabildo Eclesiástico de Puebla (A.C.E.P.), April 13, 1811.

79. Ibid., September 26, 1811, and April 29, 1813.

80. José de Lezama (1811), cited in Herrejón Peredo, *Del sermón al discurso cívico,* 296.

81. Libro de Cabildos, 80 (1811), in A.M.P.

82. A.C.E.P., June 11, 1811.

83. Libro de Cabildos, 81 (1812), in A.M.P.

84. Ibid.

85. Bringas, *Sermón que en la Reconquista de Guanaxuato,* 26.

86. José María Cos, *El General Cos, a las provincias de su mando* (1814), in C.L., vol. 312.

87. José Servando Teresa de Mier Noriega y Guerra, *The Memoirs of Fray Servando Teresa de Mier,* trans. Helen Lane (New York, 1998), 199.

88. Luis Carrasco y Enciso, *Oración Eucarística por la libertad gloriosa y feliz restitución del Rey Nuestro Señor al trono augusto de sus mayores, que en la solemne función celebrada por el batallón tercero de patriotas distinguidos de Fernando Séptimo* (México, 1815), in B.U.A.P., 54.

89. Ibid., 40, 54–57.

90. According to Juan Ortiz Escamilla, the impact of this constitution was minimal compared to the influence of the Constitution of 1812 (see Ortiz Escamilla, "Fuerzas armadas y liberalismo en México en una etapa revolucionaria, 1810–1821," in *La trascendencia del liberalismo doceañista en España y en América,* ed. Chust and Frasquet, 171–72).

91. Antonio Bergosa y Jordán, *Carta pastoral del ilustrísimo señor Don Antonio Bergosa y Jordán obispo de Oaxaca, a sus diocesanos* (Mexico City, 1815), in C.L., vol. 716, 12.

92. Timothy E. Anna, "The Buenos Aires Expedition and Spain's Secret Plan to Conquer Portugal, 1814–1820," *Americas* 34, no. 3 (January 1978), 356. The war in New Spain ultimately took between 200,000 and 400,000 lives (see ibid., "Agustín de Iturbide and the Process of Consensus," in *The Birth of Modern Mexico, 1780–1824,* ed. Christon I. Archer, [Wilmington, Del., 2003], 188).

93. Hidalgo y Costilla, *Manifiesto del Sr. Hidalgo y Costilla,* 126.

94. Simón Bolívar, *Reply of a South American to a Gentleman of this Island,* in *Selected Writings of Bolivar,* ed. Harold A. Bierck Jr. (New York, 1951), 105.

95. *El Amigo de la Patria,* no. 2, September 19, 1822.

96. *El Tribuno de la Plebe,* no. 1, 1821. The insurgency drew upon an extant paradigm in heralding their leaders as liberators. The Cortes of Cádiz had looked into establishing a commission to institute "una orden de la patria" to reward the brilliant military actions of generals "que merezcan el título de *libertadores de la patria*" (emphasis mine; D.S.C.G.E., December 18, 1810).

97. Libro de Cabildos, 89 (1820), in A.M.P.

98. Ibid.

99. José Antonio Joaquín Pérez Martínez, *Don por la divina gracia y de la santa sede apostólica, obispo de esta diócesis, del consejo de S. M. &c.,* Libro de Cabildos, 89 (1820), in A.M.P.

100. José Antonio Joaquín Pérez Martínez, *Discurso que hizo a los electores de provincia en la Catedral de la Puebla de los Angeles el Illmo. Señor Dr. Don Antonio Joaquín Pérez Martínez Obispo el día 17 de Septiembre de 1820* (Puebla, 1820), in B.U.A.P., 1–4.

101. Libro de Cabildos, 90 (1821), in A.M.P.

102. Ibid.

103. Ibid.

104. Ludovico de Lato Monte, *Catecismo de la independencia en siete declaraciones* (Mexico City, 1821), in B.U.A.P., 2–4, 16–17.

105. José de Jesús Huerta, *Sermón que en la solemne bendición de las banderas del regimiento de infantería de la milicia nacional local de Guadalajara* (Guadalajara, 1822), in C.L., vol. 1415, 16.

106. Juan de Dios María Piñera, *Sermón panegírico eucharístico que en honra de nuestro libertador el Señor D. Agustín Primero* (Guadalajara, 1822), in C.L., vol. 1415, 6–7.

107. Clavijero, in his work on the Aztec past, assigned great significance to indige-

nous tongues. He answered critics by compiling a short vocabulary of Nahuatl that demonstrated that the language clearly had words for metaphysical as well as concrete mathematical terms. The Bible could easily be translated in such a complex language, he argued. Brading concludes that Clavijero's "intentions were openly patriotic—he wrote: 'To serve my country in the best manner possible, and to restore to its splendour the truth so darkened by an incredible mob of modern writers'" (Brading, *The Origins of Mexican Nationalism,* 19–20).

108. In many ways, this charter mirrored the Constitution of 1812. Article 2 stated that Catholicism will be the religion of the state, and Article 5 declared that sovereignty emanates from the people. The final addendum stipulated that September 16 will be celebrated as Independence Day (*Sentimientos de la Nación,* in *Morelos. Documentos,* ed. Antonio Arriaga [Morelia, 1965], 33–35.

109. Cited in Earle, *The Return of the Native,* 24.

110. Brading, *The First America,* 581.

111. Huerta, *Sermón que en la solemne bendición,* 9.

112. Piñera, *Sermón panegírico eucharístico,* 5–6.

113. Francisco García Diego, *Sermón, que en la solemnísima función que hizo este colegio de N.S. de Guadalupe de Zacatecas en acción de gracias por la feliz conclusión de la independencia del imperio mejicano* (Guadalajara, 1822), in C.L., vol. 1404, 31.

114. García Diego, *Sermón, que en la solemnísima función,* 30.

115. Manuel de la Bárcena, *Sermón exhortario que en la solemne función anual, que hace la imperial orden de Guadalupe a su celestial patrona* (1823), cited in D.A. Brading, *Mexican Phoenix: Our Lady of Guadalupe: Image and Tradition across Five Centuries* (Cambridge, U.K., 2001), 239.

116. Brading, *The Origins of Mexican Nationalism,* 3.

117. Guardino, *Peasants, Politics, and the Formation of Mexico's National State,* 58.

118. Eley and Suny, "Introduction: From the Moment of Social History to the Work of Cultural Representation," 22.

CHAPTER SIX

1. José Bravo, *A la compañía patriótica, justa y benéfica de oficiales militares de Sevilla, reunidos por el sistema constitucional* (Seville, 1821), in C.D.F., vol. 977, sig. 3456. To compare and contrast, see Ascensio Nebot, *Artículo remitido* (Valencia, March 30, 1820), in B.V.; and Diego José de Cádiz, *El soldado-católico.*

2. Hobsbawm, *Nations and Nationalism since 1780,* 40.

3. Gil Novales, *El Trienio Liberal,* 5.

4. Rodríguez O., *The Independence of Spanish America,* 193–94.

5. Two opposing political traditions emerged in the aftermath of the Trienio in the former provinces of the Spanish Monarchy. The first, forged by the leaders of the war and the military, emphasized executive power, while the second, advocated by the autonomists, upheld the legislative body as the arbiter of power in the tradition of the parliamentary ideals enshrined in the Constitution of 1812. The tensions between the competing forces were played out in the political battles of the immediate postindependence years (see Rodríguez O., "The Transition from Colony to Nation").

6. Callahan, *Church, Politics, and Society in Spain,* 122–25. In Zaragoza, those who cried "Muera la libertad, viva el Rey y la Religión" were answered by chants of "Viva Riego, viva el héroe" (*Diario de la ciudad de Valencia,* no. 85, November 25, 1821). A song ridiculed *el trapense:* "Coro. Arrojad, catalanes, las armas, / Y en la fuga buscad salvación, / Porque Mina se acerca lanzando / Exterminio cual bravo león. /. . . El infame Trapense os engaña, / Os destruye el malvado Barón; / No creais á los viles traidores, / No peligra vuestra religión. /. . . Sacerdotes idiotas seducen / Vuestra fe, patriotismo y candor: / Escuchad los ministros virtuosos, / Y al momento saldreis del error. / Si Jesus la venganza detesta, / Si obediencia á las leyes mandó, / El cristiano que á ellas se opone, / A Luzbel obedece, no á Dios. /. . . Y que vivan por siglos eternos/ Dios, Rey, Patria, Ley y Religión. / Coro" ("A los Catalanes seducidos por los corifeos del bando servil," in *Colección de canciones patrióticas que dedica al ciudadano Rafael de Riego y a los valientes que han seguido sus huellas* [Valencia, 1822], in B.V.).

7. *Diario de la ciudad de Valencia,* no. 146, May 27, 1822. On the other hand, across the border from Navarre in La Rioja, residents exhibited "a decided adhesion to the constitional system," which was due in large part to the support of *exaltado* clerics in the region (see *El Espectador,* no. 398, May 17, 1822).

8. Gil Novales, *El Trienio Liberal,* 43–44. By 1822, civil strife had become endemic in parts of northern Spain. In Galicia, reports in May 1822 indicated that hundreds of anticonstitutional "facciosos," part of a *junta apostólica,* had been routed. Many were killed, including priests seeking refuge over the border in Portugal. They had not been welcomed, however, because the Portuguese were by then united with the Spaniards under the banner of constitutionalism. A revolution, begun in 1820, had been consolidated with the calling of the Cortes and a liberal constitution completed by 1822 (*Diario de la ciudad de Valencia,* no. 150, May 31, 1822; *El Espectador,* no. 403, May 22, 1822).

9. *Diario de la ciudad de Valencia,* no. 144, May 25, 1822.

10. Alberto Pujol, *Discurso que en la pompa fúnebre efectuada por decreto de S.M. en la ciudad de Barcelona, a la digna memoria del Excmo. Señor don Mariano Álvarez de Castro, gobernador que fue de la plaza de Gerona, el día 26 de octubre de 1816 en la Iglesia de Santa María del Mar* (Barcelona, 1816), in C.G.I., 17, 36.

11. See, for example, Juan Nicasio Gallego's 1808 poem *El Día Dos de Mayo: Elegia* (Cádiz, 1808), in C.G.I.

12. D.S.C.G.E., May 2, 1811. One deputy argued that religion should have been included within the text of the decree, noting that Spaniards had defended both their country and their faith against the infidel French invaders.

13. Sidro Vilarroig, *Reflexiones Cristiano-Políticas,* 3–4.

14. Alcalá Galiano, *Memorias de D. Antonio Alcalá Galiano,* in *Obras escogidas,* 2:92.

15. *Diario de la ciudad de Valencia,* no. 110, April 20, 1822.

16. Antonio Sabiñón, "Himno patriótico," in *Guerra de la Independencia,* ed. Delgado, 368.

17. Ibid., 370.

18. Don José Sabau y Blanco, *Instrucción familiar, política y moral sobre el origen, la naturaleza, propriedades, derechos y obligaciones de la sociedad civil, que comunmente se llama estado* (Madrid, 1812), in *Catecismos políticos españoles arreglados a las constituciones del siglo XIX,* 91; Villanueva, *Catecismo del estado.*

19. "Marcha nacional" (Cádiz), in C.D.F., vol. 88, sig. 367.

20. A number of songs published during the Trienio continued to denigrate the name of Napoleon, contrasting French rule with the values of "civic ardor" and a people "that want to be free" ("Protesta del Pueblo Español," in *Colección de canciones patrióticas*).

21. "Marcha nacional."

22. Bravo, *A la compañía patriótica.*

23. "Himno del Ciudadano Riego," in *Colección de canciones patrióticas.* See Carlos Serrano, *El nacimiento de Carmen: Símbolos, mitos y nación* (Madrid, 1999), 124.

24. Bravo, *A la compañía patriótica.*

25. Expedientes sobre teatro y diversiones, 172, in A.M.P. Other titles, from the dozens cited in the archive, include *Buen Labrador, Buena Esposa, Católico Recaredo, Cristóbal Colón, Destrucción de Sagunto,* and *México por Carlos quinto.*

26. Ana María Freire López, "La Guerra de la Independencia española como motivo teatral: Esbozo de un catálogo de piezas dramáticas (1808–1814)," *Investigación franco-española* 1 (1988): 127–45.

27. See, for example, the one-act play by F. Enciso Castrillón, *El sermón sin fruto o sea Josef Botellas en el ayuntamiento de Logroño,* in Emmanuel Larraz, *La Guerre d'Indépendance espagnole au théâtre, 1808–1814* (Aix en Provence, 1987), 12–42.

28. *La quema de la constitución en aldea leal por el Doct. Don Patricio Español.* This is not listed by Freire.

29. *Instrucción Popular en forma de Catecismo sobre la presente guerra: La consagra al exército y al pueblo de España un presbítero* (Seville, 1809), in C.D.F., vol. 886, sig. 3275, 15.

30. Callahan, *Church, Politics, and Society in Spain,* 61.

31. Apolinar Contoni, *Cartilla de explicación de la constitución política de la monarquía española, para la instrucción de los niños de la parroquia de Santiago de la ciudad de Baza* (Seville, 1821), in *Catecismos políticos españoles arreglados a las constituciones del siglo XIX,* 205, 208, 210.

32. López Cepero, *Lecciones políticas para el uso de la juventud española,* 141.

33. Ibid., 148.

34. Ibid., 155.

35. Ibid., 156–57. One cleric noted: "Examinad la sábia constitucion, que ha lebantado á la Inglaterra al poder colosal, que admiramos con asombro en nuestros días, y advertirémos en ellas defectos esenciales, de que está exenta la nuestra" (Ignacio María del Castillo, *Exhortación que en la Santa Iglesia Patriarchal de Sevilla hizo a los cuerpos de infantería y caballería de la milicia voluntaria local al tiempo de prestar el juramento solemne de defender la Constitución* [Seville, 1820], in C.D.F., vol. 509, sig. 1717, 23).

36. Martínez, *Discurso que en la solemnidad de jurarse la Constitución política,* 236.

37. Ibid., 234–35.

38. Luis de Borbón, *Luis de Borbón por la divina Misericordia Presbítero Cardenal de la Sta. Iglesia Romana* (Madrid, 1820), in C.D.F., vol. 508, sig. 1708, iv. In a funeral oration given for the Conde de Floridablanca in 1809, the rallying cry of "vanquish or die for the Law, the Country and the King" was raised, clearly pointing to the importance of constitutional law in liberal thought (*Elogio fúnebre en las exequias que en honor del Serenísimo Señor Presidente de la Soberana Junta Central de España e Indias y Conde de Florida-Blanca D. Josef Moñino* [Murcia, 1809], in C.D.F., vol. 35, sig. 211, 31).

39. Borbón, *Luis de Borbón por la divina Misericordia,* iv–viii.

40. Lato Monte, *Catecismo de la independencia en siete declaraciones,* 1–2.

41. Castillo, *Exhortación que en la Santa Iglesia Patriarchal de Sevilla hizo a los cuerpos de infantería,* 7–8.

42. Antonio Bernabéu, *España venturosa por la vida de la Constitución y la muerte de la Inquisición* (Madrid, 1820), in C.G.I., 206. See Emilio La Parra López, "Antonio Bernabéu: Un clérigo constitucional," *Trienio, Ilustración y Liberalismo* 3 (May 1984): 105–31.

43. Laborda y Galindo, *Oración que en el día 12 de marzo y templo metropolitano de Ntra. Sra. Del Pilar,* 10.

44. Castillo, *Exhortación que en la Santa Iglesia Patriarchal de Sevilla hizo a los cuerpos de infantería,* 20–21.

45. *Diario de la ciudad de Valencia,* no. 42, June 11, 1821.

46. Rafael de Vélez, *Instrucción pastoral que el ilustrísimo señor Don Fr. Rafael de Vélez Obispo de Ceuta dirige a sus diocesanos para precaverlos de los errores esparcidos en varios números del Liberal Africano* (Algeciras, 1822), in C.D.F., vol. 579, sig. 2110, 102.

47. Borbón, *Luis de Borbón por la divina Misericordia,* ix.

48. Callahan, *Church, Politics, and Society in Spain,* 127.

49. Cries of "Viva la Constitución, Viva el Rey por la Constitución" greeted the reinstated liberal regime in Valencia in 1820, according to the *Redactor constitucional de Valencia,* no. 6, March 16, 1820. By 1822, shouts of "viva la Nación, viva la libertad, viva la Constitución, viva el Rey constitucional" were reported during a celebration of Madrid's defense on July 7 (*Diario de la ciudad de Valencia,* no. 167, July 16, 1822). On the controversy, see Seoane, *Historia del periodismo en España,* 2:110.

50. Gil Novales, *El Trienio Liberal,* 53.

51. *Diario de la ciudad de Valencia,* no. 167, July 16, 1822.

52. Miguel Cortés y López, *Elogio fúnebre de los que murieron en Madrid el día 7 de julio de 1822 defendiendo la constitución* (Valencia, 1822), in B.V., 37.

53. Ibid., 5.

54. See León Navarro, *La pasión por la libertad,* 226.

55. Cortés y Lopez, *Elogio fúnebre de los que murieron en Madrid,* 24.

56. Ibid., 18–20.

57. Castillo, *Exhortación que en la Santa Iglesia Patriarchal de Sevilla hizo a los cuerpos de infantería,* 13, 24.

58. Pablo de Sichar, *Manifiesto del illustrísimo Señor Obispo de Barcelona* (Mexico City, 1820), in C.L., vol. 259, 1–2.

59. Antonio Romero, *Sermón predicado en la solemne fiesta del juramento de la Constitución de la Monarquía Española, que el día 22 de marzo del año de 1820 se celebró en la Santa Iglesia Catedral de Cádiz* (Cádiz, 1820), in C.G.I., 4–5.

60. Ignacio María del Castillo, *Sermón predicado en la Santa iglesia metropolitana y patriarcal de Sevilla el día 9 de marzo* (Seville, 1821), in C.D.F., vol. 535, sig. 1904, 14, 20.

61. Ibid., 21.

62. Martínez, *Discurso que en la solemnidad de jurarse la Constitución política,* 234.

63. Castillo, *Sermón predicado en la Santa iglesia metropolitana y patriarcal de Sevilla,* 21–25.

64. Álvarez Junco, *Mater dolorosa,* 38. Other historians have noted that "the idealiza-

tion of the Visigothic period by regalist ministers [in the eighteenth century] became a crucial component of their defence of monarchical aggrandizement" (see Paquette, *Enlightenment, Governance, and Reform in Spain,* 78). Clearly, different governing regimes in Spain, from the Bourbons through Franco, have employed the Visigoths and their independence from Rome as instruments with which to glorify the present and serve their own purposes.

65. Castillo, *Exhortación que en la Santa Iglesia Patriarchal de Sevilla hizo a los cuerpos de infantería,* 17.

66. *A los ilustres Comuneros,* in *Colección de canciones patrióticas.*

67. Lato Monte, *Catecismo de la independencia en siete declaraciones,* 23–24.

68. *Canción* (Mexico City, 1821), in B.P.

69. *México libre: Melodrama heroica en un acto* (Mexico City, 1821), in B.P.

70. Castillo, *Exhortación que en la Santa Iglesia Patriarchal de Sevilla hizo a los cuerpos de infantería,* 12–16.

71. *Diario de las Sesiones de Cortes,* June 26, 1820.

72. *Representación de los americanos militares residentes en la Coruña, sobre el número de representantes por las provincias de ultramar en las Córtes* (Méjico, 1820), in B.U.A.P., 2.

73. Ivana Frasquet, "El liberalismo doceañista en el México independiente, 1821–1824," in *La trascendencia del liberalismo doceañista en España y en América,* ed. Chust and Frasquet, 143.

74. *Diario de las Sesiones de Cortes,* June 4, 1821.

75. Ibid.

76. Ibid.

77. Ibid., June 5, 1821.

78. Ibid.

79. Juan de Dios María Piñera, *Sermón panegírico eucharístico que en honra de nuestro libertador el Señor D. Agustín Primero* (Guadalajara, 1822), in C.L., vol. 1415, 6. On this theme, see Earle, *The Return of the Native,* 26.

80. Piñera, *Sermón panegírico eucharístico,* 6, 8.

81. Earle, *The Return of the Native,* 41. Earle distinguishes a "double discourse" on Indians, through which nationalists simultaneously vilified contemporary indigenous populations and acclaimed pre-Conquest kingdoms.

82. *Diario de las Sesiones de Cortes,* June 25, 1821.

83. Rodríguez O., "From Royal Subject to Republican Citizen," 40.

84. Cited in Rodríguez O., *The Independence of Spanish America,* 209.

85. Frasquet, "El liberalismo doceañista en el México independiente," 147.

86. Ibid.

87. José María Hidalgo, *Que en la solemne función que celebró el ilustre ayuntamiento de Guadalajara, capital de Nueva Galicia, en la iglesia catedral de la misma ciudad el día 13 de diciembre de 1822,* in C.L., vol. 1432, 14.

88. Hidalgo, *Que en la solemne función que celebró el ilustre ayuntamiento de Guadalajara,* 4; Laborda y Galindo, *Oración que en el día 12 de marzo,* 12.

89. On "entangled history," see Eliga H. Gould, "Entangled Histories, Entangled Worlds: The English-Speaking Atlantic as a Spanish Periphery," *American Historical Review* 112 (June 2007): 764–86.

90. Centelles y Nuñez, *Efemerides ó bien sean sucesos memorables ocurridos en Valencia.*

91. "Al restablecimiento de la Constitución," in *Colección de canciones patrióticas.*

92. Cited in Álvarez Chillida, *El antisemitismo en España,* 96.

93. Castells and Moliner, *Crisis del antiguo régimen y revolución liberal en España,* 190.

94. Christopher Schmidt-Nowara, *Empire and Antislavery: Spain, Cuba, and Puerto Rico, 1833–1874* (Pittsburgh, 1999).

95. Christopher Schmidt-Nowara, *The Conquest of History: Spanish Colonialism and National Histories in the Nineteenth Century* (Pittsburgh, 2006).

96. Renato Barahona, *Vizcaya on the Eve of Carlism: Politics and Society, 1800–1833* (Reno, 1989), 218.

97. While the church attempted to break with the state and function as a separate corporate body, the state curtailed its privileges and undermined its economic organization. Payment of tithes became voluntary in 1833 under the government of Gómez Farías, and from 1835 onward, the state enjoyed the practice of national patronage. Although never officially recognized by the church, the effective conclusion of the debate reduced the powers of the church and symbolized the liberal ascendancy in Mexico (see Michael P. Costeloe, *Church and State in Independent Mexico: A Study of the Patronage Debate 1821–1857* [London, 1978]).

98. Federico Suárez, cited in Anna, "The Buenos Aires Expedition," 357.

99. For the case of Mexico, see Florencia E. Mallon, *Peasant and Nation: The Making of Postcolonial Mexico and Peru* (Berkeley and Los Angeles, 1995). Regarding mid-nineteenth-century Spain, see Castells and Moliner, *Crisis del antiguo régimen y revolución liberal en España.*

100. Lovett, *Napoleon and the Birth of Modern Spain,* 2: 848.

101. Cruz, *Gentlemen, Bourgeois, and Revolutionaries.*

102. See, for example, Ruth Harris, *Lourdes: Body and Spirit in the Secular Age* (New York, 1999).

EPILOGUE

1. See Álvarez Junco, "El nacionalismo español como mito movilizador," 38. Cries of "war, war, to vanquish or die" rang out on June 28, 1808, according to the *Gazeta de Valencia,* no. 15, July 15, 1808. There is evidence that "Viva España" was a rallying cry in 1808 as well. For example, in a play that opened in Cádiz on July 25, 1808, to celebrate the Spanish victory over the French at Bailén, a soldier in a tavern triumphantly shouts "Viva España en libertad" (*Melo-drama en un acto* [1808], in C.D.F., vol. 25, sig. 106, 7).

2. "Aguirre: Los héroes del 2 de mayo sabían muy bien lo que era España," *El Pais,* May 2, 2008.

3. Javier Ocaña, "Homenaje a una ciudad," *El Pais,* September 30, 2008; Carolyn P. Boyd, *Historia Patria: Politics, History, and National Identity in Spain, 1875–1975* (Princeton, 1997), 131; Benito Pérez Galdós, *Episodios Nacionales: El 19 de Marzo y el 2 de Mayo,* in *Obras Completas* (Madrid, 1945), 1:246.

4. Late on the evening of September 15, 2006, Mexican president Vicente Fox, in the Parroquia de Nuestra Señora de los Dolores, recited: "Mexicanas y mexicanos: ¡Viva nues-

tra Independencia! ¡Vivan los héroes que nos dieron patria y libertad! ¡Viva Hidalgo! ¡Viva Morelos! ¡Viva Allende! " He ended with "¡Viva México!" (cited in "Grito de Fox pasado por agua," *La Jornada,* September 16, 2006).

5. See Hamill, *The Hidalgo Revolt,* 121–23.

6. Carlos Fuentes, "Centenarios," *El Pais,* June 30, 2007.

7. See, for example, Rosario, *Oración fúnebre,* 37, 42.

8. Laborda y Galindo, *Oración que en el día 12 de marzo y templo metropolitano de Ntra. Sra. Del Pilar,* 14.

9. *Oración que en la misa solemne de la jura de la Constitución política de la Nación Española dixo a la Junta Superior y pueblo de Infantes el Redactor de la Gazeta de la Mancha* (1812), in C.D.F., vol. 137, signatura 552, 6–7.

BIBLIOGRAPHY

ARCHIVES

Archivo del Cabildo Eclesiástico de Puebla (A.C.E.P.)
Archivo Diocesano de Valencia (A.D.V.)
Archivo Histórico Municipal (A.H.M.), Valencia
Archivo Histórico Nacional (A.H.N.), Madrid
Archivo Municipal de Puebla (A.M.P.)
Biblioteca Palafoxiana (B.P.), Puebla
Biblioteca Universidad de Valencia (B.U.V.)
Biblioteca Valenciana (B.V.)
Colección Documental del Fraile (C.D.F.), Servicio Histórico Militar, Madrid
Colección Gómez Ímaz (C.G.I.), Biblioteca Nacional, Madrid
Colección Lafragua, la Benemérita Universidad Autónoma de Puebla (B.U.A.P.)
Colección Lafragua (C.L.), Biblioteca Nacional, Mexico City
Diario de las Sesiones de Cortes, 1820, 1821
Diario de las Sesiones de las Cortes Generales y Extraordinarias (D.S.C.G.E.), 1810–13
Diario de las Sesiones de las Cortes Generales y Extraordinarias: Sobre el Tribunal de la Inquisición, 1813

PERIODICALS

El Amigo de la Patria, 1822
Atalaya de la Mancha, 1814
El Conciso, 1810
El Despertador Americano, 1810–1811
Diario de la ciudad de Valencia, 1821–1822
Diario de Madrid, 1808
El Espectador, 1822

Gazeta de Valencia, 1808
Ilustrador Americano, 1812
Periódico de las Damas, 1822
El Procurador General de la Nación y del Rey, 1813
Redactor constitucional de Valencia, 1820
El Redactor General, 1811
El Robespierre Español, 1811
Semanario Patriótico, 1808, 1811
Semanario Patriótico Americano, 1812
El Tribuno de la Plebe, 1821
El Voto de la Nación Española, 1809–1810

BOOKS AND ARTICLES

Adelman, Jeremy. *Sovereignty and Revolution in the Iberian Atlantic.* Princeton: Princeton University Press, 2006.

Aguado, Anna. "Liberalismos y ciudadanía femenina en la formación de la sociedad burguesa." In *La trascendencia del liberalismo doceañista en España y en América,* edited by Manuel Chust and Ivana Frasquet. Valencia: Generalitat Valenciana, 2004.

Alcalá Galiano, Antonio. *Obras escogidas.* Madrid: Ediciones Atlas, 1955.

Álvarez Chillida, Gonzalo. *El antisemitismo en España: La imagen del judío (1812–2002).* Madrid: Martial Pons, 2002.

Álvarez García, Mariano. *El clero de la Diócesis de Valladolid durante la Guerra de la Independencia.* Valladolid: Diputación Provincial de Valladolid, 1984.

Álvarez Junco, José. "La invención de la Guerra de la Independencia." *Studia Histórica-Historia Contemporánea* 12 (1994): 75–99.

———. *Mater dolorosa: La idea de España en el siglo XIX.* Madrid: Taurus, 2001.

———. "El nacionalismo español como mito movilizador: Cuatro guerras." In *Cultura y movilización en la España contemporánea,* edited by Rafael Cruz and Manuel Pérez Ledesma. Madrid: Alianza Universidad, 1997.

———. "The Nation-Building Process in Nineteenth-Century Spain." In *Nationalism and the Nation in the Iberian Peninsula: Competing and Conflicting Identites,* edited by Clare Mar-Molinero and Angel Smith. Oxford: Berg, 1996.

Anderson, Benedict. *Imagined Communities: Reflections on the Origin and Spread of Nationalism.* Rev. ed. London: Verso, 1991.

Anna, Timothy E. "Agustín de Iturbide and the Process of Consensus." In *The Birth of Modern Mexico, 1780–1824,* edited by Christon I. Archer. Wilmington, Del.: Scholarly Resources, 2003.

———. "The Buenos Aires Expedition and Spain's Secret Plan to Conquer Portugal, 1814–1820." *Americas* 34, no. 3 (January 1978): 356–80.

Archilés, Ferran, and Manuel Martí. "Ethnicity, Region and Nation: Valencian Identity and the Spanish Nation-State." *Ethnic and Racial Studies* 24, no. 5 (September 2001): 779–97.

Ardit Lucas, Manuel. *Revolución liberal y revuelta campesina: Un ensayo sobre la desintegración del régimen feudal en el País Valenciano (1793–1840).* Barcelona: Editorial Ariel, 1977.

Arriaga, Antonio, ed. *Morelos: Documentos.* Morelia: Gobierno del Estado de Michoacán, 1965.

Artola, Miguel. *La burguesía revolucionaria.* Madrid: Alianza Editorial, 1973.

———. *La España de Fernando VII.* Madrid: Espasa-Calpe, 1968.

Ávila, Alfredo. "El cristiano constitucional: Libertad, derecho y naturaleza en la retórica de Manuel de la Bárcena." *Estudios de Historia Moderna y Contemporánea de México* 25 (January–June 2003): 1–41.

Aymes, Jean-René. *La Guerra de la Independencia en España (1808–1814).* Translated by Pierre Conard. Madrid: Siglo Veintiuno, 1975.

Baker, Keith Michael. "Defining the Public Sphere in Eighteenth-Century France: Variations on a Theme by Habermas." In *Habermas and the Public Sphere,* edited by Craig Calhoun. Cambridge: MIT Press, 1992.

Barahona, Renato. *Vizcaya on the Eve of Carlism: Politics and Society, 1800–1833.* Reno: University of Nevada Press, 1989.

Barbastro Gil, Luis. *Revolución liberal y reacción (1808–1833): Protagonismo ideológico del clero en la sociedad valenciana.* Alicante: Caja de Ahorros Provincial de Alicante, 1987.

Bayly, C. A. *Origins of Nationality in South Asia: Patriotism and Ethical Government in the Making of Modern India.* Delhi: Oxford University Press, 1998.

Bell, David A. *The Cult of the Nation in France: Inventing Nationalism, 1680–1800.* Cambridge: Harvard University Press, 2001.

Benson, Nettie Lee. "The Elections of 1809: Transforming Political Culture in New Spain." Edited by Kathryn Vincent. *Mexican Studies* 20, no. 1 (Winter 2004): 1–20.

Bierck, Harold A., Jr., ed. *Selected Writings of Bolivar.* New York: Colonial Press, 1951.

Bose, Sugata. "Nation as Mother." In *Nationalism, Democracy and Development: State and Politics in India,* edited by Bose and Ayesha Jalal. Delhi: Oxford University Press, 1998.

Boyd, Carolyn P. *Historia patria: Politics, History, and National Identity in Spain, 1875–1975.* Princeton: Princeton University Press, 1997.

———. "The Second Battle of Covadonga: The Politics of Commemoration in Modern Spain." *History & Memory* 14, no. 1/2 (Fall 2002): 37–64.

Brading, D. A. *The First America: The Spanish Monarchy, Creole Patriots, and the Liberal State, 1492–1867.* Cambridge: Cambridge University Press, 1991.

———. *Mexican Phoenix: Our Lady of Guadalupe: Image and Tradition across Five Centuries.* Cambridge: Cambridge University Press, 2001.

———. *The Origins of Mexican Nationalism.* Cambridge: Centre of Latin American Studies, 1985.

Breña, Roberto. *El primer liberalismo español y los procesos de emancipación de América, 1808–1824: Una revisión historiográfica del liberalismo hispánico.* Mexico City: Centro de Estudios Internacionales, Colegio de México, 2006.

Breuilly, John. *Nationalism and the State.* Manchester: Manchester University Press, 1982.

Brubaker, Rogers. *Citizenship and Nationhood in France and Germany.* Cambridge: Harvard University Press, 1992.

Burdiel, Isabel. "Myths of Failure, Myths of Success: New Perspectives on Nineteenth-Century Spanish Liberalism." *Journal of Modern History* 70 (December 1998): 892–912.

Burleigh, Michael. *Earthly Powers: The Clash of Religion and Politics in Europe, from the French Revolution to the Great War.* New York: HarperCollins, 2005.

Bushnell, David. "The Independence of Spanish South America." In *The Independence of Latin America,* edited by Leslie Bethell. Cambridge: Cambridge University Press, 1987.

Cadalso, José. *Cartas Marruecas.* Edited by S. Solé Camps and J. Palomar Ros. Madrid: Editorial Alhambra, 1986.

Callahan, William J. *Church, Politics, and Society in Spain, 1750–1874.* Cambridge: Harvard University Press, 1984.

Cañizares-Esguerra, Jorge. *How to Write the History of the New World: Histories, Epistemologies, and Identities in the Eighteenth-Century Atlantic World.* Stanford: Stanford University Press, 2001.

———. "La Ilustración hispanoamericana: Una caracterización." In *Revolución, independencia y las nuevas naciones de América,* edited by Jaime E. Rodríguez O. Madrid: Fundación Mapfre, 2005.

———. "New World, New Stars: Patriotic Astrology and the Invention of Indian and Creole Bodies in Colonial Spanish America, 1600–1650." *American Historical Review* 104, no. 1 (February 1999): 33–68.

Capitán Díaz, Alfonso. *Los catecismos políticos en España (1808–1822).* Granada: Imprenta Román, 1978.

Carr, Raymond. *Spain, 1808–1939.* Oxford: Clarendon Press, 1966.

Carrera, Magali M. *Imagining Identity in New Spain: Race, Lineage, and the Colonial Body in Portraiture and Casta Paintings.* Austin: University of Texas Press, 2003.

Castells, Irene, and Antonio Moliner. *Crisis del antiguo régimen y revolución liberal en España (1789–1845).* Barcelona: Editorial Ariel, 2000.

Catecismos políticos españoles arreglados a las constituciones del siglo XIX. Madrid: Consejería de Cultura de la Comunidad de Madrid, 1989.

Chakrabarty, Dipesh. *Provincializing Europe: Postcolonial Thought and Historical Difference.* Princeton: Princeton University Press, 2000.

Chaplin, Joyce E. "Race." In *The British Atlantic World, 1500–1800,* edited by David Armitage and Michael J. Braddick. New York: Palgrave Macmillan, 2002.

Chust, Manuel. *La cuestión nacional americana en las Cortes de Cádiz.* Valencia: Fundación Historia Social-Instituto de Investigaciones Históricas, UNAM, 1999.

———. "Un bienio trascendental: 1808–1810." In *1808: La eclosión juntera en el mundo hispano,* coord. Manuel Chust. Mexico City: Fondo de Cultura Económica, 2007.

Colley, Linda. *Britons: Forging the Nation 1707–1837.* New Haven: Yale University Press, 1992.

Connaughton, Brian. "Los curas y la feligresía ciudadana en México, siglo XIX." In *Las nuevas naciones: España y México, 1808–1850,* edited by Jaime E. Rodríguez O. Madrid: Fundación Mapfre, 2008.

———. *Ideología y sociedad en Guadalajara (1788–1853).* Mexico City: Consejo Nacional para la Cultura y las Artes, 1992.

Constitución Política de la Monarquía Española. In *Los inicios del constitucionalismo español: De las Cortes de Cádiz a la crisis de la monarquía absoluta (1808–1833).* Valencia: Instituto de Ciencias de la Educación, 1980.

Conversi, Daniele. *The Basques, the Catalans and Spain: Alternative Routes to Nationalist Mobilization.* Reno: University of Nevada Press, 1997.

Costeloe, Michael P. *Church and State in Independent Mexico: A Study of the Patronage Debate 1821–1857.* London: Royal Historical Society, 1978.

Coverdale, John F. *The Basque Phase of Spain's First Carlist War.* Princeton: Princeton University Press, 1984.

Cowans, Jon, ed. *Early Modern Spain: A Documentary History.* Philadelphia: University of Pennsylvania Press, 2003.

Cruz, Jesus. *Gentlemen, Bourgeois, and Revolutionaries: Political Change and Cultural Persistence among the Spanish Dominant Groups, 1750–1850.* New York: Cambridge University Press, 1996.

———. "Notability and Revolution: Social Origins of the Political Elite in Liberal Spain, 1800 to 1853." *Comparative Studies in Society and History* 36 (January 1994): 97–121.

Davidoff, Leonore, and Catherine Hall. *Family Fortunes: Men and Women of the English Middle Class, 1780–1850.* Chicago: University of Chicago Press, 1987.

Dawson, P. "Active Citizen." In *Historical Dictionary of the French Revolution,* edited by Samuel Scott and Barry Rothaus. Westport, Conn.: Greenwood Press, 1985.

Delgado, Sabino, ed. *Guerra de la Independencia: Proclamas bandos y combatientes.* Madrid: Editora Nacional, 1979.

Duara, Prasenjit. "Historicizing National Identity, or Who Imagines What and When." In *Becoming National,* edited by Geoff Eley and Ronald Grigor Suny. New York: Oxford, 1996.

Dufour, Gérard. *Un liberal exaltado en Segovia: El canónigo Santiago Sedeño y Pastor (1769–1823).* Valladolid: Secretariado de Publicaciones, Universidad de Valladolid, 1989.

Durkheim, Emile. *The Elementary Forms of the Religious Life.* Translated by Joseph Ward Swain. New York: Free Press, 1965.

Dym, Jordana. *From Sovereign Villages to National States: City, State, and Federation in Central America, 1759–1839.* Albuquerque: University of New Mexico Press, 2006.

———. "La soberanía de los pueblos: Ciudad e independencia en Centroamérica, 1808–1823." In *Revolución, independencia y las nuevas naciones de América,* edited by Jaime E. Rodríguez O. Madrid: Fundación Mapfre, 2005.

Earle, Rebecca. *The Return of the Native: Indians and Myth-Making in Spanish America, 1810–1930.* Durham, N.C.: Duke University Press, 2007.

Eastman, Scott. "'America Has Escaped from Our Hands:' Rethinking Empire, Identity and Independence during the *Trienio Liberal* in Spain, 1820-1823." *European History Quarterly* 41, no. 3 (2011): 428–43.

———. "Las identidades nacionales en el marco de una esfera pública católica: España y Nueva España durante las guerras de independencia." In *Las nuevas naciones: España y México, 1808–1850,* edited by Jaime E. Rodríguez O. Madrid: Fundación Mapfre, 2008.

———. "*La que sostiene la península es guerra nacional:* Identidades colectivas en Valencia y Andalucía durante la Guerra de Independencia." *Historia y Política. Ideas, procesos y movimientos sociales* 14 (November 2005): 245–70.

Eley, Geoff. "Nations, Publics, and Political Cultures: Placing Habermas in the Nineteenth Century." In *Habermas and the Public Sphere,* edited by Craig Calhoun. Cambridge: MIT Press, 1992.

Eley, Geoff, and Ronald Grigor Suny. "Introduction: From the Moment of Social History to the Work of Cultural Representation." In *Becoming National,* edited by Eley and Ronald Grigor Suny. New York: Oxford, 1996.

Elliott, J. H. "Atlantic History: A Circumnavigation." In *The British Atlantic World, 1500–1800,* edited by David Armitage and Michael J. Braddick. New York: Palgrave Macmillan, 2002.

Elorza, Antonio. "Cristianismo ilustrado y reforma política en Fray Miguel de Santander." *Cuadernos hispanoamericanos* 214 (October 1967): 73–107.

———. *La ideología liberal en la Ilustración española.* Madrid: Editorial Tecnos, 1970.

Esdaile, Charles. *Fighting Napoleon: Guerrillas, Bandits and Adventurers in Spain 1808–1814.* New Haven: Yale University Press, 2004.

———. *The Peninsular War: A New History.* New York: Palgrave Macmillan, 2003.

———. *Spain in the Liberal Age: From Constitution to Civil War, 1808–1939.* Oxford: Blackwell, 2000.

Etienvre, Françoise, ed. *Centinela contra franceses: Edición, con introducción, notas y apéndices documentales por Françoise Etienvre.* London: Tamesis, 1988.

Farriss, Nancy M. *Crown and Clergy in Colonial Mexico: The Crisis of Ecclesiastical Privilege.* London: Athlone Press, 1968.

Fernández Sebastián, Javier. "España, monarquía y nación: Cuatro concepciones de la comunidad política española entre el Antiguo Régimen y la Revolución liberal." *Studia Histórica-Historia Contemporánea* 12 (1994): 45–74.

Fitzsimmons, Michael P. "The National Assembly and the Invention of Citizenship." In *The French Revolution and the Meaning of Citizenship,* edited by Renée Waldinger, Philip Dawson, and Isser Woloch. Westport, Conn.: Greenwood Press, 1993.

Florescano, Enrique. *National Narratives in Mexico: A History.* Norman: University of Oklahoma Press, 2006.

Flórez Estrada, Álvaro. *Introducción para la historia de la Revolución de España.* London: Imprenta de R. Juigné, 1810.

Fontana, Josep. *La quiebra de la monarquía absoluta 1814–1820.* Barcelona: Ariel, 1971.

Ford, Caroline. *Creating the Nation in Provincial France: Religion and Political Identity in Brittany.* Princeton: Princeton University Press, 1993.

Fox, E. Inman. *La invención de España.* Madrid: Cátedra, 1998.

Fradera, Josep M. *Colonias para después de un imperio.* Barcelona: Edicions Bellaterra, 2005.

———. "El proyecto liberal catalán y los imperativos del doble patriotismo." *Ayer* 35 (1999): 87–100.

Frasquet, Ivana. "El liberalismo doceañista en el México independiente, 1821–1824." In *La trascendencia del liberalismo doceañista en España y en América,* edited by Manuel Chust and Ivana Frasquet. Valencia: Generalitat Valenciana, 2004.

Freire López, Ana María. "La Guerra de la Independencia española como motivo teatral: Esbozo de un catálogo de piezas dramáticas (1808–1814)." *Investigación franco-española,* no. 1 (1988): 127–45.

Fuentes, Juan Francisco. "Concepto de *pueblo* en el primer liberalismo español." *Trienio, Ilustración y Liberalismo* 12 (November 1988): 176–209.

Fusi, Juan Pablo. *España: La evolución de la identidad nacional.* Madrid: Ediciones Temas de Hoy, 2000.

———. "Revisionismo crítico e historia nacionalista (A propósito de un artículo de Borja de Riquer)." *Historia Social* 7 (Spring–Summer 1990): 127–35.

Gallardo, Bartolomé. *Diccionario crítico-burlesco: Diccionario razonado manual para inteligencia de ciertos escritores que por equivocación han nacido en España.* Madrid: Manuel Bueno, 1820.

Gellner, Ernest. *Nations and Nationalism.* Ithaca: Cornell University Press, 1983.

Giddens, Anthony. *The Consequences of Modernity.* Stanford: Stanford University Press, 1990.

Gil Novales, Alberto. *El Trienio Liberal.* Madrid: Siglo Veintiuno, 1980.

Godineau, Dominique. *The Women of Paris and Their French Revolution.* Translated by Katherine Streip. Berkeley and Los Angeles: University of California Press, 1998.

Gould, Eliga H. "Entangled Histories, Entangled Worlds: The English-Speaking Atlantic as a Spanish Periphery." *American Historical Review* 112 (June 2007): 764–86.

Greenfeld, Liah. *Nationalism: Five Roads to Modernity.* Cambridge: Harvard University Press, 1992.

Guardino, Peter F. *Peasants, Politics, and the Formation of Mexico's National State: Guerrero, 1800–1857.* Stanford: Stanford University Press, 1996.

———. *The Time of Liberty: Popular Political Culture in Oaxaca, 1750–1850.* Durham, N.C.: Duke University Press, 2005.

Guedea, Virginia. *En busca de un gobierno alterno: Los Guadalupes de México.* Mexico City: Universidad Nacional Autónoma de México, 1992.

Guerra, François-Xavier. "Forms of Communication, Political Spaces, and Cultural Identities in the Creation of Spanish American Nations." In *Beyond Imagined Communities: Reading and Writing the Nation in Nineteenth-Century Latin America,* edited by Sara Castro-Klarén and John Charles Chasteen. Washington, D.C.: Woodrow Wilson Center Press, 2003.

———. *Modernidad e independencias: Ensayos sobre las revoluciones hispánicas.* Mexico City: Editorial Mapfre, 1992.

Habermas, Jürgen. *The Structural Transformation of the Public Sphere: An Inquiry into a Category of Bourgeois Society.* Translated by Thomas Burger. Cambridge: MIT Press, 1989.

Hamill, Hugh, Jr. *The Hidalgo Revolt: Prelude to Mexican Independence.* Gainesville: University of Florida Press, 1966.

Hamnett, Brian R. "Puebla: City and Province during the Independence Period, 1800–1824." In *La ciudad y el campo en la historia de México,* edited by Ricardo Sánchez, Eric Van Young, and Gisela Von Wobeser, 161–72. Mexico City: Universidad Autónoma de México, 1992.

———. *Roots of Insurgency: Mexican Regions, 1750–1824.* Cambridge: Cambridge University Press, 1986.

Harris, Ruth. *Lourdes: Body and Spirit in the Secular Age.* New York: Viking, 1999.

Heiberg, Marianne. "Basques, Anti-Basques, and the Moral Community." In *Becoming National,* edited by Geoff Eley and Ronald Grigor Suny. New York: Oxford, 1996.

Hernández y Dávalos, J. E., ed. *Colección de documentos para la historia de la Guerra de Independencia de México.* 6 vols. Liechtenstein: Kraus Reprint, 1968.

Herr, Richard. *The Eighteenth-Century Revolution in Spain.* Princeton: Princeton University Press, 1958.

———. "Flow and Ebb 1700–1833," In *Spain: A History,* edited by Raymond Carr. Oxford: Oxford University Press, 2000.

———. *Rural Change and Royal Finances in Spain at the End of the Old Regime.* Berkeley and Los Angeles: University of California Press, 1989.

———, ed. *Memorias del cura liberal don Juan Antonio Posse con su Discurso sobre la Constitución de 1812.* Madrid: Centro de Investigaciones Sociológicas, 1984.

Herrejón Peredo, Carlos. *Del sermón al discurso cívico: México, 1760–1834.* Zamora, Michoacán: El Colegio de Michoacán, 2003.

Herrero, Javier. *Los orígenes del pensamiento reaccionario español.* Madrid: Editorial Cuadernos para el Diálogo, 1971.

Herzog, Tamar. *Defining Nations: Immigrants and Citizens in Early Modern Spain and Spanish America.* New Haven: Yale University Press, 2003.

———. "Early Modern Spanish Citizenship: Inclusion and Exclusion in the Old and the New World." In *New World Orders: Violence, Sanction, and Authority in the Colonial Americas,* edited by John Smolenski and Thomas J. Humphrey. Philadelphia: University of Pennsylvania Press, 2005.

Hobsbawm, E. J. *Nations and Nationalism since 1780: Programme, Myth, Reality.* 2nd ed. Cambridge: Cambridge University Press, 1992.

Hocquellet, Richard. *Résistance et révolution durant l'occupation napoléonienne en Espagne 1808–1812.* Paris: Boutique de l'histoire, 2001.

Holguín, Sandie. *Creating Spaniards: Culture and National Identity in Republican Spain.* Madison: University of Wisconsin Press, 2002.

Jacobson, Stephen. "'The Head and Heart of Spain': New Perspectives on Nationalism and Nationhood." *Social History* 29, no. 3 (August 2004): 393–407.

Kagan, Richard L. "Prescott's Paradigm: American Historical Scholarship and the Decline of Spain." *American Historical Review* 101, no. 2 (1996): 423–46.

Kamen, Henry. *The Spanish Inquisition: A Historical Revision.* New Haven: Yale University Press, 1997.

Kohn, Hans. *The Idea of Nationalism: A Study in Its Origins and Background.* New York: Macmillan, 1944.

Kramer, Lloyd. "Habermas, History, and Critical Theory." In *Habermas and the Public Sphere,* edited by Craig Calhoun. Cambridge: MIT Press, 1992.

La Parra López, Emilio. "Antonio Bernabéu: Un clérigo constitucional." *Trienio, Ilustración y Liberalismo* 3 (May 1984): 105–31.

———. *El primer liberalismo español y la iglesia: Las Cortes de Cádiz.* Alicante: Instituto de Estudios Juan Gil-Albert, 1985.

Landes, Joan B. *Women and the Public Sphere in the Age of the French Revolution.* Ithaca: Cornell University Press, 1988.

Larraz, Emmanuel. *La Guerre d'Indépendance espagnole au théâtre, 1808–1814.* Aix en Provence: Université de Provence, 1987.

León Navarro, Vicente. *La pasión por la libertad: Miguel Cortés y López (1777–1854).* Valencia: Biblioteca Valenciana, 2003.

Liehr, Reinhard. *Ayuntamiento y oligarquía en Puebla, 1787–1810.* 2 vols. Mexico City: Secretaría de Educación Pública, 1976.

Lipsett-Rivera, Sonya. "Language of Body and Body as Language: Religious Thought and Cultural Syncretism." In *Religion in New Spain,* edited by Susan Schroeder and Stafford Poole. Albuquerque: University of New Mexico Press, 2007.

Llorente, Juan Antonio. *The History of the Inquisition of Spain.* Philadelphia: James M. Campbell and Co., 1843.

Lovett, Gabriel H. *Napoleon and the Birth of Modern Spain.* 2 vols. New York: New York University Press, 1965.

Lynch, John. *Bourbon Spain 1700–1808.* Oxford: Blackwell, 1989.

———. *The Spanish American Revolutions 1808–1826.* 2nd ed. New York: Norton, 1986.

Mallon, Florencia E. *Peasant and Nation: The Making of Postcolonial Mexico and Peru.* Berkeley and Los Angeles: University of California Press, 1995.

Maravall, José Antonio. "El sentimiento de nación en el siglo XVIII: la obra de Forner." *La Torre* (Puerto Rico), 15, no. 57 (1967): 25–56.

———. "Sobre orígenes y sentido del catolicismo liberal en España." In *Homenaje a Aranguren.* Madrid: Ediciones de la Revista de Occidente, 1972.

Marichal, Carlos. *Spain (1834–1844): A New Society.* London: Tamesis, 1977.

Martínez, María Elena. "Guardian of the Christian Society: The Holy Office of the Inquisition—Racism, Judaizing, and Gambling." In *Religion in New Spain,* edited by Susan Schroeder and Stafford Poole. Albuquerque: University of New Mexico Press, 2007.

Marx, Anthony W. *Faith in Nation: Exclusionary Origins of Nationalism.* Oxford: Oxford University Press, 2003.

Mier Noriega y Guerra, José Servando Teresa de. *The Memoirs of Fray Servando Teresa de Mier.* Translated by Helen Lane. New York: Oxford University Press, 1998.

Miles, Robert, and Malcolm Brown. *Racism.* 2nd ed. London: Routledge, 2003.

Morales Moya, Antonio. "Los conflictos ideológicos en el siglo XVIII español." *Revista de Estudios Políticos* 80 (1993): 7–37.

Moreno Alonso, Manuel. *Los españoles durante la ocupación napoleónica: La vida cotidiana en la vorágine.* Málaga: Editorial Algazara, 1997.

———. *Sevilla napoleónica.* Seville: Ediciones Alfar, 1995.

Morgan, Edmund S. *Inventing the People: The Rise of Popular Sovereignty in England and America.* New York: Norton, 1988.

Morodo, Raul, and Elías Díaz. "Tendencias y grupos políticos en las Cortes de Cádiz y en las de 1820." *Cuadernos Hispanoamericanos* 201 (1966): 637–75.

Mosse, George L. *The Nationalization of the Masses: Political Symbolism and Mass Movements in Germany from the Napoleonic Wars through the Third Reich.* New York: H. Fertig, 1975.

Nadal, Jordi. "A Century of Industrialization in Spain, 1833–1930." In *The Economic Modernization of Spain, 1830–1930,* edited by Nicolás Sánchez-Albornoz; translated by Karen Powers and Manuel Sañudo. New York: New York University Press, 1987.

Napier, W. F. P. *History of the War in the Peninsula and in the South of France, from the Year 1807 to the Year 1814.* London: Thomas and William Boone, 1832.

Noel, Charles C. "Clerics and Crown in Bourbon Spain, 1700–1808." In *Religion and Politics in Enlightenment Europe,* edited by James E. Bradley and Dale K. Van Kley. Notre Dame, Ind.: Notre Dame University Press, 2001.

Núñez Seixas, Xosé M. *Historiographical Approaches to Nationalism in Spain.* Saarbrücken: Breitenbach, 1993.

———. "The Region as *Essence* of the Fatherland: Regionalist Variants of Spanish Nationalism (1840–1936)." *European History Quarterly* 31, no. 4 (2001): 483–518.

Ormsby, James Wilmot. *An Account of the Operations of the British Army, and of the State and Sentiments of the People of Portugal and Spain, during the Campaigns of the Years 1808 & 1809. Vol. 2.* London: James Carpenter, 1809.

Ortiz Escamilla, Juan. "Fuerzas armadas y liberalismo en México en una etapa revolucionaria, 1810–1821." In *La trascendencia del liberalismo doceañista en España y en América,* edited by Manuel Chust and Ivana Frasquet, 169–86. Valencia: Generalitat Valenciana, 2004.

O'Toole, Rachel. "Castas y representación en Trujillo colonial." In *Más allá de la dominación y la resistencia: Estudios de historia peruana, siglos XVI–XX,* edited by Paulo Drinot and Leo Garofalo. Lima: Instituto de Estudios Peruanos, 2005.

Pacho Polvorinos, Alberto. "Original proyecto de Cruzada presentado por el P. Manuel de Traggia a la Junta Central." In *La Guerra de la Independencia (1808–1814) y su momento histórico,* vol. 2. Santander: Institución Cultural de Cantabria, 1982.

Paquette, Gabriel B. *Enlightenment, Governance, and Reform in Spain and Its Empire, 1759–1808.* New York: Palgrave Macmillan, 2008.

Payne, Stanley G. *Basque Nationalism.* Reno: University of Nevada Press, 1975.

Pérez Galdós, Benito. *Episodios nacionales.* In *Obras completas.* Madrid: M. Aguilar, 1945.

Pérez Garzón, Juan Sisinio. "Curas y liberales en la revolución burguesa." In "El Anticlericalismo." Edited by Rafael Cruz. *Ayer* 27 (1997): 67–100. Madrid: Marcial Pons.

Pérez Moreda, Vicente. "Spain's Demographic Modernization, 1800–1930." In *The Economic Modernization of Spain, 1830–1930*, edited by Nicolás Sánchez-Albornoz; translated by Karen Powers and Manuel Sañudo. New York: New York University Press, 1987.

Philip, Kavita. *Civilizing Natures: Race, Resources and Modernity in Colonial South India*. New Brunswick, N.J.: Rutgers University Press, 2004.

Plaza Prieto, Juan. *Estructura económica de España en el siglo XVIII*. Madrid: Confederación Española de Cajas de Ahorros, 1975.

Portero, José Antonio. *Púlpito e ideología en la España del siglo XIX*. Zaragoza: Libros Pórtico, 1978.

Portillo Valdés, José María. *Revolución de nación: Orígenes de la cultura constitucional en España, 1780–1812*. Madrid: Boletín Oficial del Estado, 2000.

Pradt, Domenique de. *Europe and America, in 1821*. Translated by J. D. Williams. London: G. Cowie and Co., 1822.

Prakash, Gyan. "Subaltern Studies as Postcolonial Criticism." *American Historical Review* 99, no. 5 (December 1994): 1475–90.

Quirós, Vicente Bernaldo de. *Sermón que en la función solemne celebrada por el ilustrísimo cabildo eclesiástico y el M.I. ayuntamiento constitucional, de la M.N.Y.L. ciudad de Motril, el día 23 de julio de 1820*. Granada: Imp. de Nicolás Moreno, 1820.

Revuelta González, Manuel. "Actitudes opuestas de dos obispos santanderinos ante la Guerra de la Independencia." In *La Guerra de la Independencia (1808–1814) y su momento histórico*, vol. 2. Santander: Institución Cultural de Cantabria, 1982.

Rico, Juan. *Memorias históricas sobre la revolución de Valencia, que comprehenden desde el 23 de mayo de 1808 hasta fines del mismo año, y sobre la causa criminal formada contra el P. F. Juan Rico, el Brigadier D. Vicente González Moreno, el Comisario de Guerra D. Narciso Rubio, y otros*. Cádiz: D. Manuel Santiago de Quintana, 1811.

Ringrose, David. *Spain, Europe and the "Spanish Miracle" 1700–1900*. New York: Cambridge University Press, 1996.

Riquer i Permanyer, Borja de. "La débil nacionalización española del siglo XIX." *Historia Social* 20 (Fall 1994): 97–114.

———. "Sobre el lugar de los nacionalismos-regionalismos en la historia contemporánea española." *Historia Social* 7 (Spring–Summer, 1990): 105–26.

Rodríguez O., Jaime E. "From Royal Subject to Republican Citizen: The Role of the Autonomists in the Independence of Mexico." In *The Independence of Mexico and the Creation of the New Nation*, edited by Rodríguez O. Los Angeles: UCLA Latin American Center Publications, 1989.

———. *The Independence of Spanish America*. Cambridge: Cambridge University Press, 1998.

———. "'Ningun pueblo es superior a otro': Oaxaca y el federalismo mexicano." In

Poder y legitimidad en México, siglo XIX. Instituciones y cultura política, edited by Brian Connaughton. Mexico City: Universidad Autónoma Metropolitana, Miguel Porrúa, 2003.

———. "The Origins of Constitutionalism and Liberalism in Mexico." In *The Divine Charter: Constitutionalism and Liberalism in Nineteenth-Century Mexico,* edited by Rodríguez O. Lanham, Md.: Rowan and Littlefield, 2005.

———. *"Rey, religión, yndependencia y unión": El proceso de la independencia de Guadalajara.* Mexico City: Instituto José María Luis Mora, 2003.

———. "The Transition from Colony to Nation: New Spain, 1820–1821." In *Mexico in the Age of Democratic Revolutions, 1750–1850,* edited by Rodríguez O. Boulder: Lynne Rienner, 1994.

Rousseau, Jean-Jacques. *On the Social Contract.* Translated by Donald A. Cress. Indianapolis: Hackett, 1987.

Rugeley, Terry. *Yucatán's Maya Peasantry and the Origins of the Caste War.* Austin: University of Texas Press, 1996.

Ryan, Mary P. "Gender and Public Access: Women's Politics in Nineteenth-Century America." In *Habermas and the Public Sphere,* edited by Craig Calhoun. Cambridge: MIT Press, 1992.

Sahlins, Peter. *Boundaries: The Making of France and Spain in the Pyrenees.* Berkeley and Los Angeles: University of California Press, 1989.

———. "The Nation in the Village: State-Building and Communal Struggles in the Catalan Borderland during the Eighteenth and Nineteenth Centuries." *Journal of Modern History* 60 (June 1988): 234–63.

Santander, Miguel de. *Doctrinas y sermones para misión.* 2nd ed. Madrid: La Administración del Real Arbitrio de Beneficencia, 1802.

———. *Sermones dogmáticos.* Vol. 1. Madrid: Imprenta de D. Josef del Collado, 1805.

———. *Sermones panegíricos de varios misterios, festividades y santos.* Vol. 2. Madrid: Imprenta de la viuda de Aznar, 1814.

Saugnieux, Joël, ed. *La Ilustración católica en España: Escritos de Antonio Tavira (1737–1807).* Salamanca: Ediciones Universidad de Salamanca, 1986.

Schmidt-Nowara, Christopher. *The Conquest of History: Spanish Colonialism and National Histories in the Nineteenth Century.* Pittsburgh: University of Pittsburgh Press, 2006.

———. *Empire and Antislavery: Spain, Cuba, and Puerto Rico, 1833–1874.* Pittsburgh: University of Pittsburgh Press, 1999.

Schulte, Henry F. *The Spanish Press 1470–1966: Print, Power, and Politics.* Urbana: University of Illinois Press, 1968.

Seed, Patricia. "'Are These Not Also Men?': The Indians' Humanity and Capacity for Spanish Civilization." *Journal of Latin American Studies* 25, no. 3 (October 1993): 629–52.

Seoane, María Cruz. *Historia del periodismo en España: 2. El siglo XIX.* Madrid: Alianza Editorial, 1983.

———. *El primer lenguaje constitucional español (Las Cortes de Cádiz).* Madrid: Editorial Moneda y Crédito, 1968.

Serrano, Carlos. *El nacimiento de Carmen: Símbolos, mitos, nación.* Madrid: Taurus, 1999.

Serrano Ortega, José Antonio. "El discurso de la unión: El patriotismo novohispano en la propaganda realista durante el movimiento insurgente de Hidalgo." *Estudios de Historia Novohispana* 14 (1994): 157–77.

Shubert, Adrian. *A Social History of Modern Spain.* London: Unwin Hyman, 1990.

Sieyès, Emmanuel Joseph. "What Is the Third Estate?" In *The Old Regime and the French Revolution,* edited by Keith Michael Baker. Chicago: University of Chicago Press, 1987.

Silverblatt, Irene. *Modern Inquisitions: Peru and the Colonial Origins of the Civilized World.* Durham, N.C.: Duke University Press, 2004.

Smith, Theresa Ann. *The Emerging Female Citizen: Gender and Enlightenment in Spain.* Berkeley and Los Angeles: University of California Press, 2006.

Sobrevilla Perea, Natalia. "Batallas por la legitimidad: constitucionalismo y conflicto político en el Perú del siglo XIX (1812–1860). *Revista de Indias* 69, no. 246 (2009): 101–28.

Solís, Ramón. *El Cádiz de las Cortes: La vida de una ciudad en los años de 1810 a 1813.* Madrid: Sílex, 2000.

Spivak, Gayatri Chakravorty. "Can the Subaltern Speak?" In *Marxism and the Interpretation of Cultures,* edited by Cary Nelson and Lawrence Grossberg. Urbana: University of Illinois Press, 1988.

Suárez, Federico. *Las Cortes de Cádiz.* Madrid: Ediciones Rialp, 1982.

Sullivan, John. *ETA and Basque Nationalism: The Fight for Euskadi 1890–1986.* London: Routledge, 1988.

Tanck de Estrada, Dorothy. "Los catecismos políticos: De la revolución francesa al México independiente." In *La revolución francesa en México,* edited by Solange Alberro, Alicia Hernández Chavez and Elías Trabulse. Mexico City: El Colegio de México: Centro de Estudios Mexicanos y Centroamericanos, 1992.

Taylor, William B. *Magistrates of the Sacred: Priests and Parishioners in Eighteenth-Century Mexico.* Stanford: Stanford University Press, 1996.

———. "The Virgin of Guadalupe in New Spain: An Inquiry into the Social History of Marian Devotion." *American Ethnologist* 14, no. 1 (February 1987): 9–33.

Terán Fuentes, Mariana. *El artificio de la fe.* Zacatecas: Universidad Autónoma de Zacatecas, 2002.

———. "De nación española a federación mexicana: La opinión pública en la formación de la nación." In *Las nuevas naciones: España y México, 1808–1850,* edited by Jaime E. Rodríguez O. Madrid: Fundación Mapfre, 2008.

Tilly, Charles, ed. *Citizenship, Identity and Social History.* Cambridge: Cambridge University Press, 1996.

Tone, John Lawrence. *The Fatal Knot: The Guerrilla War in Navarre and the Defeat of Napoleon in Spain.* Chapel Hill: University of North Carolina Press, 1994.

———. "Spanish Women in the Resistance to Napoleon, 1808–1814." In *Constructing Spanish Womanhood: Female Identity in Modern Spain,* edited by Victoria Lorée Enders and Pamela Beth Radcliff. Albany: State University of New York Press, 1999.

Toreno, José María Queipo de Llano, Conde de. *Historia del levantamiento, guerra y revolución de España.* Madrid: Ediciones Atlas, 1953.

Townsend, Joseph. *A Journey through Spain in the Years 1786 and 1787.* London: C. Dilly, 1792.

Traslosheros, Jorge E. "Santa María de Guadalupe: Hispánica, novohispana y Mexicana: Tres sermones y tres voces. 1770–1818." *Estudios de Historia Novohispana* 18 (1998): 83–103.

Twinam, Ann. *Public Lives, Private Secrets: Gender, Honor, Sexuality, and Illegitimacy in Colonial Spanish America.* Stanford: Stanford University Press, 1999.

Valencina, Ambrosio de. *Los capuchinos de Andalucía en la guerra de la independencia.* Seville: Establecimiento Tipográfico de "El Adalid Seráfico," 1910.

Van Kley, Dale. *The Religious Origins of the French Revolution: From Calvin to the Civil Constitution, 1560–1791.* New Haven: Yale University Press, 1996.

Van Young, Eric. *The Other Rebellion: Popular Violence, Ideology, and the Mexican Struggle for Independence 1810–1821.* Stanford: Stanford University Press, 2001.

Varela, Javier. "Nación, patria y patriotismo en los orígenes del nacionalismo español." *Studia Histórica-Historia Contemporánea* 12 (1994): 31–43.

Varela Suanzes-Carpegna, Joaquín. *La teoría del estado en los orígenes del constitucionalismo hispánico (Las Cortes de Cádiz).* Madrid: Centro de Estudios Constitucionales, 1983.

Vicens Vives, J. *Historia de España y América social y económica.* Vol. 4, *Los Borbones: El siglo XVIII en España y América.* Barcelona: Editorial Vicens-Vives, 1977.

Vilar, Pierre. *Hidalgos, amotinados y guerrilleros: Pueblo y poderes en la historia de España.* Barcelona: Editorial Crítica, 1982.

Villanueva, Joaquín Lorenzo. *Catecismo del estado según los principios de la religión.* Madrid: Impr. Real, 1793.

Voekel, Pamela. *Alone before God: The Religious Origins of Modernity in Mexico.* Durham, N.C.: Duke University Press, 2002.

Weber, Eugen. *Peasants into Frenchmen: The Modernization of Rural France, 1870–1914.* Stanford: Stanford University Press, 1976.

Weber, Max. *The Protestant Ethic and the Spirit of Capitalism.* Translated by Talcott Parsons. New York: Scribner's, 1976.

White, José Blanco. *Cartas de España*. Madrid: Alianza Editoria, 1972.

Wilson, Kathleen. *The Island Race: Englishness, Empire and Gender in the Eighteenth Century*. London: Routledge, 2003.

Zaret, David. "Religion, Science, and Printing in the Public Spheres in Seventeenth-Century England." In *Habermas and the Public Sphere*, edited by Craig Calhoun. Cambridge: MIT Press, 1992.

INDEX